# African American Women's Life Issues Today

# African American Women's Life Issues Today

## Vital Health and Social Matters

*Catherine Fisher Collins, Editor*

*Foreword by Julianne Malveaux*

 PRAEGER

AN IMPRINT OF ABC-CLIO, LLC
Santa Barbara, California • Denver, Colorado • Oxford, England

**Library of Congress Cataloging-in-Publication Data**

African American women's life issues today : vital health and social matters / Catherine Fisher Collins, editor ; foreword by Julianne Malveaux.
    pages cm
    Includes bibliographical references and index.
    ISBN 978-1-4408-0297-3 (hardcopy : alk. paper) — ISBN 978-1-4408-0298-0 (ebook)   1. African American women—Health and hygiene.   2. African American women—Diseases.   3. African American women—Social conditions.   I. Collins, Catherine Fisher, editor of compilation.
    RA778.4.A36A325   2013
    613'.04244—dc23       2013006761

ISBN: 978-1-4408-0297-3
EISBN: 978-1-4408-0298-0

17   16   15   14   13       1   2   3   4   5

This book is also available on the World Wide Web as an eBook.
Visit www.abc-clio.com for details.

Praeger
An Imprint of ABC-CLIO, LLC

ABC-CLIO, LLC
130 Cremona Drive, P.O. Box 1911
Santa Barbara, California 93116-1911

This book is printed on acid-free paper ∞

Manufactured in the United States of America

This book is dedicated to my children, Clyde A. Collins, MD, and Laura Harris, Elementary School Principal.

You are the loves and my life,
I am so blessed to have you call me mom

# Contents

## SECTION II: MENTAL HEALTH

## SECTION III: ENVIRONMENTAL FACTORS

# Foreword: Sick, Tired, and Healing

When I write about African American women, my work is focused on our economic status, on the number of African American women in poverty, head households, or raise children alone. I also focus on the levels of income and wealth that African American women experience. While these data tell an important story about the nature of inequality in our nation and the ways it especially affects African American women, there are other data that are equally important in describing the status of African American women.

Dr. Catherine Fisher Collins has assembled an impressive volume of voices to speak of these other issues, among them depression, health disparities, domestic violence, and incarceration. In reading these chapters, I was reminded of Fannie Lou Hamer, the amazing Mississippi civil rights leader who declared that she was "sick and tired of being sick and tired." Hamer experienced economic inequality and paid an economic price for her activism (she was evicted from the plantation where her husband and daughters lived because she registered to vote). Still, her sickness and her tiredness came from attempting to dismantle a patently unjust political and economic system, her frustration at the slow pace of progress, and at the propensity to make compromises that she found unacceptable. She may also have been sick and tired of the health effects of the beating she took in 1963 in Winona, Mississippi. One of her eyes was badly damaged and she never regained full health after that beating.

Hamer died at 59 of heart failure. She also battled diabetes and last-stage breast cancer. Her health care was inadequate—she may have been a beneficiary of President Obama's Patient Protection and Affordable Care Act had our legislators been more progressive at that time. Thirty-five years after Hamer's death, too many African American women still face challenges in accessing health care—for physical, dental (which is often treated differently from other physical health issues), or mental health issues. Too many part-time workers have no access to health care, and too many full-time workers have less than they should because of high co-payments or long waiting periods when they take on new jobs. In any case, the income and employment inequities of African American women directly impact health inequities.

In his 1967 speech "The Casualties of the War in Vietnam," Dr. Martin Luther King said:

> Of all the good things in life, the Negro has approximately one half of those of whites, of the bad he has half that of whites. Thus, half of all Negroes live in substandard housing and Negroes have half the income of whites. When we turn to the negative experiences of life the Negro has a double share. The infant mortality rate is double that of whites. There are twice as many Negroes in combat in Vietnam at the beginning of 1967 and twice as many Negro soldiers died in action in proportion to their numbers in the population as whites.

Things have improved somewhat for African American people, but African American women still have a fraction (perhaps a bit more than half) of the good things that White women have (income, college attendance), and a multiple (perhaps less than double) of the negatives (unemployment, single parenthood, breast cancer, incarceration) that White women experience. Collins and her colleagues capture that differential in this fine set of chapters.

Insufficient attention has been paid to African American women's life issues; yet, these health and social issues shape the quality of life for African American women. Like Hamer, too many are overworked, underpaid, and burdened with responsibilities of both elders and youth. These members of the "sandwich generation" have less assistance and more responsibilities to similarly situated White women. Too often, these women take care of everyone except themselves and this shows up in their health and social interactions. Both health and social issues can be partly addressed by public policy, but the other part of closing these gaps is a shift in community attitudes about health and social matters.

In taking care of others and ignoring self, African American women put themselves at risk of an array of health challenge and undermine their own contribution to social and economic equity. Imagine what our world would be like if Fannie Lou Hamer had lived past age 59; if we had her input in an array of issues; or if she, like Dorothy Irene Height, who lived to be 98 years old; maintained leadership and elder status among African American women. She would have provided us with a gravitas that would have forced us to shrug off some of the trappings of class division among African American women in the spirit of her statement "Whether we are PhDs or no D's, we are all in this together."

Hamer sacrificed her body and her spirit for the civil rights movement. *African American Women's Life Issues Today: Vital Health and Social Matters* captures the ways that African American women can both be effective and self-caring. This is a rich collection of chapters that speaks both to the challenges that African American women face and to ways we might remedy them.

—Julianne Malveaux

# Preface

This book will begin with a commentary, a brief overview of the health and social status of African American women. Several questions are raised about the causes of these women's poor health and social status, and why that status remains so very poor. There are three sections comprising nine dynamic chapters and commentary written by African American women scholars who are experts in their respective professions. Each author addresses a different risk factor that negatively impacts the African American female populace.

The first section "Physical Health" contains chapters discussing the issues of heart disease, sickle cell anemia, cervical cancer, breast cancer, and obesity.

Chapter 1 presents the number one killer of women, especially African American women—heart disease. When you compare the data, you see that heart disease is an equal-opportunity killer. However, you also see the disproportionate impact it has on Black women. It also discusses why women are just now beginning to comprehend the seriousness of this disease. Also presented are psychosocial cultural factors, American Heart Association guidelines, and the health belief model—one of the first, and best known, social cognition models relating to health behavior changes.

The focus of Chapter 2 is on sickle cell anemia, a disease that has no cure. Among the many issues connected to this disease are a historical stigma and discrimination that continues to affect those who are affected. Also presented are the most recent statistics, physical manifestations, psychosocial implications, inheritance patterns, the impact of reproductive decisions, and treatment options.

Cancer hits African American women with a disproportionate impact. When it comes to cancer, Black women have the highest death rate and shortest survival rate of any racial and ethnic group in America, despite the fact that, with proper screening and follow-up care, the disease's impact can be mitigated. Chapters 3 and 4 explore this deadly scourge and its disproportionate impact. Cervical cancer is explored in Chapter 3, which includes the "why" of that disproportionate impact, as well as latest guidelines regarding preventive screening. Breast cancer is explored in Chapter 4, which includes a discussion of the author's personal family experience with this deadly disease. Also included are the subjects of access issues, health professionals' responsibilities, and the impact of social and public policy needs.

Chapter 5 addresses obesity, a subject that First Lady Michelle Obama has brought to the forefront of the health discussion in America. Although her focus is on child obesity, children grow up, and many of them carry that extra weight—or more—into adulthood. The chapter addresses biological, psychological, and societal factors related to obesity in African American women and includes a discussion on how African American men view overweight and obese women.

The second section covers issues of mental health, specifically depression, dementia, trauma, and hope.

Chapter 6 deals with depression, a very common mental illness afflicting the African American community, and yet one that is rarely discussed. To speak of any mental health problems, even in light of the scientific advances made to manage such illnesses, remains a taboo in the Black community. The multiple roles that African American women must play as caregiver to "every one" coupled with the daily experiences of racism and sexism only elevates the effects of depression.

Chapter 7 is a discussion on dementia, a chronic progressive disorder of an individual's cognitive function. Thoroughly presented are the various types of dementia, including Alzheimer's, risk factors, treatment options, and the important and demanding role placed on African American caregivers. Also included are the latest guidelines regarding preventive screening.

The final section examines environmental factors that negatively impact African American women's health, including domestic violence and the experience of being imprisoned.

Chapter 8 addresses how community violence, including domestic violence, impacts intimate partner relationships. This chapter is one of the first to explore the seriousness of how street violence impacts every aspect of urban communities, including personal relationships.

Our final chapter, Chapter 9, presents the health status and challenges facing African American women who are incarcerated in America's prisons.

Often, these women enter correctional system in poor health, and often leave in the same poor condition.

These dynamic and informative chapters challenge the status quo of the health professions, act as a starting point to guide debate, and hopefully facilitate the formation of policies designed to address the issues presented.

# Acknowledgments

There are so many to thank, but I must first begin with the Almighty—Thanks be to God.

This book would not have been possible without the assistance of contributing authors Drs. Fumni Aiyegbo, Patricia K. Bradley, Shuana K. Tucker, Dense M. Linton, Mattie L. Rhodes, Jamesetta A. Newland, Portia Johnson, Lisa M. Loury-Lomas, Lorraine E. Peeler, and Yvonne Wesley. There is only one word to describe your commitment and that word is "outstanding!"

To my wonderful parents, the late Herman and Catherine Fisher: I thank you, Dad, for instilling the joy of reading. I love and miss you both.

My children, Principal Laura Harris (of Buffalo, New York) and Clyde A. Collins, MD and Gastroenterologist (of Knoxville, Tennessee): You are the love of my life. How do I thank you for being my children!

My sincere appreciation is extended to the following:

Dr. Vivian Pinn, former director of the Department of Health and Human Services' Office on Women's Health, for writing the forewords to *African American Women's Health and Social Issues* (1996) and *African American Women's Health and Social Issues* (2006). Your assistance is greatly appreciated.

My colleagues at State University of New York's Empire State College: Thank you.

Marnetta Malcolm, Lisa Brocato, and Kevin Carr, my colleagues at WWWS 1400 AM, who provide support for my Women's Health Radio Program: I wouldn't be able to air the program without you, and your technical assistance is greatly appreciated.

Melvin Bankhead III: Your support and technical assistance is also deeply appreciated.

Members of For Women Only and The Buffalo Links, Inc.: Thank you.

And, finally, to everyone that I missed: Know that you are all very special in my life and have helped to inspire this book.

# Introduction on the Health and Social Status of African American Women

## *Catherine Fisher Collins*

Each time I write a commentary on the health and social status of African American women, I want to believe that at the end of my research, I will find some extensive measurable improvement. With the enormous amount of health-care expenditures and research into the causes of such glaring disparities, one would assume that there would be some improvement in their health and social status. Once again, here I can only report a very slight improvement.

This commentary briefly presents some of the health disparities experienced by African American women. Some of these health and social disparities are discussed in more detailed in the chapters that follow.

Research has been done on how social issues like racism (Collins, 2006, pp. 122, 123), poor education (Hahn, Teutsch, Franks, Chang, & Lloyd, 2008, p. 451), poverty (McCord & Freeman, 2009, p. 30; Almgren & Lindhorst, 2012, 73), diet (Beckles & Truman, 2011, p. 13), and the environment (Brown, 2009, p. 69) affect health status. This is well documented, but then why haven't we fixed our urban schools, stopped the dumping of waste in poor urban communities, curbed the effect of the poor poverty diet, stopped cutting infant and children programs, curbed the school dropout rate, and served the sickest community that are mostly living in close proximity to large public/community hospitals?

Life expectancy is one measurement that defines how well a particular group of people are doing. In other words, life expectancy "describes the likelihood of surviving to a given age at a given time in history" (Harper & Lambert, 1994, p. 16). In order to measure how well African American women are doing in terms of life expectancy, they must be compared with someone who has optimal health status—in this case, with other women, particularly White and Hispanic women. Therefore, in Table I.1, I present the life expectancy of women by race and ethnicity for 1960–2007.

## Table I.1
### Life Expectancy of Women by Race and Ethnicity, 1960–2007

| Race/Ethnicity | 1960 | 1970 | 1980 | 1990 | 2000 | 2001 | 2002 | 2003 | 2004 | 2005 | 2006 | 2007 |
|---|---|---|---|---|---|---|---|---|---|---|---|---|
| White | 74.1 | 75.6 | 78.7 | 79.4 | 80.5 | 79.9 | 79.9 | 80.0 | 80.4 | 80.4 | 80.6 | 80.8 |
| Black | 66.3 | 68.3 | 72.5 | 73.6 | 76.1 | 74.7 | 75.4 | 75.6 | 76.0 | 76.1 | 76.5 | 76.8 |
| Hispanic | n/a | n/a | n/a | n/a | n/a | n/a | n/a | 83.7 | n/a | n/a | n/a | 83.1 |

*Sources:* Data source for 1960–1990 statistics from C. F. Collins, ed. (2006), *African American women health and social issues* (2nd ed.), Westport, CT: Praeger.

Data source for 2003 statistics for Hispanic women from NIH (2002), *Women of color health data book: Adolescent to seniors* (3rd ed.), Bethesda, MD: Office of Research on Women's Health.

Data source for 2007 statistics for Hispanic women from CDC (2010), United States life tables by Hispanic origin, *Vital and Health Statistics, 2*(132).

Data source for African American and White women 2001–2007 from NCHS (2011), *Health, United States, 2010: With special features on death and dying*, Hyattsville, MD: U.S. Department of Health and Human Services.

Life expectancy can also be affected by diseases that an individual group may succumb to, like heart diseases, cancer, stroke, and diabetes, all of which seriously affect the health status of African American women. For the African American community, when a segment of the population (e.g., women) makes up 50 percent of a deadly disease, as with HIV/AIDS, that can have devastating effect on the total population. Just how many women are we talking about? Figure I.1 shows how many women are in American population.

As you can see in Figure I.1, African American women make up a very small percentage of the total American female population, yet in some health/social categories, they make up 50 percent of those incarcerated, living in poverty, and affected disproportionately by certain health diseases like HIV/AIDS and by substance abuse. Therefore, this is a drain on the African American female population who are needed to take care of their children and elderly parents and provide social and economic resources to many improvised communities. Please keep this in mind when reviewing the following disparity categories, which once again are very destructive to the African American community.

Now that you have seen how many females are in the American population, let's turn our attention to which diseases are killing them. There have been some changes in the lineup of the 10 leading causes of death. For example, in 1995 and 1999, the fifth leading cause of death for African

**Figure I.1**
**Black Females as Percent of Population**

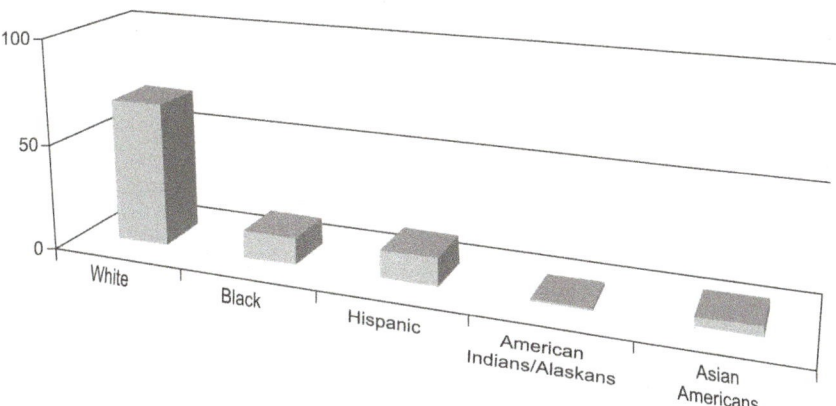

*Source:* Adapted from NIH (2002), *Women of color health data book: Adolescent to seniors* (3rd ed.), Bethesda, MD: Office of Research on Women's Health, Figure 24: Distribution of Women by Race and Ethnicity 2004, p. 91.

American women was accidents (Collins, 2003, p. 7; 2006, p. 6), and in 2002, the fifth leading cause of death was nephritis/kidney syndrome (NIH, 2002, p. 69). Table I.2 presents the 10 leading causes of death for Black, White, and Hispanic women.

As you can see, heart disease is the leading cause of death among Black, White, and Hispanic females. However, as you can see from Table I.3, African American women's health disparities for heart and cancer deaths are extremely poor.

From 1995 to 2002, their death rate for heart continued to rise from 165.5 to 263.0. For White females as well, heart death rate also plummeted from 100.0 to 192.1. However, in 2007, there was some notable improvement for African American women whose death rate per 100,000 dropped to 204.5, while their White counterparts dropped to 153.3.

**Table I.2**
**Ten Leading Causes of Death for Black, White, and Hispanic Women by Race and Ethnicity, 2002**

| Black | White | Hispanic |
| --- | --- | --- |
| Diseases of the heart | Diseases of the heart | Diseases of the heart |
| Malignant neoplasms | Malignant neoplasms | Malignant neoplasms |
| Cerebrovascular diseases | Cerebrovascular diseases | Cerebrovascular diseases |
| Diabetes mellitus | Diabetes mellitus | Diabetes mellitus |
| Nephritis, nephritic syndrome | Nephritis, nephritic syndrome | Chronic liver disease and cirrhosis |
| Accidents (unintentional injuries | Accidents (unintentional injuries | Accidents (unintentional injuries |
| Chronic lower respiratory diseases | Chronic lower respiratory diseases | Chronic lower respiratory diseases |
| Septicemia | Septicemia | Certain conditions originating in prenatal period |
| Pneumonia and influenza | Pneumonia and influenza | Pneumonia and influenza |
| Human immuno-deficiency virus | Alzheimer disease | Alzheimer disease |

*Source:* Adapted from NIH (2002), *Women of color health data book: Adolescent to seniors* (3rd ed.), Bethesda, MD: Office of Research on Women's Health, Table 4 Leading Causes of Death for Women by Race/Ethnicity, 2002, p. 69.

Table I.3

Age-Adjusted Death Rates from Heart Disease and Cancer Rate per 100,000 for African American and White American Females

| Cause of Death | Black | | | White | | |
|---|---|---|---|---|---|---|
| | 1995[a] | 2002[b] | 2007[c] | 1995 | 2002 | 2007 |
| Heart | 165.5 | 263.0 | 204.5 | 100.0 | 192.1 | 153.3 |
| Cancer | 136.5 | 190.3 | 175.2[d] | 111.3 | 162.4 | 150.6[d] |

*Sources:*

[a] C. F. Collins, ed. (1996), *African American women health and social issues*, Westport, CT: Praeger, Table 1.3, p. 7.

[b] Adapted from NIH (2002), *Women of color health data book: Adolescent to seniors* (3rd ed.), Bethesda, MD: Office of Research on Women's Health, Figure 6, p. 70.

[c] NIH, (2012), *Women of color health information collection: Cardiovascular diseases*, NIH Publication No. 12-7680, Bethesda, MD: Office of Research on Women's Health.

[d] U.S. Cancer Statistics Working Group (2010), *United States cancer statistics: 1999–2007 incidence and mortality web-based report*, Atlanta, GA: U.S. Department of Health and Human Services.

Furthermore, "In 2009 nearly 11 percent of African American women suffered from heart disease, while over 35 percent had high blood pressure" (NIH, 2012, p. 10). Hypertension, diabetes, and obesity are three of the major risk factors for cardiovascular diseases.

In addition and equally troubling, as African American women age, their mortality also increases. Elderly African American women death rates are as poor as younger African American in age group 45–54. For example, in the 65–84 age group, the death rate was 734 per 100,000, and for 75–84, the death rate was 1,822 per 100,000; however, White women in the 85-year-old age group had the worst of all at 5,351 per 100,000 (NIH, 2002, p. 70; see additional discussion in Chapter 1). In addition, Perry-Bottinger presents how gender and ethnic disparities have a bearing on the outcome for African American women. She states:

> There are cases of patients being sent home while having a heart attack. One study found the likelihood of this happening is highest if the patient is an African American woman. Nonwhite women younger than 55 are the most likely patients to be sent home from the emergency room. During a heart attack . . . Women are less likely to be referred for life-saving treatment and for rehabilitation. (Collins, 2006, pp. 23, 24)

Let's turn our attention to the second leading cause of death for African American, White, and Latino women—cancer. According to American Cancer Society's *Cancer facts & figures for African Americans 2011–2012,*

"African Americans have the highest death rate and shortest survival of any racial and ethnic group in the US for most cancers [p. 1]; about 168,900 new cases are expected to be diagnosed among African Americans [p. 4] and in 2011 about 65,540 African Americans are expected to die from cancer [p. 5]." When you couple heart disease with cancer death, these diseases would certainly have an impact on African Americans' life expectancy (see Table I.1).

The National Cancer Institute (NCI) notes that the most frequent cancers affecting African American women are breast (34%), lung (13%), and colorectal cancer (11%; ACS, 2011, p. 4). Figure I.2 shows in 2007, 121.0 out of 100,000 White women were diagnosed with breast cancer, followed by 117.0 Black and 88.2 Hispanic women (U.S. Cancer Statistics Working Group, 2010).

Breast cancer is the most frequently diagnosed cancer for all women. Specifically to African American women, the major cancer affecting them is breast cancer, surpassed only by lung cancer. In 2011, it was estimated that 26,840 new cases of breast cancer occurred among African American women (ACS, 2011, p. 7).

Even though breast cancer is diagnosed more frequently among Black and White women, Black women have a higher death rate from breast cancer. "Furthermore, premenopausal African American women appear to be at particular risk for basal-like breast cancer (i.e., triple-negative cancers), an

**Figure I.2**
**Cancer Diagnosed in 2007 among Hispanic, White, and Black Women per 100,000**

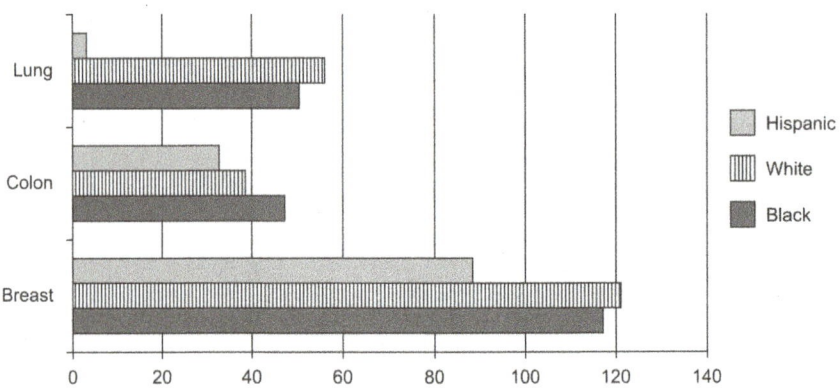

*Source:* U.S. Cancer Statistics Working Group (2010), *United States cancer statistics: 1999–2007 incidence and mortality web-based report.* Atlanta, GA: U.S. Department of Health and Human Services.

aggressive subtype of breast cancer associated with shorter survival" (ACS, 2011, p. 8). However, according to Beatrice Motamedi (2000), the survival rate for Black women jumps to 89 percent if the cancer is diagnosed before it has spread. Yet, 44 percent of newly diagnosed breast cancers found in African American women have spread to areas beyond the breast compared with 35 percent of their White counterparts.

Other factors that may affect their survival are longer time intervals before their next scheduled mammogram and the lack of follow-up of suspicious result, which may also affect their survival. Preventive measures are so very important, and reducing risk factors like "avoiding weight gain and obesity engaging in regular physical activity, and minimizing alcohol intake" (ACS, 2011, p. 8) may contribute to increased longevity.

Another cancer that affects African Americans' health is that of the cervix. "Although mortality rates have declined steadily over the past several decades due to the prevention and early detection . . . African American women remain twice as likely to die from cervical cancer as white women" (ACS, 2011, p. 9). With the primary infection for cervical cancer of the human papillomavirus (HPV) and FDA's approval of the use of the vaccines (Ganlisil and Cevarix) for the prevention of the most common HPV infections, which cause about 70 percent of cervical cancers, I am hopeful that we will eventually see a dramatic decline of cervical cancers among the African American female population.

Colon and rectal cancers among African Americans in 2011 are estimated to be 16,650 cases. This is the third most common cancer among African American women and men. Some factors that increase risk for colorectal cancer include physical inactivity, obesity, high consumption of red or processed meats, and smoking (ACS, 2011, p. 10). Smoking as a risk factor for African American women is particularly devastating for a population that is so needed to see themselves in a positive manner on television, movies, and ads. When all you see in the media are negative images or no positive images, of African American women, even when she is seen smoking, no matter how detrimental to her health, it may be worth the risk. As Moodie-Mills presents in her article "Sound-off: A slow sweet death" (2011), "As the younger sibling, I longed to be 'cool,' and smoking was the easiest way into that 'club.' The harshness of the smoke had me hacking my brains out. But no matter how painful it was, I couldn't get the images of beautiful Black women with long 'elegant' cigarettes hanging between their polished nails out of my mind. They had me thinking to myself, 'I want to be sophisticated like them.' " Certainly, the cigarette industry must have analyzed the weaknesses and violability of this community and designed their marketing approach to sell their product to this African American community—and it worked. In fact, "the tobacco industry spends $1 million each hour marketing its products" (Precious, 2012, p. 1). A community with a high school dropout rate would further be a target—uneducated, need to be accepted in a positive light. A defect in health knowledge would be a prime target. This is supported by results of the American Lung Association study: "In 2008 smoking rates are . . . much higher in African American females over age 25 years old who have less than a high school education (23.2%) compared to those with a college education (9.5%)" (American Lung Association, www.lung.org/stop-smoking/about-smoking/facts-figures/African-Americas-and-tobacco. html). Therefore, the American Lung Association recognizes that education is a significant predictor of smoking behavior of African American women.

The Surgeon General in March 2012 released over 900-page report: *Preventing tobacco use among youth and young adults*, from which I have chosen to present some of the highlights that are relevant to my prior discussion:

- Tobacco is the leading cause of preventable and premature deaths, which kills an estimated 443,000 Americans a year.
- Each day in the United States, over 3,800 young people under 18 years of age smoke their first cigarette, and over 100 youths under the age of 18 become daily cigarette smokers.
- The tobacco industry spends an estimated $10 billion a year to market its products (p. 3).
- The adolescents most likely to begin to use tobacco and progress to regular users are those who have lower academic achievement (p. 10).

Closely linked to heart disease and hypertension is the third leading cause of death among African American women—stroke. According to Sacks (2012), there were about 800,000 strokes per year in the United States alone, which annually cost $41 billion in U.S. health-care cost (p. 7).

Strokes occur when there is a blockage of an artery (by a blood clot), intracerebral hemorrhage, or subarachnoid hemorrhage that deprives the brain of needed oxygen and leads to loss of vision, numbness or weakness on one side of the body, speech impairment, or dropping lips. Sadly, "black women have the highest prevalence of stroke of any group . . . a higher incident rate of stroke than white women in every age group" (http://www.womensheart.org/content/stroke/what_is_a_stroke.asp). In addition, research has shown in Non-Whites dementia is higher following a stroke (Gorelick, 1998).

High blood pressure is the number one risk factor for stroke, and one in three African American women suffers from high blood pressure. The Black community is full of hypertension. Also, smoking doubles the risk of a stroke, and people with diabetes (discussed next) have very high incidents of stroke. Social factors like racism or racial encounters can further precipitate an increase in blood pressure (Collins, 2003, pp. 12–14).

Like smoking, the number of persons with hypertension varies with levels of education. Between 1999 and 2002, 43 percent of Blacks had hypertension as compared with 28 percent of Whites, and for those African American women with a high school diploma and higher education, the prevalence of hypertension was 37 percent, and for those who had less education, the prevalence was 51 percent (NIH, 2002, p. 12). There has also been some research that suggests that dark-skinned African Americans experienced more attacks than light-complected African Americans and may be a stressor that precipitates a spike in blood pressure. The constant barrage of racist attacks provoked by White females showed a rise in blood pressure (Derrick, 1997, p. 37).

The fourth leading cause of death for African American, White, and Latino women is diabetes. According to the Centers for Disease Control and Prevention's (CDC) *National diabetes fact sheet 2011*, diabetes affects 25.8 million Americans, of which (i.e., 8.3%) 4.9 million (i.e., 18.7%) are African Americans. In 2007, African American women had the highest diabetes prevalence rate (12.7%) as compared with White (6.1%) and Hispanic (10.9%) women (NIH, 2010, p. 8). Diabetes is a disease of the endocrine system where the pancreas fails to produce enough insulin to metabolize a person's intake of sugar. Therefore, the body has high levels of sugar in blood, which is harmful to other body systems. This sugar or blood glucose affects the body's ability to heal and is the leading cause of kidney diseases/renal failure, amputations, and blindness, all of which disproportionately affect African Americans. In cost to the health-care system, it's in the millions. In 2007, the estimated cost of diagnosis of diabetes was $174 million—$116 million in direct medical cost and $58 million in indirect costs (NIH, 2010, p. 13).

Now that you have seen how leading cause's diseases affect African American women's health, let's take a look at how African American women's *behavior* and other *factors* affect their health status. There are some illnesses that have their roots/foundation in how one behaves as they engage and interact in their respective communities. I have chosen to present a small sample of those health conditions that fall into these categories: STD (sexually transmitted disease), obesity, and smoking (previously discussed).

However, before I begin the STD discussions, there are a range of social factors that also contribute to the large number of African Americans high STD infections. The CDC's *Fact sheet: African Americans and sexually transmitted diseases* reports that "blacks represent just 14 percent of the US population, yet account for approximately half of all reported Chlamydia and syphilis cases and almost three-quarters of all reported gonorrhea cases" (April 2011, p. 1).

Some of these factors include economic bondage. If an African American female is uneducated or have minimal saleable skills, she is relegated to low-income housing because she can't afford to move to a more affluent neighborhood. Therefore, her male companions that she may have sex with are also limited. Her social environment—where she shops, have her hair done, and walk in the park—is where she will draw her companions from. In addition, the high incarceration of African American males who may have engaged in sex with other STD-infected inmates may be a *pathway* for the spread of STDs. Further, the mistrust of the medical system may also lead to a delay in individual seeking treatment before engaging in sexual relations (discussed next), and the lack of health insurance too can delay seeking needed treatment.

I begin this discussion with a look at the following STDs: syphilis, gonorrhea, chlamydia, herpes simplex virus type 2 (HSV-2), and HIV/AIDS. STDs have been a serious problem for the African American community since the infamous 1932 government sponsored "Tuskegee Study of Untreated Syphilis in Negro Men"—the federal government funded a long-term study of syphilis, seeking to learn how syphilis affected Blacks, as opposed to Whites. The study withheld treatment (see section on "Health Disparities in Black and White Women" regarding treatments like bypass withheld from African American women with heart disease) from the 400 poor Black men involved in the study, who were only told that they were being treated for "bad blood." Forty years later, a newspaper exposed the experiment to the public, and the government ended the study. By the end of the experiment, 28 of the men had died directly of syphilis, 100 were dead of related complications, 40 of their wives had been infected, and 19 of their children had been born with congenital syphilis (Collins, 2006, p. 85). Because of this experiment that further received attention through a theater production "Mrs. Evers' Boys," African Americans have been very suspicious of the medical community's medical treatment of them.

It is hard to measure how the early introduction of syphilis into the African American community in the 1930s as the initial pathway continues to plague the community in the 20th century. I'll let you be the judge.

While STDs affect all women, African American women are particularly plagued by higher rates of syphilis, chlamydia, and gonorrhea, and so are their Black male counterparts. In 2010, the primary and secondary syphilis rate per 100,000 population for Black women was 6.4, and for Black men, it was 28.2. For gonorrhea, the rate for Black women was 430.8 and for Black men was 443.6. For Chlamydia, it was 761.8 for Black males and 1,536.5 for Black females (CDC, 2011, pp. 73–75).

We must keep in mind that the higher number of STDs among African American women and men may also be attributable to where they receive care. People without health insurance (later discussed) mostly receive care at public government-funded clinics, where all STDs must be reported to state health department who reports to the CDC. In contrast, those who have private insurance and a private doctor and a long-standing patient/client relationship may or may not report. There are some STDs by state law that must be reported, like HIV/AIDS. Annually, there are 19 million new cases of STDs reported at an annual cost $17 billion to health-care cost system.

In 1981, when AIDS was first reported, the racial makeup of the cases was 60 percent White, 25 percent Black, and 14 percent Hispanic; 90 percent of the cases were among men and by male-to-male contact (Valdiserri, 2011, p. 488). Today, there has been a total shift with the burden of this illness once again among minorities, primarily among Blacks. According to the CDC, in 2009, the racial make was 49 percent Black, 20 percent Hispanic, and 28 percent White (CDC, 2011, *HIV Surveillance report*, 2009). In addition, "between 1985 and 2004, the proportion of all reported AIDS cases occurring among women increased from 8 to 31 percent, with the disease disproportionately affecting women of color" (NIH, 2002, p. 127). Further, according to CDC report *HIV among women*:

> At some point in her lifetime, 1 in 139 women will be diagnosed with HIV infection. Black and Hispanic/Latina women are at increased risk of being diagnosed with HIV infection (1 in 32 black women and 1 in 106 Hispanic/Latina women will be diagnosed with HIV, compared with 1 in 182 Native Hawaiian/other Pacific Islander women; 1 in 217 American Indian/Alaska Native women; and 1 in 526 for both white and Asian women).

African American women who engage in unprotected sexual intercourse are at risk of contracting HIV/AIDS. Syphilis has been reported to have increased 134 percent in the past 5 years among Black men who have sex with other men (MSM), and there was a sharp increase in HIV in this population (CDC, http://www.cdc.gov/stdstat10/trends.htm). In addition, in 2009, Black men accounted for 70 percent of the estimated new HIV infections among all Blacks, and Black MSM represented an estimated 73 percent of new infections among all Black men and 37 percent among all MSM (CDC Fact Sheet, *HIV and AIDS among African Americans*, November 2011, p. 1), which places Black women at severe risk of HIV infection if she does not know that her partner is as they say "swings both ways" or have multiple female partners. Further, the presence of one STD will compromise a Black woman's immune system (some women can be treated for four or more STDs and some may not know they have an STD), which make her even more vulnerable to infections.

Other STDs worth mention and have health consequences for a Black female health status are trichomoniasis, HSV-2, and HPV. Trichomoniasis is another common STD that affects 3.7 million in the United States and 180 million worldwide. This disease is transmitted from person to person by a parasite through sexual contact. As reported by the CDC, "In women, the most commonly infected part of the body is the lower genital tract (vulva, vagina, or urethra), and in men, the most commonly infected body part is the inside of the penis (urethra). During sex, the parasite is usually transmitted from a penis to a vagina, or from a vagina to a penis, but it can also be passed from a vagina to another vagina" (CDC, *Trichomoniasis stat*). Among African American women, the prevalence of 13.3 percent is relatively high when compared with White and Mexican women, which are 1.3 and 1.8 percent, respectively. Most women do not have symptoms that make it imperative that African American women have a yearly checkup.

Another STD that a woman may have and not know until a sore appears is HSV-2—which is the main cause of genital herpes, an incurable treatable but not curable disease. In America nationwide, the prevalence of this disease is 16.2 percent (14–49 age), which is about 1 in 6 in this age group. It is more common in women than men and the infection of another can occur even when there are no symptoms, making this an insidious, very dangerous disease that can unknowingly be spread in the African American community. The HSV-2 virus is the genital type and HSV-1 is the oral type that resides in the mouth and on the lips and is commonly referred to as a "fever blister." In a CDC study (March 9, 2010), "the study finds that women and blacks were most likely to be infected. HSV-2 prevalence was nearly twice as high among women (20.9 percent) than men (11.5 percent), and was more than three times higher among blacks (39.2 percent) than whites (12.3 percent). And once again the most affected group was black women, with a prevalence rate of 48 percent."

"The United States spends more than any other country but has the eighth-lowest life expectancy. . . . Japan, meanwhile, spends $2,878 per person—about $5,000 less than the United States—and has the highest life expectancy among developed nations" (Sauter & Stockdale, 2012, p. 1). The United States is a leading spender for health care ($2.7 trillion spent in 2012), then why are there so much health disparities, particularly among African Americans?

In general, health disparity has always existed for African American people since the first 16 landed on the shores of Virginia in 1619. The Emancipation Proclamation nor the Civil Rights Act of 1964 guaranteed that African Americans would be treated fairly, health wise or otherwise.

When I began to look at other health disparities, I could not believe that the maternal mortality (mothers dying from childbirth) for American women was so awful. Amnesty International released a report, *The maternal health care crisis in the USA*, that stated, "It's more dangerous to give birth in the United States than 49 other countries and African American women are almost four times greater risk than Caucasian" (Amnesty International, 2010, p. 30).

What is America's maternal mortality? According to *Women of color health data book* (3rd edition, n.d., p 104), African American mothers are more likely to die from pregnancy complications and child birth than White or Hispanic mothers (p. 104). Maternal mortality rate per 100,000 live births was 6 for Whites, 7 for Hispanic, and 25 for African American mothers, which is four times higher. It gets worse for older pregnant African American mothers (those 35 years of age and older); it was 34.8, 9.1, and 10.2 for African American, White, and Hispanic mothers, respectively (p. 104). Kung, Hoyert, Xu, and Murphy (2008) reported that, "the maternal mortality rate for 2005 was 15.1 deaths per 100,000 live births. Black women have a substantially higher risk of maternal death than white women. The maternal mortality rate for black women was 36.5 deaths per 100,000 live births, roughly 3.3 times the rate for white women" (11.1 deaths per 100,000 live births; p. 13).

Americans, particularly African American women, are eating themselves into sickness. The number of obese women in America is staggering. "Among adults, overweight and obesity are identified using the Body Mass Index (BMI), a measure that adjusts body weight for height. Overweight generally is defined as a BMI of 25 and above, while obesity is defined as having a BMI of 30 and above" (NIH, 2002, p. 73). According to NIH Office of Research on Women's Health, Science Series 2010, 80 percent of African American, 70 percent of Hispanic, and 50 percent of white women are obese. Research has shown that "across racial/ethnic groups, women of lower socioeconomic status . . . are 50 percent more likely to be obese than women of higher socioeconomic status" (NIH, 2002, p. 74). The poverty diet is high in fats, sugar, and carbohydrates and low in lean meats, fish, vegetables, and fruits because the individual lacks the funds to purchase the latter—foods that have greater nutritional value will certainly not add the unwanted pounds. Also to a poor diet, inactivity due to neighborhood violence like drive-by shootings can interfere with an African American woman's ability to include an inexpensive exercise program like walking. When you add these barriers to other challenges like rent and transportation, trying to reach a healthy weight may be too stressful to deal with.

## HEALTH DISPARITIES IN BLACK AND WHITE

In their article, Truman et al. (2011) state, "health disparities as defined by U.S. federal law and commonly used in the U.S. public health literature to refer to gaps in health between segments of the population" (p. 3). Also, in their article, Giscombe and Black (2010) states that the National Institutes of Health (NIH) define health disparities as "differences in the incidence, prevalence, mortality, and burden of diseases and other adverse health conditions that exist among specific population groups in the United States" and NIH designated the following populations: Black/African American, Hispanics/Latino, Native Americans, Alaskan Natives, Asian American, Native Hawaiians, Pacific islanders, and the medically underserved (p. 116).

As you have seen from prior discussion, African American women fit the description as their mortality is extremely poor when compared with other segments of the population and they carry the burden with the highest rate of cardiovascular disease, diabetes, STDs, AIDS, and numerous other diseases. An explanation for health disparities includes access to health services and substandard quality care (Giscombe and Black, 116).

As you have seen from this prior discussion, among African American women, there are many health disparities. What should the health-care industry do to rid these women of these disparities that would lead to improve their health?

One social disparity that impacts Americans is poverty. Poverty is defined, "in its most basic sense, . . . about living in a state of deprivation from whatever it is that is deemed essential" (Almgren & Lindhorst, 2012, p. 43) like a physician, nurse, social worker, dentist, or caregivers that have some racial/ethnic connection with them, health insurances, and access to health-care provider services (hospital/clinics).

In 2008, the U.S. overall poverty was 13.3 percent; however, among African Americans, it was 24.7 percent, and 23.2 percent among Hispanics (Almgren & Lindhorst, 2012, p. 50). Now fast-forward to 2010, where the overall poverty is 15.1 percent (1 in 7 was poor), the highest since 1993. However, among African Americans, it was 27.4 percent, for Hispanics 26.6 percent, and for Whites 9.9 percent (Trisi, Sherman, & Broaddus, 2011, p. 9).

Two key and necessary components that appear to affect disparity are access to health services (a competent medical provider) and money to purchase health insurances.

We have already established that the burden of mortality, morbidity, and health disparities fall heavily on the backs of African American women and this may be due to access. Then assuming once an African American woman gains access to hospital or clinic services, this would eliminate the health disparity. However, according to Almgren and Lindhorst (2012), "hospital systems in American cities, very much like the public school system, function as a separate and unequal system of care for African Americans . . . not through the mechanism of overt racism, but through racial and ethnic disparities in health insurance coverage and entrenched patterns of health access." (p. 128).

This system is easily maintained because between 2007 and 2008, 86.7 million people who were uninsured, and among these, there were a significant number of African Americans and Hispanics. As reported by Families USA (2009), "more than half of Hispanics/Latinos (55.1 percent), two out of five African Americans (40.3 percent) and one third of other racial minorities (34 percent) were uninsured as compared to one-quarter Whites (25.8 percent)" (p. 1). With this number of uninsured who must seek health care in charity or county/government-run hospitals established to serve the poor, they will have an endless stream of uninsured clients who will continue to perpetuate this well-established health delivery system for the uninsured and poor African American females. Regrettably, "there is strong evidence that African Americans living in cities where there are high levels of racial segregation are more likely to be admitted to inferior hospitals with high mortality rates" (Almgren & Lindhorst, 2012, p. 128).

Now that we have seen how the uninsured and disparities are linked, let's take a look at how hands-on health provider may also have a link to African American women health disparities.

I have previously presented how some African American women are less likely to be referred for advanced needed cardiac procedures, like bypass and stents. On the flip side, when care is offered, as in the study by Rodriguez-Gomez and Salas-Serrano and reported by Almgren and Lindhorst (2012) who state that "African Americans and other minorities experience more misdiagnosis and inappropriate services" (p. 311), once again health disparities in the hands of the professionals are questioned. Also, the majority of health care for African American women and other minorities are provided by nonminorities (see Figure I.3).

**Figure I.3**

**Percentage of Health-Care Professionals and Occupations by Race and Ethnicity, 2008**

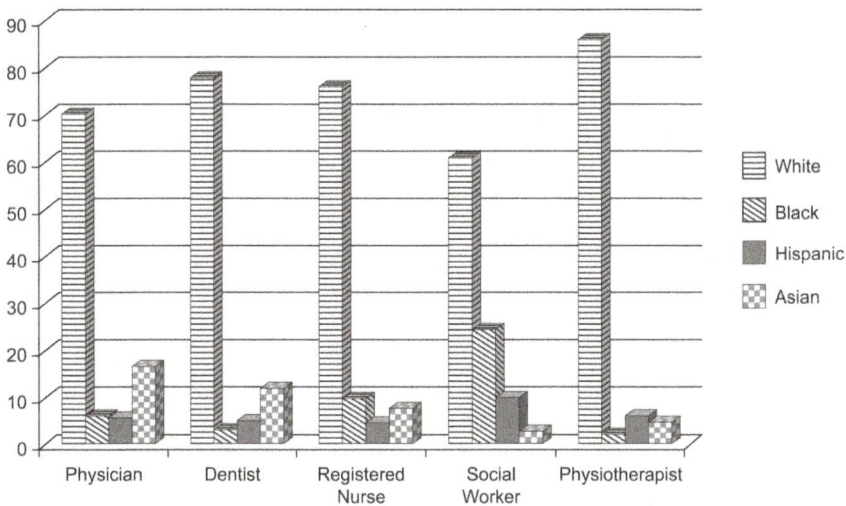

*Source:* Adapted from G. R. Almgren, & T. Lindhorst (2012), *The safety-net health care system: Health care at margins.* New York: Springer Publishing Company, Table 4.1, p. 123.

This would make you question if this has a bearing on health disparities for African American women. There have been several reports that investigated health disparities: AHRQ 2009 National Health Care Disparities Report, Institute of Medicine 2003, Committee on Understanding and Eliminating Racial and Ethnic Disparities in Health Care and number of federal and state reports have attempted to address health disparities among African Americans. Yet, these disparities continue to exist. As far back as the early Model City Programs, the federal government has attempted to eliminate health disparities in the African American community. Yet, they still exist. When you look at health disparities in African Americans, it's like you expect them to be present because we may have unknowingly normalized them as a condition that will always exist among that group, and therefore it's a normal occurrence. Just think for a minute, it's normal for 80 percent of African American women to be obese, have more diseases like HIV/AIDS and diabetes, and die in childbirth. If it wasn't normal, then why hasn't this population health status improved? The providers of health care—doctors, nurses, social workers, and hospital administrators—depend on sick people to make a living. So if that's the case, then it's normal for them to be sick and some others to be "normally" sick.

Whatever you may think about this notion of normalized sickness, at least I have peaked your interest.

## REFERENCES

ACS. (2011). *Cancer facts & figures for African Americans 2011–2012*. Atlanta, GA: ACS. Retrieved from http://www.cancer.org/acs/groups/content/@epidemiologysurveilance/documents/document/acspc-027765.pdf

Almgren, G. R., & Lindhorst, T. (2012). *The safety-net health care system: Health care at margins*. New York: Springer Publishing Company.

Amnesty International. (2010). *Deadly delivery: The maternal health care crisis in the USA*. London: Amnesty International. Retrieved from http://www.amnestyusa.org/sites/default/files/pdfs/deadlydelivery.pdf

Beckles, G. L., & Truman, B. I. (2011, January 14). Education and income—United States, 2005 and 2009. *Centers for Disease Control and Prevention's Morbidity and Mortality Weekly Report, 60*, S13–S17. Retrieved from http://www.cdc.gov/mmwr/pdf/other/su6001.pdf

Brown, P. (2009). Popular epidemiology: Community response to toxic waste-induced diseases. In P. Conrad (Ed.), *The sociology of health and illness: Critical perspective* (8th ed., pp. 69–77). New York: Worth Publishers.

CDC. (2010). Sexually Transmitted Diseases Surveillance 2010. Retrieved from http://ww.cdc.gov/std/stats

CDC. (2011). *HIV surveillance report, 2009*. Vol. 21. Retrieved www.cdc.gov/hiv/topics/surveillance/resources/reports/

CDC. (2012). *Preventing tobacco use among youth and young adults: A report of the Surgeon General*. Atlanta, GA: U.S. Department of Health and Human Services. Retrieved from http://www.cdc.gov/tobacco/data_statistics/sgr/2012/consumer_booklet/pdfs/consumer.pdf

CDC Fact Sheet. (2011). HIV and AIDS Among African Americans: A snapshot, November 2, 2011. Retrieved from www.cdc.gov/nchhstp/. . ./docs/FastFacts-AA-Final508Comp.pdf

CDC Fact Sheet. (2011). African American and Sexually Transmitted Diseases, The Health Consequences of Sexually Transmitted Diseases, April 2011. Retrieved from www.cdc.gov/nchhstp/newsroom/docs/AA-and STD-Fact-Sheet.pdf

Collins, C. (2003). *Sources of stress and relief for African American women*. Westport, CT: Praeger.

Collins, C. F. (2006). Commentary on the health and social status of African American women. In C. F. Collins (Ed.), *African American women health and social issues* (2nd ed.). Westport, CT: Praeger.

Derrick, R. C. (1997). Healing the wounds of racism. *Essence, 27*(11), 37.

Families USA. (2009). *Health care reform: Critical to closing the gap for communities of color*. Retrieved from http://www.familiesusa.org/assets/pdfs/health-reform/closing-the-gap.pdf

Gorelick, P. B. (1998, February 5–7). *Cerebrovascular diseases in African Americans*. Presidential symposium address presented at the 23rd International Joint Conference on Stroke and Cerebral Circulation, Orlando, FL. Retrieved from http://stroke.ahajournals.org/content/29/12/2656.full

Hahn, R. A., Teutsch, S. M., Franks, A. L., Chang, M.-H., & Lloyd, E. E. (2008). The prevalence of risk factors among women in the United States. In P. Conrad (Ed.), *The sociology of health and illness: Critical perspective* (8th ed., pp. 451–459). New York: Worth Publishers.

Harper, A. & Lambert, L. (1994). *The health of the population: An introduction*, 2nd ed. New York: Springer.

Kung, H.-C., Hoyert, D. L., Xu, J., & Murphy, S. L. (2008). Deaths: Final data for 2005. *National Vital Statistics Report, 56*(10), 25. Retrieved from www.cdc.gov/nchs/data/nvsr/nvsr56/nvsr_10.pdf

McCord, C., & Freeman, H. P. (2008). Excess mortality in Harlem. In P. Conrad (Ed.), *The sociology of health and illness: Critical perspective* (8th ed., pp. 30–37). New York: Worth Publishers.

Motamedi, B. (2000). *Cancer and black women*. Retrieved from Women.WebMD.com/feature/black-women-cancer

Moodie-Mills, D. (2011, May 11). Sound-off: A slow sweet death. *Essence*. Retrieved from http://www.essence.com/2011/05/12/slow-sweet-death-black-women-smoking-menthol-cigarettes-sound-off/

NCI. *Health disparities defined*. Retrieved from http://crchd.cancer.gov/disparities/defined.html

NIH. (2002). *Women of color health data book: Adolescent to seniors* (3rd ed.). Bethesda, MD: Office of Research on Women's Health.

NIH. (2010). *Women of color health information collection: Diabetes mellitus.* NIH Publication No. 10-6780. Bethesda, MD: Office of Research on Women's Health. Retrieved from http://orwh.od.nih.gov/resources/policyreports/pdf/ORWH-HIC-Diabetes-Mellitus.pdf

NIH. (2012). *Women of color health information collection: Cardiovascular diseases.* NIH Publication No. 12-7680. Bethesda, MD: Office of Research on Women's Health.

Precious, T. (2012, March 9). Smoking a "Pediatric Epidemic." *Buffalo News,* p. 1.

Rodriguez-Gomez, J. R. & Salas-Serrano, C. C. (2006). Treatment adherence in ethnic minorities: Particularities and alternatives. In W. T. O'Donahue & E. R. Levensky (Ed.), *Promoting treatment adherence: A practical handbook for health care provider* (pp. 393–400). Thousand Oaks, CA: Sage Publishers.

Sacks, D. (2012). Who should treat stroke? *Journal of NeuroInterventional Surgery, 4*(1), 1–7.

Sauter, M. B., & Stockdale, C. B. (2012, March 29). Countries that spend the most on health care. *24/7 Wall Street.* Retrieved from http://www.foxbusiness.com/industries/2012/03/29/countries-that-spend-most-on-health-care/

Trisi, D., Sherman, A., & Broaddus, M. (2011, September 14). Poverty rate second-highest in 45 years: Record numbers lacked health insurances, lived in deep poverty. *Center on Budget and Policy Priorities.* Retrieved from http://cbpp.org/files/9-14-11pov.pdf

Truman, B. I., Smith, C. K., Roy, K., Chen, Z., Moonesingh, R., Zhu, J., Crawford, C. G., & Zaza, S. (2011, January 14). Rationale for regular reporting on health disparities and equalities—United States. *Morbidity and Mortality Weekly Report, 60,* 3–10.

U.S. Cancer Statistics Working Group. (2010). *United States cancer statistics: 1999–2007 incidence and mortality web-based report.* Atlanta, GA: U.S. Department of Health and Human Services. Retrieved from www.cdc.gov/uscs.

Valdiserri, R. (2011). Thirty years of AIDS in America: A story of infinite hope. *Aids Education & Prevention, 23*(6), 479–494.

Woods-Giscombe, C., & Black, A. (2010). Mind-body interventions to reduce risk for health disparities related to stress and strength among African American women: The potential of mindfulness-based stress reduction, loving, kindness and the NTU therapeutic framework. *Complement Health Practice Review, 15*(3), 115–131.

# SECTION I

## PHYSICAL HEALTH

# 1

## Health Disparities and Cardiovascular Disease in African American Women

### Mattie L. Rhodes

Cardiovascular disease (CVD) is the number one cause of adult morbidity and mortality for African American (AA), Caucasian American (CA), and Hispanic American males and females, as well as males and females of most ethnicities in the United States today (Minino, Murphy, Xu, & Kochanek, 2009). Heart disease is described as any abnormal functioning of the heart or blood vessels that prevents the heart from functioning normally. It includes all diseases of the circulatory system. The most common type of heart disease is coronary heart disease (CHD) or cardiovascular disease (CVD), in which the arteries of the heart slowly narrow, reducing blood flow to the heart muscle. While the most common symptom of a heart attack is chest pain or discomfort, women are more likely than men to have other symptoms, such as shortness of breath, nausea and vomiting, and back or jaw pain (AHA, 2012). Types of CVD include hypertension, congestive heart failure, stroke, atrial fibrillations, congenital cardiovascular defects, and hardening of the arteries (atherosclerosis) of blood vessels.

More than 2,200 Americans die of CVD each day, an average of 1 death every 39 seconds (AHA, 2012 update). Coronary artery disease (CAD) kills more women than all cancers combined, and is the leading killer of women in the United States. Even though much attention has been given to breast cancer, far more women die of heart disease than breast cancer. Statistics show that 1 in 3 women die of heart disease versus 1 in 30 of breast cancer (AHA, 2011). There are additional concerns regarding the disparities facing women of color with heart disease and are complicated by differential access and use patterns evident between White women and women of color. The Institute of Medicine defines disparity as differential treatment provided to members of racial or ethnic groups that are not justified by health condition differences or treatment preference. Even though CVD remains the number one killer for all males and females in the United States, there are notable gender and racial disparities that impact health outcomes for AA women.

## BACKGROUND

In 2008, CVD caused one death per minute among women in the United States (Lloyd-Jones et al. 2010; AHA, 2011). Since 1984, the number of CVD deaths for females has gradually increased and exceeded those for males (AHA, 2012). In the United States, based on 2008 figures, 811,940 people of all ages die each year from CVD (over 1 in 3) or 36.2 percent of American adults have one or more types of CVD (Table 1.1). Among males, 37.4 percent have some form of CVD and 35 percent of females have some form of heart disease. Although the death rates from CVD have declined, 51 percent of females across the board are dying each year from heart disease (Table 1.1). There are significant gender differences worth noting.

### Gender Differences

Although heart disease is commonly perceived as a problem for males, gender differences reveal that annually, in the United States, more women than men die from CVD: 419,730 and 392,210, respectively (AHA, 2011). CVD is the leading cause of death and disability in women (Table 1.2).

Heart disease is the leading cause of death in women in every major developed country and emerging economy (Gholizadeh, 2008). According to the World Health Organization (WHO, 2011), not only is heart disease a concern in the United States, but also more than 50 percent of women in developed countries die of CVD including myocardial infarction (MI), heart failure, and strokes.

Table 1.1

**Prevalence and Mortality of Cardiovascular Diseases for All Ages in 2008**

| Population Group | Prevalence, 2008—Age ≥20 Years | Mortality, 2008—All Ages |
|---|---|---|
| Both sexes | 82,600,000 (36.2%) | 811,940 |
| Males | 39,900,000 (37.4%) | 392,210 (48.3%) |
| Females | 42,700,000 (35.0 %) | 419,730 (51.7%) |

*Source:* Adapted from AHA (2012), Heart disease and stroke statistics—2012 updates: Prevalence, *Circulation, 125,* e2–e220.

Table 1.2

**Leading Causes of Death in U.S. Females of Age 18 and Older in 2007 by Percentage**

| Condition | All | Black | White | Hispanic |
|---|---|---|---|---|
| Heart disease | 25.5 | 26.0 | 25.6 | 23.8 |
| Cancer | 22.4 | 22.7 | 22.3 | 23.2 |
| Stroke | 6.8 | 7.0 | 6.7 | 5.7 |

*Source:* Adapted from U.S. Health Resources and Services Administration (2010), *Women's health USA 2010*, Rockville, MD: U.S. Department of Health and Human Services. Retrieved from http://mchb.hrsa.gov/whusa10/more/references.html#II5

In 2007–2008, Black males have the highest death rates and have shown the greatest decline, while White females have the lowest death rates (Table 1.3). Women of color have lower rates than White males and have shown the next highest decline. They suffer disproportionately from heart disease and are the focus, specifically AAs and Hispanics/Latinos. Statistics have shown that one in five women have some form of CVD. Women, generally, are diagnosed later than men, generally are sicker, suffer more from comorbidities such as diabetes and hypertension, and consequently have a higher mortality rate (AHA, 2009). There has also been an increase in CVD death rates among U.S. women in 35 to 54 years of age, which is likely because of the effects of the obesity epidemic.

Table 1.3

**Age-Adjusted Death Rates per 100,000 from Cardiovascular Disease**

| Race, Sex, and Origin | 2007 | 2008 |
|---|---|---|
| All | 190.9 | 186.5 |
| All males | 237.7 | 232.3 |
| All females | 154.0 | 150.4 |
| Black male | 305.9 | 295.6 |
| Black female | 204.5 | 197.5 |
| Hispanic male | 165.0 | 151.9 |
| Hispanic female | 118.8 | 104.6 |
| White male | 234.8 | 229.9 |
| White female | 147.2 | 150.2 |

*Source:* Adapted from National Center for Health Statistics (2012), *Health, United States, 2011: With special feature on socioeconomic status and health*, Hyattsville, MD: U.S. Department of Health and Human Services. Retrieved from http://www.cdc.gov/nchs/hus/contents2011.htm#030

Clearly, heart disease is the number one killer of women, but, historically, women have not perceived themselves at risk for morbidity and mortality from heart disease. This lack of accurate risk perception prevents women from appreciating the need for early preventive behaviors and the importance of seeking early lifesaving interventions in the presence of active cardiovascular symptoms. Most American females believe that breast cancer is their major health threat despite the fact that heart disease kills six times more than breast cancer (AHA, 2011). Until recently, women largely have been excluded from past research on the diagnosis and treatment of heart disease. A 2006 national survey conducted by American Heart Association (AHA) reports that 27 percent of women cited breast cancer as their greatest threat and only 21 percent cited CVD. Progress has however been made in the incidence of CVD in women.

Sharito and Swan (2010) conducted an evidentiary systematic review regarding "Factors Accounting for Gender Differences in Managing Cardiovascular Disease in Women"—results are shown in Table 1.4. Factors found were grouped in four categories: (1) perception and early recognition, (2) misperceptions and presenting symptoms, (3) treatment, and (4) heart-related quality of life outcomes. Abuful, Gidron, and Henkin (2005) found that physicians are more likely to classify women at lower risk for CVD than men. There has been a perception by health-care providers that women are not at risk for heart disease and therefore may not be monitored for early recognition of signs and symptoms. Women may then delay seeking care for cardiac-related concerns and subsequently may not be treated as aggressively as males (DeVon, Ryan, Ochs, & Shapiro, 2008). Mosca et al. (2005) reported results of a 2004 study that indicated that less than 20 percent of physicians were aware of CVD as the number one cause of death for women.

**Table 1.4**
**Factors Accounting for Gender Differences in Managing Coronary Artery Disease in Women**

| | |
|---|---|
| **Perception and Early Recognition** | Gender bias in the utilization of diagnostic and therapeutic interventions (Levy et al., 2007, Narins et al., 2006, Shaw et al., 2006). |
| | No such bias after correcting for differences in severity of illness at presentation, age, and comorbidity (Bigi & Cortigiani, 2005, Manson et al., 2002). |
| | The perception that women are at lower risk for the disease than men. This may translate into a lack of attention to early symptoms and signs of coronary artery disease in women. Abuful, Gidron, and Henkin (2005) found physicians are more likely to classify women at lower risk for cardiovascular disease than men despite similar calculated risk. |

*(Continued)*

**Table 1.4** *(Continued)*

| | |
|---|---|
| **Misperception and Presenting Symptoms** | Symptoms experienced by females often differ from the descriptions reported by males. Women may not be diagnosed with CAD as quickly as men. Women thus may delay seeking care, or when they do seek care, may not be treated as aggressively as men (DeVon et al., 2008). |
| **Treatment** | • Gender differences are also evident in success rates of interventions meant to improve coronary circulation (myocardial revascularization). Differences in the prognosis for men and women with heart disease (Redberg, 2005a, 2005b).<br>• Women have 56% excess risk for early mortality following transmural myocardial infarction. One reason for this prognosis may be women's likelihood of receiving care from primary care physicians who fail to prescribe beta blockers and aspirin as a cardiologist would.<br>• The evidence for benefit in secondary prevention among women is much stronger than the evidence for primary prevention:<br>　○ Aspirin treatment reduced risk of cardiovascular events by about 25% (Ridker, 2001).<br>　○ Lipid lowering therapy also appears to provide substantial benefit in secondary prevention in women (Albert et al., 2005). |
| **Heart-Related Quality of Life Outcomes (HRQOL)** | Women with CAD are older, have a higher burden of co-morbid illnesses, are more often widowed, are more likely to live alone, have more depressive symptoms, have poorer psychosocial adjustment following a CAD event, and demonstrate lower referral/participation in cardiac rehabilitation programs compared to men (Norris, Saunders et al., 2004).<br><br>Two studies of women with coronary artery disease found general lack of data comparing men and women with CAD for differences with respect to health-related quality-of-life (HRQOL) outcomes (Norekval et al., 2007; Rutledge et al., 2006).<br><br>Norris, Ghali and colleagues (2004) found differences between men and women with CAD have great relevance when addressing secondary prevention programs. For example, women are less likely to be prescribed beta blocker therapy after MI, and they are less likely to be prescribed statins and angiotensin converting enzyme inhibitors. |

*Source:* Adapted from S. Sharito, & Swan, B. A. (2010), Women and cardiac disease: An evidentiary review, *Medsurg Nursing, 19*(5), 282–306.

Norris, Saunders et al. (2004) found that when considering heart-related quality of life outcomes, women with CVD have poorer health outcomes, are generally older, have more comorbidities, have more symptoms of depression, and have lower referral and participation in cardiac rehabilitation programs compared to men. It is clear that heart disease is more deadly in women. Once a woman is diagnosed, she will be more likely to die from the disease than a man (Holly, 2010). Much of this is because women are usually older and more likely to suffer more comorbidities and acute illnesses.

There are differences in secondary-prevention programs between women and men. Women are less likely to be prescribed beta blocker therapy after an MI and are less likely to be prescribed statins and angiotensin-converting enzyme inhibitors (Norris, Ghali et al., 2004). A contributing factor to disparities in mortality rates for CVD is that women, in addition to being seven years older than men, tend to have MI when they have entered menopause and have lost the benefit of estrogen (Lloyd-Jones et al., 2010). Being older, women tend to have more comorbid conditions such as diabetes, systolic hypertension, and obesity at time of diagnosis (Thom et al, 2006).

Some believe that estrogen may be protective from cholesterol deposits in the vessels. It has been reported by some that a woman's risk of CVD rises significantly after menopause, which may be due to the loss of endogenous estrogen (Maturana, Irigoyen, and Spritzer, 2007). This loss of endogenous estrogen after menopause has been associated with endothelial dysfunction as well as detrimental changes in cholesterol levels and vascular remodeling (Maturana et al., 2007).

### Racial Differences

According to the U.S. Census Bureau, women comprise 51 percent of the U.S. population of 307 million residents: Black comprise about 6.5 percent, Hispanic 7.6 percent, and White 40 percent of the population (Table 1.5).

Previous research on CVD has focused on White middle-class males and the assumption has been made that such findings apply to females as well. Overall, compared with White women, women of color have the higher mortality rate (Table 1.3) and have the highest risk-factor burden for developing CVD due to potent CVD risk factors, such as hypertension and obesity (Dennison and Hughes, 2010; Kaiser Family Foundation, 2005; Lloyd-Jones et al., 2010).

CVD rates in the United States are significantly higher for Black females compared with their White counterparts (286.1/100,000 versus

**Table 1.5**

**2009 U.S. Resident Population Estimate by Sex, Race, and Origin**

| Race | Total U.S. Population | Percentage of Total Population | Female Population | Percentage of Female Population |
|---|---|---|---|---|
| Total U.S. population | 307,006,550 | 100 | 155,557,060 | 50.67 |
| White | 246,978,393 | 79.6 | 124,425,000 | 40.08 |
| Hispanics | 48,419,324 | 15.6 | 23,362,405 | 7.6 |
| Black | 41,000,060 | 13.3 | 21,384,000 | 6.5 |

*Source:* Adapted from National Center for Health Statistics (2012), *Health, United States, 2011: With special feature on socioeconomic status and health,* Hyattsville, MD: U.S. Department of Health and Human Services. Retrieved from http://www.cdc.gov/nchs/hus/contents2011.htm#001

205.7/100,000; National Center for Health Statistics, 2012). AA women tend to have more morbidity and mortality from CVD than Whites. For AA women, the mortality rate is disproportionately high. AA women are especially at risk, with a 49.0 percent prevalence of CVD compared to 35.0 percent in White women (WW; AHA, 2009). Reports from the Institute of Medicine found that in a study of cardiologists, for example, these physicians referred White male, Black male, and White female hypothetical "patients" (actually videotaped actors who displayed the same symptoms of cardiac disease) for cardiac catheterization at the same rates (approximately 90 percent for each group), but were significantly less likely to recommend catheterization procedures for Black female patients exhibiting the same symptoms.

Data from HERS (Heart and Estrogen/Progestin Replacement Study) reports that AA women were at a 50 percent increased risk of having a cardiac event and an almost 80 percent increased risk of having a nonfatal MI than White women (Johnson, 2005). This disparity parallels the substantially lower rate of awareness of heart disease and stroke that has been documented among Black versus White women (Lloyd-Jones et al., 2010).

Studies have shown that CVD is also the leading cause of death for AA women 20 years of age and older (National Center for Health Statistics, 2006). The incidence of CHD is low however among premenstrual women possibly due to estrogen, which has been reported to provide a level of protection for younger women. Among women under the age of 35, mortality from CHD is rare, about 3.2 per 100,000 or less than one-third that of men in the same age group.

### Risk Factors

AA women are at increased risk for morbidity and mortality from CVD compared with White women because of their higher prevalence of CVD risk factors and lower socioeconomic status (AHA, 2012). According to the Centers for Disease Control (Casper et al., 2000), AA women are nearly 40 percent more likely to die of CVD than Caucasian women. The major risk factors for CVD in women are cigarette smoking, hypertension (including isolated systolic hypertension), dyslipidemia, diabetes mellitus, obesity, sedentary lifestyle, and poor nutrition. Diabetes, smoking, high blood pressure, high blood cholesterol, physical inactivity, overweight/obesity, and family history of heart disease are all greatly prevalent among AAs and are major risk factors for CVD, including stroke.

### Access to Health Care

Differential access to quality health care is an overriding issue especially for AA women. Both AA men and women have had a long history of poor access to health care, which continues even today. The Institute of Medicine reported that there is much evidence to suggest that bias, prejudice, and stereotyping on the part of health-care providers may contribute to the differences in care. Access to health care can include limited health literacy and knowledge, financial resources and insurance coverage, contact with the health-care system, ability to receive specialty and follow-up treatment, availability of support services such as transportation and child-care services, and relationships with providers. This "lack of" or "limited" access to care can also be related to poor distribution of health-care providers and availability of services.

Lack of knowledge regarding risks and access to health care is a strong contributing factor to these negative outcomes experienced by AA women. Fewer than half of AA women (41%) however consider themselves well informed about CVD. According to AHA, even though AA women are at greater risk for CVD than any other ethnic group, they are less likely than White women to know that they may have major risk factors and are not aware of their susceptibility. Results showed that adjusting for age and education level, AA and Hispanic women were significantly less likely to be aware that heart disease/heart attack is the leading cause of death, compared with White women (Mosca, Mochari-Greenberger, Dolor, Newby, & Robb, 2010). In a national survey study conducted by AHA, awareness that heart disease/heart attack is the leading cause of death has approximately doubled among White and Hispanic women and tripled among Black women between the first survey in 1997 and the current survey (Mosca et al., 2010).

Even then there still remains racial/ethnic disparity in the proportion aware by race/ethnic group (Mosca et al., 2010).

According to the Agency for Healthcare Research and Quality, AA women are much more likely to lack a usual source of care and to encounter other difficulties in obtaining needed care. AA women, despite their higher risk of heart disease, were 10 percent less likely to receive aspirin and 27 percent less likely to receive cholesterol-lowering drugs (Jha et al., 2003). There is a failure by health-care providers to understand patients' communication challenges as they struggle to relay their symptoms in a language other than their own (Mosca et al., 2010). AA women are less likely to receive health care. When they do get care, they are more likely to get it late, which delays early diagnosis and treatment. Their heart disease may be discovered late, and opportunities for early and preventive treatment may have been compromised, or the chance to prevent or delay heart disease or diabetes is lost.

Data from the *2001 Kaiser women's health survey*, a nationally representative survey of nearly 4,000 women between the ages of 18 and 64, report that one-third of Latinas (32%) and AA women (32%) report delaying or forgoing needed care in the past year, as did one-quarter of White women. Women of color have markedly more difficulty seeing a specialist when needed. In particular, Latinas (22%) were significantly more likely to report difficulties accessing specialist care. Continuity of care, including having a regular health-care provider, promotes access to needed preventive services and generally facilitates entrée into the health-care system. Latinas have less stable connections with health-care providers, and both Latinas and AA women are more likely than White women to receive routine care in clinics and health centers. Other contributing factors to these negative outcomes experienced by AA and Latino women are genetics, environment, lifestyle, as well as lack of knowledge regarding risks and access to health care.

Researchers have reported the disparity in mortality rates for CHD between AA and CA women for several decades. All too often, the health of AA women is impacted by high poverty rates, the tendency for low levels of education, and limited access to adequate health care, all of which may increase the risk for mortality. Generations of racism also play a part as does mistrust in the medical system, cultural differences, problems accessing care, and a lack of knowledge about the importance of tests to screen for major health problems. For some diseases, genetics also may contribute to risk. There are a variety of access factors that makes it difficult for AA to gain control of heart disease risks. Included among these is limited health literacy. CVD rates in the United States are significantly higher for Black females compared with their White counterparts, which parallels the substantially lower rate of awareness of heart disease and stroke that has been documented among Blacks (Mosca et al., 2010). Knowledge that CVD is the leading cause of death among women varied with racial groups. Knowledge and awareness of CVD risk has been linked to taking preventive action by some (Mosca et al., 2010).

## HEALTH BELIEF MODEL AND PREVENTATIVE HEALTH-PROMOTING BEHAVIORS

There are other areas to consider when identifying the factors contributing to disparities in health care for women of color. Even though we live in a multicultural society, there still exist variations and lack of understanding of health beliefs, cultural values, and preferences. The root causes of disparities include variations and lack of understanding of these health beliefs, cultural values and preferences, and patients' inability to communicate symptoms in a language other than their own. Clinicians also should be familiar with patients' socioeconomic status, which may make attaining a healthy lifestyle and using medications more difficult. Differences in incidence and mortality from heart disease in AA women and Caucasian women may be reflected in health beliefs that serve to guide health-promoting behaviors. Health beliefs serve to influence the individual's initiation of preventive health behavior. Health attitudes and opinions are a reflection of one's health beliefs. Health beliefs regarding heart disease, in particular, may have an effect on the likelihood of taking preventive action in order to reduce risk.

Many models have dealt with health-seeking or preventive behavior. The health belief model (HBM) is a model of health behavior change (Maiman & Becker, 1974; Rosenstock, 1974b). Rosenstock's model of health beliefs helps to form the foundation for the assessment of the variability related to women's health behavior (Maiman & Becker, 1974). This model was developed to explain how perceptions about health and illness could predict decisions to take preventive action. Other important variables to the HBM include cues to action and modifying factors. Modifying factors condition an individual's perceptions about the benefits of preventive health action (Rosenstock, 1974a). Cues to action provide the stimulus to participate within a preventive health activity. These cues may include demographic (age, sex, race), sociopsychological (personality, class), and structural (knowledge of disease) elements. The HBM is based on Lewinian field theory (Rotter, 1954), which purports that each individual has his or her own perceptions and personal values or regions (Figure 1.1). This theory views health as a positive value region and disease or illness as a negative value region. Taking action against a disease involves individual perceptions of (1) susceptibility of disease, (2) seriousness of disease,

(3) threat of disease, and (4) perceived benefits of and barriers to preventive actions. The individual must perceive susceptibility to the threat of disease. Once susceptibility is determined, then the perception of the seriousness of the disease and of contracting it is determined. Perceptions or beliefs can be modified and developed as a result of sociocultural background, heritage and socialization process, increased knowledge, and cues to action.

The modifying background factors can be antecedents of the perceptions of the individuals. The way individuals perceive the world around them determines their behavior in many situations. Psychological readiness for action consists of perceived vulnerability and perceived seriousness. The individual must perceive that he or she is susceptible to a health threat.

This model can be applied to women and heart disease, and women of color in this case. Women must perceive that CHD is a threat to them in order

**Figure 1.1**
**Health Belief Model of Women and Heart Disease**

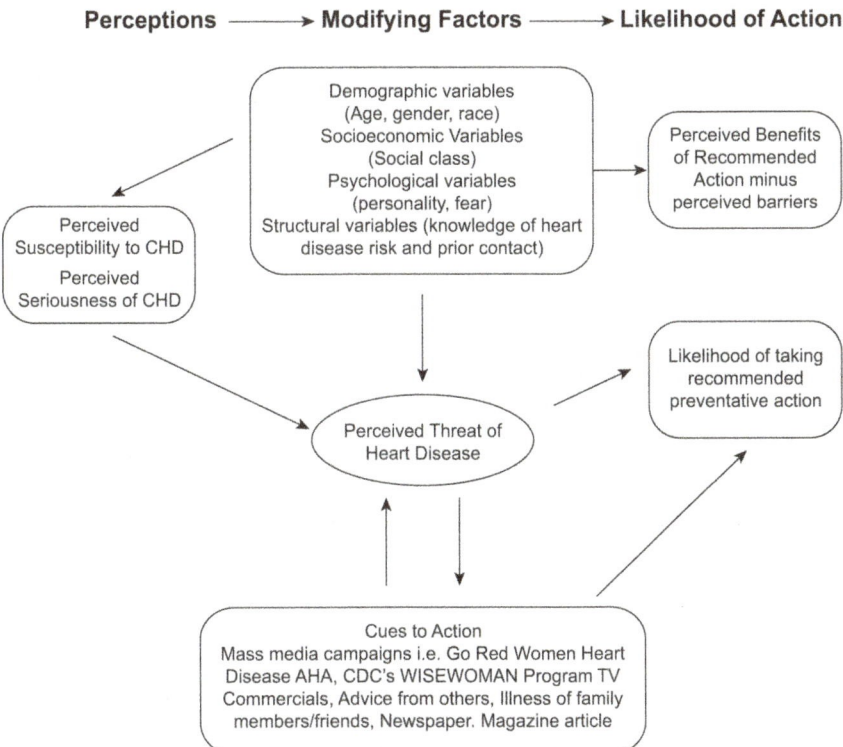

*Source:* Adapted from I. M. Rosenstock (1974a), The health belief model and preventive health behavior, *Health Education Monographs, 2,* 354–386.

to take action and practice prevention. Women's perception is impacted by level of knowledge regarding CHD and its risks and individual susceptibility. Since much of research has focused on middle-class Caucasian males, many females and minorities view CVD as a Caucasian male disease. CVD is not portrayed in the media as a female disease. For these reasons, AA and Latino females have not perceived CHD as a threat to them and therefore have not attributed their symptoms to CHD.

Readiness for action implies that the perceived benefits of a course of action to prevent the threat of heart disease must be evident. Individuals must perceive that there is a relative absence of barriers to taking action. Barrier factors for women are the lack of research, care and treatment regimen based on the male model, stereotypes regarding female sick complaints, and subsequently not being taken seriously and therefore being misdiagnosed. Environmental barriers in underserved populations are access to healthy foods, recreational facilities, and nutrition labels (Mosca et al., 2010). A previous study by the AHA has documented numerous barriers to heart health in women; chief among them was confusion by mixed messages from the media. Other barriers that health-care providers can address were as follows: 36 percent of women did not perceive themselves to be at risk, 25 percent said their health-care provider did not say heart health was important, and 1 in 5 said health-care providers did not clearly explain how they could change their risk status. Physicians have cited lack of insurance coverage as a barrier to assisting their patients with lifestyle changes.

In the HBM, mass media campaigns and governmental programs are one way to overcome barriers and heighten awareness of heart disease. In spite of an extensive education campaign aimed at American women and their health-care providers, a national survey by the AHA documented that knowledge levels about CVD were still low, although some improvement was noted in White and AA women compared to earlier surveys (Mosca, Ferris, Fabunmi, & Robertson, 2004).

Much of the change in this trend has been primarily through efforts of programs targeted for women of color: AHA's "Go Red for Women" campaign and Centers for Disease Control and Prevention's (CDC's) WISEWOMAN program. These educational efforts have been successful in promoting awareness. Go Red for Women is the AHA's nationwide movement to recognize heart disease risks in women. It bands women together in order to combat heart disease. The color red and the red dress have communicated symbolically the risk of heart disease in women. The WISEWOMAN program is a lifestyle intervention program funded by CDC and is administered through CDC's Division for Heart Disease and Stroke Prevention (CDC, 2012). It bands women together in order to combat heart disease. It provides low-income uninsured women (age 40–64) with chronic disease risk factor screenings, lifestyle modification interventions, and referral services to prevent CAD and promote health (Finkelstein, Khavjou, and Will, 2006).

### Health Locus of Control

The health locus of control (HLC) construct is also associated with preventive health behaviors (Wallston, Maides, and Wallston, 1976). The focus in this construct is on the kind and the extent of control individuals perceive that they have over their health once they feel they have a susceptibility. According to Rotter's (1954) social learning theory, an individual's behavior is a function of what he or she expects the value of specific actions to be. Individual beliefs about the HLC over their health can influence their preventive health behavior.

HLC is the expectation of individuals regarding the effects of their behavior on their health. Individuals who believe in internal control believe that their own behavior will influence outcomes. Internal locus of control is regarded as the degree individuals perceive that events, which happen in their lives, are the result of their own actions, internal control. Those with beliefs in external control expect and believe that their actions have little influence over what happens to them; rather, outside forces beyond their control such as chance or fate, or powerful others, exert most control over outcomes. When people feel they have the means to influence or modify a noxious event, they cope better with these events. The individual's expectations are based on prior experiences.

### Recommendations for Preventive Behavior of CVD in Women

Once women of color have increased awareness of risk of heart disease, taking action is needed. Recommendations for preventive behavior are in line with the AHA (Table 1.6). These guidelines address the following:

1. Lifestyle interventions: They include smoking cessation; physical activity program; rehabilitation; healthy dietary intake rich in vegetables, whole grain, oily fish, and high-fiber foods; and weight maintenance/reduction that includes balance of weight management, physical activity, and behavior modification.
2. Major risk interventions: They include optimal blood pressure level of 120/80 mm Hg and pharmacotherapy for blood pressure over 140/90 mm Hg or other major illnesses such as chronic renal failure. These may include pharmacotherapy for managing LDL or HDL and lipid-lowering drugs such as the statins or other appropriate therapy, blockers, and/or ACE inhibitors/ARBs, with addition of other drugs such as thiazides as needed to achieve goal blood pressure.
3. Preventive drug interventions: They may include aspirin, blockers, and ACE inhibitors.

**Table 1.6**

**Guidelines for Prevention of CVD in Women: Clinical Recommendations**

Lifestyle interventions

### Cigarette smoking

Women should not smoke and should avoid environmental tobacco smoke. Provide counseling, nicotine replacement, and other pharmacotherapy as indicated in conjunction with a behavioral program or formal smoking-cessation program.

### Physical activity

Women should accumulate a minimum of 30 minutes of moderate-intensity physical activity (e.g., brisk walking) on most, and preferably all, days of the week.

Women who need to lose weight or sustain weight loss should accumulate a minimum of 60–90 minutes of moderate-intensity physical activity (e.g., brisk walking) on most, and preferably all, days of the week.

### Rehabilitation

A comprehensive risk-reduction regimen—such as cardiovascular or stroke rehabilitation, or a physician-guided home, or community-based exercise training program—should be recommended to women with a recent acute coronary syndrome or coronary intervention, new-onset or chronic angina, recent cerebrovascular event, peripheral arterial disease or current/prior symptoms of heart failure, and an LVEF 40% .

### Dietary intake

Women should consume a diet rich in fruits and vegetables; choose whole grains and high-fiber foods; consume fish, especially oily fish, at least twice a week; and limit intake of saturated fat to 10% of energy (and if possible to 7%), cholesterol to 300 mg/d, alcohol intake to no more than 1 drink per day, and sodium intake to 2.3 g/d (approximately 1 tsp salt). Consumption of *trans*-fatty acids should be as low as possible (e.g., 1% of energy).

### Weight maintenance/reduction

Women should maintain or lose weight through an appropriate balance of physical activity, caloric intake, and formal behavioral programs when indicated to maintain/achieve a BMI between 18.5 and 24.9 kg/m$^2$ and a waist circumference 35 in.

### Omega-3 fatty acids

As an adjunct to diet, omega-3 fatty acids in capsule form (approximately 850–1,000 mg of EPA and DHA) may be considered in women with CHD, and higher doses (2–4 g) may be used for treatment of women with high triglyceride levels.

(Continued)

**Table 1.6** (*Continued*)

**Depression**

Consider screening women with CHD for depression and refer/treat when indicated (Class IIa, Level B).

### Major risk factor interventions

**Blood pressure—optimal level and lifestyle**

Encourage an optimal blood pressure of 120/80 mm Hg through lifestyle approaches such as weight control, increased physical activity, alcohol moderation, sodium restriction, and increased consumption of fresh fruits, vegetables, and low-fat dairy products.

**Blood pressure—pharmacotherapy**

Pharmacotherapy is indicated when blood pressure is 140/90 mm Hg or at an even lower blood pressure in the setting of chronic kidney disease or diabetes (130/80 mm Hg). Thiazide diuretics should be part of the drug regimen for most patients unless contraindicated or if there are compelling indications for other agents in specific vascular diseases. Initial treatment of high-risk women should be with -blockers and/or ACE inhibitors/ARBs, with addition of other drugs such as thiazides as needed to achieve goal blood pressure.

**Lipid and lipoprotein levels—optimal levels and lifestyle**

The following levels of lipids and lipoproteins in women should be encouraged through lifestyle approaches: LDL-C 100 mg/dL, HDL-C 50 mg/dL, triglycerides 150 mg/dL, and non-HDL-C (total cholesterol minus HDL cholesterol) 130 mg/dL (Class I, Level B). If a woman is at high risk or has hypercholesterolemia, intake of saturated fat should be 7% and cholesterol intake 200 mg/d.

**Lipids—pharmacotherapy for LDL lowering, high-risk women**

Utilize LDL-C–lowering therapy simultaneously with lifestyle therapy in women with CHD to achieve an LDL-C 100 mg/dL (Class I, Level A) and similarly in women with other atherosclerotic CVD or diabetes mellitus or 10-year absolute risk 20%.

A reduction to 70 mg/dL is reasonable in very-high-risk women with CHD and may require an LDL-lowering drug combination.

**Lipids—pharmacotherapy for LDL lowering, other at-risk women**

Utilize LDL-C–lowering therapy if LDL-C level is 130 mg/dL with lifestyle therapy and there are multiple risk factors and 10-year absolute risk 10%–20% (Class I, Level B). Utilize LDL-C–lowering therapy if LDL-C level is 160 mg/dL with lifestyle therapy and multiple risk factors even if 10-year absolute risk is 10% (Class I, Level B). Utilize LDL-C–lowering therapy if LDL 190 mg/dL regardless of the presence or absence of other risk factors or CVD with lifestyle therapy.

*(Continued)*

## Table 1.6 (*Continued*)

### Lipids—pharmacotherapy for low HDL or elevated non–HDL, high-risk women

Utilize niacin or fibrate therapy when HDL-C is low or non-HDL-C is elevated in high-risk women after LDL-C goal is reached.

### Lipids—pharmacotherapy for low HDL or elevated non-HDL, other at-risk women

Utilize niacin or fibrate therapy when HDL-C is low or non-HDL-C is elevated after LDL-C goal is reached in women with multiple risk factors and a 10-year absolute risk 10%–20%.

### Diabetes mellitus

Lifestyle and pharmacotherapy should be used as indicated in women with diabetes (Class I, Level B) to achieve an HbA1C 7% if this can be accomplished without significant hypoglycemia.

*Source:* Downloaded from http://circ.ahajournals.org/. Accessed via the Learning Library on July 26, 2012.

### Preventive drug interventions

### Aspirin, high risk

Aspirin therapy (75–325 mg/d) should be used in high-risk women unless contraindicated.

If a high-risk woman is intolerant of aspirin therapy, clopidogrel should be substituted.

### Aspirin—other at-risk or healthy women

In women 65 years of age, consider aspirin therapy (81 mg daily or 100 mg every other day) if blood pressure is controlled and benefit for ischemic stroke and MI prevention is likely to outweigh risk of gastrointestinal bleeding and hemorrhagic stroke (Class IIa, Level B), and in women 65 years of age when benefit for ischemic stroke prevention is likely to outweigh 94 adverse effects of therapy.

### Blockers

They should be used indefinitely in all women after MI, acute coronary syndrome, or left ventricular dysfunction with or without heart failure symptoms, unless contraindicated.

### ACE inhibitors/ARBs

They should be used (unless contraindicated) in women after MI and in those with clinical evidence of heart failure or an LVEF 40% or with diabetes mellitus. In women after MI and in those with clinical evidence of heart failure or an LVEF 40% or with diabetes mellitus who are intolerant of ACE inhibitors, ARBs should be used instead.

## CONCLUSION

Heart disease is a very serious risk to women, especially women of color. Women of color suffer disproportionately with many of the risk factors known to be precursors of cardiovascular. Health providers have been remiss in recognition and acceptance of this and have not been proactive in provision of care. Too often, many women of color face considerable challenges in accessing even basic health-care services. In particular, Latinas and AA women are more likely to experience certain barriers to health care than White women. Disparities are evident across several areas, such as health status, health insurance coverage rates, access to physicians, coping with health-care costs, transportation and childcare availability, use of preventive services, perceptions of quality, and knowledge related to CVD. Socioeconomic variables identify subgroups in this population where the knowledge and awareness levels are less than favorable. Research and many national educational initiatives and programs have emerged to impact and to attempt to eliminate racial and ethnic disparities in health care for women. Efforts such as AHA's Go Red for Women and CDC's WISEWOMAN have been proposed and continue to evolve. Though much success has been reported with national initiatives, continued efforts are needed to educate and raise awareness of heart disease in women of color. Continued development of programs specifically targeted to high-risk segments of populations of women of color and their health-care providers are crucial. These programs should focus on the sociocultural and economic variables involved.

It is crucial for health-care providers to understand sociocultural aspects of health beliefs that have an impact on the likelihood of taking preventive action. HBM reports that when individuals perceive that they are susceptible to the development of heart disease and that it is a danger to them, they will take action. Increased access in communities of color to knowledge of heart disease and related risks factors is important and necessary to improve preventive action. It is crucial that health-care providers appropriately implement approved guidelines such as *AHA guidelines for prevention of CVD in women: Clinical recommendations* when providing for women of color.

## REFERENCES

Abuful, A., Gidron, Y., & Henkin, Y. (2005). Physicians' attitudes toward preventive therapy for coronary artery disease: Is there a gender bias? *Clinical Cardiology, 28*(8), 389–393.

AHA. (2009). *Heart disease and stroke statistics—2009 update.* Dallas, TX: AHA.

AHA. (2011). *Heart disease and stroke statistics—2011 update.* Dallas, TX: AHA.

AHA. (2012). Heart disease and stroke statistics—2012 updates: Prevalence. *Circulation, 125*, pp. e2–e220.

Albert, M. A., Glynn, R. J., Wolfert, R. L., & Ridker, P. M. (2005). The effect of statin therapy on lipoprotein associated phospholipase A2 levels." *Atherosclerosis, 182*(1), 193–198.

Andersen, H. (2010). Tailor education on heart to women. *Case Management Advisor, 21*(9), 105–107.

Bigi, R., & Cortigiani, L. (2005). Stress testing in women: Sexual discrimination or equal opportunity?" *European Heart Journal, 26*(5), 423–425.

Casper, M. L., Barnett, E., Halverson, J. A., Elmes, G. A., Braham, V. E., Majeed, Z. A., Bloom, A. S., and Stanley, S. (2000). *Women and heart disease: An atlas of racial and ethnic disparities in mortality* (2nd ed.). Atlanta, GA: CDC. Retrieved from ftp://ftp.cdc.gov/pub/Publications/womens_atlas/00-atlas-all.pdf

CDC. (2012). *WISEWOMAN.* Retrieved from http://www.cdc.gov/WISEWOMAN/

Dennison, C. R., Hughes, S. (2010). Alarming trends in prevalence of low cardiovascular risk factor burden. *Journal of Cardiovascular Nursing, 25*(1), 5–6.

DeVon, H. A., Ryan, C. J., Ochs, A. L., & Shapiro, M. (2008). Symptoms across the continuum of acute coronary syndromes: Differences between women and men. *American Journal of Critical Care, 17*(1), 14–25.

Finkelstein, E. A., Khavjou, O. A., Mobley, L. R., Haney, D. M., Will, J. C. (2004). Racial/ethnic disparities in coronary heart disease risk factors among WISEWOMAN enrollees. *Journal of Women's Health, 13,* 503.

Gholizadeh, L., & Davidson, P. (2008). More similarities than differences: An international comparison of CVD mortality and risk factors in women. *Health Care Women International, 29*(1), 3–22.

Jha, A. K., Varosy, P. D., Kanaya, A. M., Hunninghake, D. B., Hlatky, M. A., Waters, D. D., Furberg, C. D., & Shlipak, M. G. (2003). Differences in medical care and disease outcomes among black and white women with heart disease. *Circulation, 108*(9), 1089–1094.

Johnson, P. (2005/July). CAD in women: Special consideration. *Journal Family Practice,* S1, S3. Retrieved from http://www.ncbi.nlm.nih.gov/pubmed/16134553

Lloyd-Jones, D., Adams, R. J., Brown, T. M., et al. (2010). Heart disease and stroke statistics—2010 update: A report from the American Heart Association Statistics Committee and Stroke Statistics Subcommittee. *Circulation, 121*(7), e46–e215.

Maiman, L. A., & Becker, M. H. (1974). The health belief model: Origins and correlates in psychological theory. *Health Education Monographs, 2,* 336–353.

Manson, J. E., Greenland, P., LaCroix, A. Z., Stefanick, M. L., Mouton, C. P., Oberman, A., Peri, M. G., Sheps, D. S., Pettinger, M. B., & Siscovick, D. S. (2002). Walking compared with vigorous exercise for the prevention of cardiovascular events in women. *The New England Journal of Medicine, 347*(10), 716–725.

Maturana, M. A., Irigoyen, M. C., & Spritzer, P. M. (2007). Menopause, estrogens, and endothelial dysfunction: current concepts. *Clinics (Sao Paulo), 62*(1): 77–86.

Minino, A. M., Murphy, S. L., Xu, J., & Kochanek, K. D. (2009). Deaths: Final data for 2008. *National Vital Statistics Report, 59*(10).

Mosca, L., Ferris, A., Fabunmi, R., & Robertson, R. M. (2004). Tracking women's awareness of heart disease: An American Heart Association national study. *Circulation, 109, 573–579.*

Mosca, L., Linfante, A. H., Benjamin, E. J., Berra, K., Hayes, S. N., Walsh, B. W., Fabunmi, R. P., Kwan, J., Mills, T., & Simpson, S. L. (2005). National study of physician awareness and adherence to cardiovascular disease prevention guidelines. *Circulation, 111*(4), 499–510.

Mosca, L., Mochari-Greenberger, H., Dolor, R. J., Newby, L. K., & Robb, K. J. (2010). Twelve-year follow-up of American women's awareness of cardiovascular disease risk and barriers to heart health." *Circulation Cardiovascular Quality Outcomes, 3*(2), 120–127.

Narins, C. R., Ling, F. S., Fischi, M., Peterson. D. R., Bausch, J., & Zareba, W. (2006). In hospital mortality among women undergoing contemporary elective percutaneous coronary intervention: A re-examination of the gender gap." *Clinical Cardiology, 29*(6), 254–258.

National Center for Health Statistics. (2012). *Health, United States, 2011: With special feature on socioeconomic status and health.* Hyattsville, MD: U.S. Department of Health and Human Services.

Norris, C. M., Ghali, W. A., Galbraith, P. D., Graham, M. M., Jensen, L. A., & Knudtson, M. L. (2004). Women with coronary artery disease report worse health-related quality of life outcomes compared to men. *Health and Quality of Life Outcomes, 2*(1), 21.

Norris, C. M., Saunders, L. D., Ghali, W. A., Brant, R., Galbraith, P. D., Graham, M. M., & Knudtson, M. L. (2004). Health-related quality of life outcomes of patients with coronary artery disease treated with cardiac surgery, percutaneous coronary intervention or medical management. *The Canadian Journal of Cardiology, 20*(12), 1259–1266.

Redberg, R. F. (2005a). Gender, race, and cardiac care: Why the differences? *Journal of the American College of Cardiology, 46*(10), 1852–1854.

Redberg, R. F. (2005b). Revascularization for everyone? *European Heart Journal, 26*(5), 525.

Ridker, P. M. (2001). Should statin therapy be considered for patients with elevated C-reactive protein? The need for a definitive clinical trial. *European Heart Journal, 2*(23), 2135–2137.

Rosenstock, I. M. (1974a). The health belief model and preventive health behavior. *Health Education Monographs, 2,* 354–386.

Rosenstock, I. M. (1974b). Historical origins of the health belief model. In M. H. Becker (Ed.), *The health belief model and personal behavior.* Thorofare, NJ: Slack, Inc.

Rotter, J. B. (1954). *Social learning and clinical psychology.* Englewood Cliffs, NJ: Prentice-Hall.

Salganicoff, A., Ranji, U. R., & Wyn, R. (2005). *Women and health care: A national profile.* Menlo Park, CA: Henry J. Kaiser Family Foundation.

Sharito, S., & Swan, B. A. (2010). Women and cardiac disease: An evidentiary review. *Medsurg Nursing, 19*(5), 282–306.

Shaw, L. J., Merz, C. N., Pepine, C. J., Reis, S. E., Bittner, V., Kip, K. E., Kelsey, S. F., Olson, M., Johnson, B. D., Mankad, S., Sharaf, B. L., Rogers, W. J., Pohost, G. M., & Sopko, G. (2006). The economic burden of angina in women with suspected ischemic heart disease: Results from the National Institutes of Health— National Heart, Lung, and Blood Institute—sponsored women's ischemia syndrome evaluation. *Circulation, 114*(9), 894–904.

Thom, T., Haase, N., Rosamond, W., Howard, V., Rumsfeld, J., Manolio, T., et al. (2006). Heart disease and stroke statistics—2006 Update: A report from the American Heart Association statistics committee and stroke statistics committee. *Circulation, 113*, E85–E151.

Wallston, K. A. (1991). The importance of placing measures of health locus of control beliefs in a theoretical context. *Health Education Research, 6*(2), 251, 252.

WHO. (2011). *Global Atlas on Cardiovascular Disease Prevention and Control.* S. Mendis, P. Puska, & B. Norrving (Eds.). Geneva: World Health Organization.

# 2

# African American Women: Living with Sickle Cell Disease

## *Jamesetta A. Newland*

Sickle cell disease (SCD) derives its name from the sickle, "an agricultural implement consisting of a curved metal blade with a short handle fitted on a tang" (Merriam-Webster, 2012). Many of the red blood cells (RBCs) of individuals with SCD are "peculiar elongated and sickle-shaped," first described by Dr. James Herrick in 1910 (Figure 2.1). Before this condition was assigned a name based on scientific research and knowledge, however, it was commonly referred to as *bad blood* and associated predominantly with the Negro or Black race, descendents of the slaves brought from Africa. Prejudice and ignorance about the science of SCD created a social and medical system that fostered discrimination and inequality for African Americans (Bediako, Lavender, & Yasin, 2007; Wailoo, 1997; Wailoo & Pemberton, 2006). As science and technology advanced and the structure of genes and genetic variations were discovered, knowledge about SCD also increased. No universal cure is yet available to all affected by the disease. Confusion about the distinctions between SCD and sickle cell trait continues among the lay population, while misconceptions about patients with SCD and treatment options continue among medical professionals (Mann-Jiles & Morris, 2009).

The completion of the Human Genome Project in 2003 prompted hope among scientist that the mapping of the entire human genome would lead the way to new treatment options and cures for genetic disorders, including SCD. Issues related to inadequate knowledge among affected vulnerable persons, inadequate resources, and limited access to genetic services perpetuate the disparities in health care and health status for individuals affected by SCD.

**Figure 2.1**
Comparison of a Sickle Tool, a Normal Red Blood Cell, and a Sickle-Shaped Cell

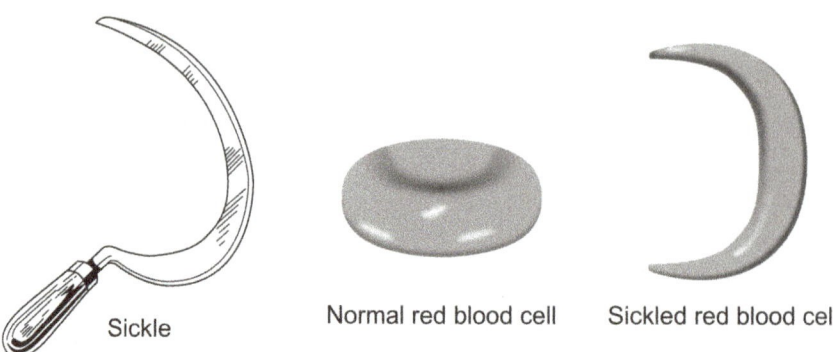

Sickle          Normal red blood cell          Sickled red blood cell

As genetic testing becomes more a part of standard care, it is important for researchers and medical professionals to be prepared to help individuals with SCD acquire the knowledge they need to make informed decisions, within the context of their support systems that include family members, social services, and the community (Norman & Miller, 2011; Wailoo & Pemberton, 2006). The Genetic Information Nondiscrimination Act of 2008 or GINA was created to safeguard against discrimination based on a person's genetic information (Hudson, Holohan, & Collins, 2008).

## PURPOSE

Women with SCD or sickle cell trait face many decisions regarding their own health or the health of a child or other family member affected by SCD. They are often the designated caretaker, responsible for all aspects of caring for a family member with SCD, and sometimes themselves too. In this chapter, an overview of SCD is presented to increase awareness of issues surrounding the historical stigma and discrimination associated with the diagnosis and that continue today, the variability and uncertainty in SCD, physical manifestations and psychosocial implications, inheritance pattern and influence on reproductive decisions, self-care, and treatment options. No startling new discoveries have occurred since this information was previously shared (Newland & Dobson, 2006), but it is always practical to remind African American women that SCD still exists; it has not been eradicated. Thus, being proactive will facilitate making decisions that could affect their personal or family health and quality of life.

## BACKGROUND

The history of the discovery of SCD in the United States reveals stigma attached to SCD from the beginning. Lebby (1846) noted on autopsy that a Black slave who had been murdered was missing a spleen. Slave owners often noticed that some slaves appeared to be sickly and were not able to endure as other slaves, leading to pronunciations of weakness and inferiority in the African race. Dr. Herrick (1910) established the clinical diagnosis of sickled cells by describing the shape of the RBCs in a young dental student from the West Indies. Crude methods of laboratory diagnosis for SCD then prevailed for decades, creating inaccurate diagnosis and beliefs that the disease, finally named sickle cell anemia, was transmitted from only one parent to a child. The distinction between the disease SCA and nondisease (sickle cell trait) was made from observations of differences in clinical symptoms and physical findings (Lessin & Jensen, 1974; Wailoo 1991, 1997).

SCD was the first molecular disease discovered (Pauling et al., 1949) and the first disease for which the genetic mutation was recognized in 1957. The actual gene was isolated in 1977 (Wailoo, 1997). All these firsts, however, did not reverse the notion that Negros had bad blood. Issues of access and discrimination continued.

Interest in SCD flourished in the 1970s after Congress passed the National Sickle Cell Anemia Control Act (1972); widespread national educational campaigns resulted often with misinformation and scare tactics. Comprehensive Sickle Cell Centers (CSCCs) were created in areas of the United States with concentrated numbers of persons with SCD. Since 2004 in the Maternal and Child Health Bureau, Health Resources and Service Administration has administered SCD programs for direct care and for newborn screening. CSCCs no longer exist with funding from the National Institutes of Health (NIH), but the NIH is part of a six federal partners collaborative in the Sickle Cell Disease Initiative, launched in 2011by the U.S. Department of Health and Human Services (NHLBI, 2011). The overarching goal is to improve the health of people with SCD.

## MORTALITY AND MORBIDITY

SCD is no longer a "disease of childhood" as was the case 50 years ago. Individuals now are able to survive well into the fourth and fifth decades and beyond depending on genotype. Age of death increased to 14 years for persons with SCD-SS by the early 1970s (Diggs, 1973) and 95 percent of individuals with SCD-SC survived to the age of 20 years on average. Platt et al. (1994) reported that the median age of death for individuals with

SCD-SS had increased to 42 years for males and 48 years for females, and 60 years and 68 years, respectively, for males and females with SCD-SC. Hassell (2010) used CDC (Centers for Disease Control and Prevention) mortality data in reporting estimated numbers of individuals with SCD in the United States—not specified by genotype or gender, however. The mean age of death was 39 years in 2006. Other statistics noted that 9 percent of SCD-related deaths occurred before the age of 20 years, 28 percent between the ages of 35 and 44 years, and 35 percent at ages greater than 45 years. Treatments such as preventive penicillin, hydroxyurea, and transfusion for stroke prevention have contributed to reduced mortality. The longer life span of persons with SCD has created a need for transition programs to move these individuals effectively from pediatric to adult care while maintaining optimal health (McPherson, Thaniel, & Minniti, 2009; Newland, 2008; Quinn, Rogers, McCavit, & Buchanan, 2010; Wojciechowski, Hurtig, & Dorn, 2002). But with the improved care for children with SCD, the highest risk group for early mortality is now young adults (Quinn et al., 2010).

## PREVALENCE AND INCIDENCE

SCD affects individuals of ancestries from Africa, South or Central America (especially Panama), Caribbean islands, Mediterranean countries (such as Turkey, Greece, and Italy), India, and Saudi Arabia. Reported numbers of people affected by SCD varies widely, but the National Heart Lung and Blood Institute (NHLBI) provides the following estimates for the United States (NHLBI, 2009):

- 70,000 to 100,000 have sickle cell anemia, mainly African Americans.
- 1 out of every 500 African American newborn has SCD.
- 1 out of every 36,000 Hispanic American newborn has SCD.
- 1 in 12 African Americans has sickle cell trait.
- More than 2 million Americans have sickle cell trait.

Hassell (2010) estimated national and state SCD populations based on the 2008 U.S. Census, using data from the National Newborn Screening Information System. Included was birth-cohort disease prevalence of African Americans and Hispanics. Mortality data from the CDC were included in the calculations. The estimated numbers were 104,000 to 138,900, which dropped to 72,000 to 98,100 when adjusted for early mortality associated with SCD. Hassell looked at only sickle cell types: HbSS (60%),

HbSC (30%), and HbSβthal (+ and 0). SCD does affect Caucasians but at a much lower rate. Several state health departments and sickle cell associations have estimated the incidence of SCD to be 1 in every 58,000 to 60,000 live births and the trait at 1 in every 400 to 600 live births (New Jersey Department of Health and Senior Services, 2005; Washington State Department of Health, n.d.) or about 1000 babies each year (SCDAI, 2012).

## DEFINITION AND ETIOLOGY

SCD is classified in the category of hemoglobinopathies or conditions of abnormal hemoglobin. It is characterized by the production of abnormal hemoglobin S, anemia, and acute and chronic tissue damage secondary to blockage in blood vessels by the abnormally shaped sickled cells. Formerly referred to as sickle cell anemia, the term "SCD" encompasses the wider spectrum of the phenotypic expression associated with SCD given the multiple possibilities for genetic combinations.

SCD is the most common hemoglobinopathy in individuals of African descent worldwide. The presence of malaria in Africa most likely contributed to the growth in the number of persons with sickle cell trait, which appeared to be protective against malaria. Individuals with the trait did not die as a result of infection by the *Anopheles* mosquito as those with SCD, who succumbed to the complications of malaria such as dehydration, vaso-occlusion, and hyperhemolysis (increased rupturing of RBCs). Therefore, individuals with sickle cell trait lived to reach reproductive age and pass on the abnormal gene to their children (Edelstein, 1986; Roberts & Williams, 2003).

## GENETICS

The gene is the basic unit of inheritance and is located on chromosomes, which are the structures in cells containing complex DNA codes (string of proteins). Each person has 46 chromosomes in every cell, receiving 23 from each parent. The predominant protein in RBCs is the hemoglobin molecule, consisting of four polypeptide chains—two alpha ($\alpha$) and two beta ($\beta$) chains. If genes are regulated normally, an individual has two normal $\beta$ genes and four normal $\alpha$ genes. Hemoglobin is responsible for transporting oxygen in RBCs to the organs and other structures in the body. During replication of the hemoglobin molecule in RBCs, the substitution of amino acid with glutamic acid on chromosome 11 at position 6 of the $\beta$-globulin chain results in SCD (Mankad, 1995).

An allele is one of the possible alternative forms of a gene. Multiple alleles may exist for one gene, but individuals carry only two alleles of a particular gene. Genotype refers to the specific allelic makeup of an individual for some characteristic. The composition of normal adult hemoglobin is more than 95 percent hemoglobin A, 1.5 to 3.5 percent hemoglobin A2, and no hemoglobin S, F, or C. The four most common genotypes for SCD in the United States have been classified by CDC, as reported by Platt, Rosenstock, and Espeland (1984, p. 8):

SCD-SS: S, F, A2 (<4 percent)—two hemoglobin S genes or homozygous (the same alleles)

SCD-SC: S, C—one each of hemoglobin S and C

SCD-S$\beta^+$: S, F, A, A2—one hemoglobin S and decreased production in $\beta$ chains

SCD-S$\beta^0$: S, F, A2 ($\geq$4 percent)—one hemoglobin S and no production in $\beta$ chains

The original designation was hemoglobin followed by SS or SC; the SCD prefix was later approved for addition to certain genotypes (Pass et al., 2000). There are many other types of SCD by genotype not discussed here. Thalassemia, the second most common hemoglobin disorder in the world, is characterized by reduced quantities but normal structure. Heterozygous disease, or sickle cell trait (SA), is not classified as a form of SCD and individuals generally exhibit no clinical signs or symptoms of disease; they have primarily normal hemoglobin A. Hereditary persistence of fetal hemoglobin (HPFH) also is not classified as SCD, but it does appear to provide some benefit in individuals with SCD.

The expression of the disease, or phenotype, of the person varies widely. Why this occurs is still a puzzle to scientists, and investigators are always seeking answers to why individuals with the same genotype do not have the same signs and symptoms of SCD, even within the same family.

## TRANSMISSION

SCD is transmitted as an autosomal recessive trait, meaning that a child must receive one abnormal hemoglobin gene from each parent to have SCD. Table 2.1 illustrates several possibilities based on the parents' genotypes. The chances of producing a child with a particular genotype are the same for each pregnancy (Table 2.1).

Table 2.1

Transmission of Sickle Cell Disease Depending on Parent Genotype

| | Mother SA trait | | | | Mother AA normal | |
|---|---|---|---|---|---|---|
| Father SA trait | S | A | | Father SA trait | A | A |
| S | SS | SA | | S | SA | SA |
| A | AS | AA | | A | AA | AA |
| 25% chance of having a child with SCD **with every pregnancy** | | | | 50% chance of having a child with sickle cell trait **with every pregnancy** | | |
| | Mother SS disease | | | | Mother AA normal | |
| Father SA trait | S | S | | Father SS disease | A | A |
| S | SS | SS | | S | SA | SA |
| A | AS | AS | | S | SA | SA |
| 50% chance of having a child with SCD **with every pregnancy** | | | | All pregnancies (100%) will result in a child with sickle cell trait | | |

## DIAGNOSIS

A blood test is needed to diagnose SCD. Early identification and intervention significantly improve morbidity and reduce mortality. The common methods of testing are hemoglobin electrophoresis, isoelectric focusing, high-performance liquid chromatography, and DNA analysis. These four tests analyze hemoglobin in RBCs and can distinguish between sickle cell trait, SCD, and no SCD; they are equally accurate. The method used will depend on local availability and cost. Tests that should not be used for diagnosis are solubility tests, such as Sickledex and sickling tests, which were used extensively in the early years. These two tests recognize only that hemoglobin S is present in the blood and not other genetic variants. Solubility tests are highly inaccurate in newborns who have a high concentration of hemoglobin F and in individuals with severe anemia. Other tests that should not be used in diagnosis are the blood count and blood smear (Children's Hospital of Philadelphia, 2006; Wethers, 2000a). Testing both parents of a child, if possible, can help with diagnosis. Other factors, such as family history and clinical symptoms, should be taken into account before a diagnosis is made. DNA analysis where the genes are studied remains the most definitive, but is costly.

### Newborn Screening

The latest report from the National Newborn Screening and Genetics Resource Center indicates that *all* 50 states and the District of Columbia screen *all* newborns for hemoglobin disorders—SS, SA, and SC and not just infants thought to be high risk because of ancestry (NNSGRC, 2012). Recommendation to include SCD as part of the panel of metabolic and genetic disorders in the already regulated mandatory state newborn screening programs was facilitated by a report from the U.S. Preventive Services Task Force (USPSTF, 2007). Only five years earlier, all states were not screening for SCD. Early identification, parental education, and initiation of prophylactic penicillin for infants had demonstrated reduced morbidity and mortality (Wong, Powars, & Overturf, 1995). The most popular technique continues to be capillary blood specimen from a heel stick set onto filter paper before the baby leaves the hospital. States are generally responsible for the testing so there is great variation in newborn screening services across the country (Therrell, Johnson, & Williams, 2006). Efforts are coordinated through the Sickle Cell Disease and Newborn Screening Program funded through the Health Resources and Services Administration's Maternal and Child Health Bureau. Each state has a notification system to parents when an infant has a positive result and a referral system to trained sickle cell providers. Initial positive results should be confirmed no later than two months after birth. Therrell, Johnson, and Williams (2006) identified issues in general with programs related to specimen storage practices, privacy of personal genetic information, educational programs about newborn screening for parents and health professionals, and resources for follow-up. Knowing the practices and policies in your state will help you navigate the health-care system with a child diagnosed with SCD.

### Pathophysiology

The normal RBC lives approximately 120 days. Figure 2.1 shows the difference between a normal disc-shaped cell and an abnormal sickle-shaped cell. Normal RBCs are soft and pliant and easily move through the lumen of blood vessels. Sickled cells on the other hand are irregularly shaped and often become sticky through a process of polymerization and clump together in the small blood vessels, creating blockages. This vaso-occlusion compromises blood flow by reducing the amount of oxygen being delivered. Pain is the symptom a person feels when a structure does not receive adequate oxygen.

Function is compromised and the resulting damage to tissues and organs can be temporary or permanent.

### Physical Manifestations and Complications

Physical manifestations and complications of SCD vary between affected persons and can be related to complications listed in Table 2.2 (Ballas et al., 2010; Bloom, 1995; Serjeant & Serjeant, 2001). Signs and symptoms might include mild to severe pain anywhere in the body but particularly in the limbs with swelling in the joints, headache, coldness in the hands and feet, paler than normal skin or mucous membranes, jaundice, dizziness, shortness of breath especially with activity, and lack of energy. With the advent of penicillin prophylaxis for children under the age of two years with SCD, infections no longer were the leading cause of death in young children (Wong, Powars, & Overturf, 1995). Complications that most commonly affect children with SCD are infection, acute splenic sequestration crisis, aplastic crisis, acute chest syndrome, stroke, gall bladder disease, renal complications, and pain (Wethers, 2000b). Some of these continue into adulthood and become chronic, such as pain (Smith et al., 2008), while others manifest in adulthood, such as leg ulcers.

Table 2.2
**Complications of Sickle Cell Disease**

| Body System/Organ | Complications |
| --- | --- |
| Musculoskeletal/Skin | Dactylitis or hand-foot syndrome in infancy |
| | Avascular necrosis (of hip) |
| | Osteomyelitis |
| | Osteopenia/osteoporosis |
| | Chronic leg ulcers |
| Pulmonary | Acute chest syndrome, resulting in chronic lung disease |
| | Pulmonary hypertension |
| Abdomen/ Gastrointestinal | Splenic sequestration or "bleeding into the spleen," leading to the removal of spleen |
| | Functional asplenia |
| | Gall stones, leading to removal of gall bladder |
| Blood | Chronic anemia, causing easy fatigability |

(*Continued*)

**Table 2.2  (Continued)**

| Body System/Organ | Complications |
| --- | --- |
| | Aplastic anemia, leading to fatal cessation of blood forming process |
| | Transfusions that place individuals at risk for blood-borne infectious diseases, such as HIV/AIDS and hepatitis B and C |
| Renal/ Genitourinary | Acute kidney failure |
| | Chronic kidney failure, leading to need for hemodialysis |
| | Priapism or painful penile erection, leading to impotence |
| | Urinary tract and kidney infections |
| Heart | Cardiomegaly or cardiomyopathy |
| | Congestive heart failure |
| | Hypertension |
| Neurologic | Cerebral vascular accident or stroke |
| | Mini-infarcts, causing cognitive deficits and learning disabilities |
| | Seizure |
| Eyes | Sickle cell retinopathy, leading to blindness |
| | Retinal detachment |
| | Glaucoma |
| Ears | Sensorineural hearing loss |
| Other | Vaso-occlusion, causing acute and chronic pain |
| | Fever in children |
| | Infections |
| | Delayed growth and development |
| | Transfusion and iron overload |

*Sources:* S. K. Ballas, S. Lieff, L. J. Benjamin, C. D. Dampier, M. M. Heeney, C. Hoppe, C. S. Johnson, Z. R. Rogers, K. Smith-Whitley, W. C. Wang, & M. J. Telen (2010), Definitions of the phenotypic manifestations of sickle cell disease, *American Journal of Hematology*, 85(1), 6–13.
M. Bloom (1995), *Understanding sickle cell disease*, Jackson, MS: University Press of Mississippi.
G. R. Serjeant, & B. E. Serjeant (2001), *Sickle cell disease* (3rd ed.), New York: Oxford University Press.

Although a majority of children experience developmental delays in skeletal growth, they do eventually achieve normal adult height, if not weight. A healthy diet is important for growth and development; children with SCD need 20 percent more calories per day to maintain weight and provide energy to produce enough RBCs (Platt & Sacerdote, 2002).

Some people still might believe that sickle cell trait can turn into SCD; this is genetically impossible. Unnecessary restrictions or special precautions are often imposed on individuals with the trait. Controversy surrounds the practice of mandatory screening of military recruits and athletes for sickle cell trait because of the potential stigma and discrimination associated with the discovery. Stress on the body during training related to heat exposure, dehydration, and intense physical activity may increase the risk of sudden death 10 to 30 times greater than in individuals without sickle cell trait (Bonham, Dover, & Brody, 2010). Harris, Haas, Eichner, & Maron (2012) in reviewing deaths of young athletes suggest that a subset of African American college football players may be at greater risk for a catastrophic event during early conditioning because of undefined and unpredictable genetic, physiological, or environmental factors.

The phenotypic expression of a SCD genotype is variable even within the same genotype. The unpredictability of living with SCD makes it difficult for affected individuals and their caregivers to look to any day with certainty. The physical manifestations are obvious, but the psychosocial implications of the disease may be more subtle and more challenging.

### Psychosocial Implications

Parents of children with SCD often feel guilty for passing a defective gene to their child; they have created a situation in which they may have limited control. The chronic illness of a child places additional stressors on the entire family—emotional, financial, and physical—and particularly the primary caregiver, who is often the mother. Although children with SCD are now able to live well into adulthood with expert medical care, the unpredictability of the disease creates uncertainty and helplessness for the parents. But the child must remain the central focus in order to foster normal personal and social development into adulthood. Erik Erikson's eight stages of man offer a framework from which to view the psychosocial development of the individual with SCD. The life stages are sequential but a person might move forward and then regress and then move forward again. Challenges are not mutually exclusive to the category in which they are listed. Table 2.3 summarizes the challenges during the stages of the life cycle, according to Erikson (1985). During the life span of a person with SCD, family support and support from other sources such as school, health professionals, community, and religious affiliates are very important.

### Legislation Related to SCD Treatment

Federal legislation has made it possible for researchers to study various areas of SCD and for health-care professionals to provide services in the management of SCD. The Sickle Cell Anemia Control Act of 1972 was followed almost 30 years later by the Sickle Cell Treatment Act of 2003. In 2008, the NHLBI reorganized its support and funding for the then 10 recognized CSCCs across the nation by creating instead many more SCD treatment centers It has developed guidelines for the management of SCD since 1984; the fourth edition was published in 2002. Currently, it is leading the development of new evidence-based guidelines through collaboration of individuals with SCD, community-based organizations that serve the sickle

**Table 2.3**
**Psychosocial Development of the Individual with Sickle Cell Disease**

| Erikson Stage | Age | Task | Challenges |
|---|---|---|---|
| I | Infant (birth to <2 years) | Basic trust versus basic mistrust | Parental feelings of guilt<br>Separation from family for frequent hospitalizations<br>Multiple caregivers inhibit attachment<br>Not having basic needs met (e.g., for food, shelter, and touch) |
| II | Toddler (>2–3 years) | Autonomy versus shame and doubt | Too restrictive an environment<br>Lack of control and structure in environment<br>Lack of positive reinforcement |
| III | Young child (4–5 years) | Initiative versus guilt | Imaginary thinking (e.g., they are to blame for illness as punishment)<br>Awareness of difference from other children of same age<br>Acting out behaviors, refusing to cooperate |
| IV | School-age child (6–11 years) | Industry versus inferiority | Absences from school, so does not make and keep friends easily<br>Academic/cognitive difficulties<br>Decreased energy levels secondary to anemia, leading to low self-esteem<br>Overprotective parenting |

*(Continued)*

**Table 2.3 (Continued)**

| V | Adolescent (12–18 years) | Identity versus role confusion | Delayed puberty<br>Poor body image<br>Low self-esteem<br>Need for peer acceptance<br>Drive for independence versus dependence<br>Ambivalence over sexual identity<br>Anxiety and fear of death<br>Feelings of stigma |
|---|---|---|---|
| VI | Young adult (19–25 years) | Intimacy versus isolation | Finding a mate and developing relationships<br>Making decisions about having children<br>Concerns over starting a career or leaving home for school or work<br>Depression over chronic nature of SCD<br>Feelings of stigma |
| VII | Adult (26–40 years) | Generativity versus stagnation | Anxiety and depression related to ability or inability to work consistently<br>Family pressures for productivity<br>Looking to the future<br>Multiple chronic complications of SCD |
| VIII | Adults over 40 years | Ego integrity versus despair | Planning for future generations of family<br>Satisfaction with one's life and achievements<br>Sustained close relationships |

*Sources:* S. Day, & E. Chismark (2006), The cognitive and academic impact of sickle cell disease, *The Journal of School Nursing, 22*(6): 330–335.

E. H. Erikson (1985), *Childhood and society*, New York: W. W. Norton & Company, Inc.

A. F. Platt, & A. Sacerdote (2002), *Hope and destiny: The patient's and parent's guide to sickle cell disease and sickle cell trait*, Roscoe, IL: Hilton Publishing Company.

M. J. Treadwell, & K. M. Gil (1994), Psychosocial aspects, in S. H. Embury, R. P. Hebble, N. Mohandas, & M. H. Steinberg (Eds.), *Sickle Cell Disease: Basic Principles and Clinical Practice* (pp. 517–529), New York: Raven Press.

cell population, and representatives from the health-care community. These guidelines, when released in, will be aimed at patients and their primary-care practitioners primarily, but also useful to hematologists worldwide. Six agencies of the U.S. Department of Health and Human Services through the Office of Minority Health were also charged in 2011 by Secretary Sebelius to improve the health of people with SCD by improving health monitoring, evidence-based guidelines for care, access, dissemination of information, re-search efforts, and national and community advocacy (NHLBI, 2011, 2012; SCDAA 2012).

It is important that all persons with SCD have health insurance; costs associated with managing SCD over a lifetime are high. Social security and state- and federally sponsored programs are available for anyone with-out private coverage. Individuals and families have to make the effort to be informed of resources available to them from local, state, and national agencies.

## THERAPY FOR SCD

### Medical

Medical management of SCD is targeted in three main areas: diagnosis and counseling, health maintenance, and treatment of acute and chronic complications. A child is usually diagnosed at birth, but it is possible for an individual to grow to adulthood before learning that they have sickle cell trait or even one of the milder forms of SCD with no obvious phe-notypic expressions. Any adult with physical manifestations suggestive of SCD should be evaluated for disease. The most appropriate health profes-sionals to care for a person with SCD have special training in diseases of the blood and work on interprofessional teams that include hematologists, family physicians (pediatricians or internists), nurses, nurse practitioners and physician assistants, genetic counselors, nutritionists, social workers, and the religious. Medical specialists are consulted for special problems related to complications of the disease (NHLBI, 2002; Platt & Sacerdote, 2002). Care is optimized when provided in a facility with staff that are familiar with SCD or that has a referral network for needed access. All persons with SCD will have frequent contact with the health-care system through regularly scheduled appointments with someone on the team. Standard care includes frequent visits for physical examination, which might be as often as every two to three months; routine laboratory tests to assess anemia status; and other special studies to detect early damage to organs or systems so interventions can be initiated to prevent further progression. These tests might include X-rays, ultrasounds, computed tomography or magnetic resonance imaging, bone scans, transcranial doppler, pulmonary function tests, and eye and hearing tests.

All children receive daily prophylactic penicillin from as early as two months of age through five years. This practice has reduced mortality by controlling the incidence of bacterial infections. Folic acid supplementation may be given daily throughout childhood to stimulate RBC production.

Frequent tests or treatments might necessitate the placement of a more permanent intravenous access device. Transfusion therapy is used to treat severe anemia, (or prevent) a stroke, acute chest syndrome, splenic sequestration, and priapsim. There are risks to consider related to chronic transfusion—fluid overload, iron overload, sensitization, and infection. Surgery is often needed to resolve a complication of SCD, such as removal of the gall bladder or spleen. Complications are addressed if and when they appear through consultation with and referral to the appropriate member of the interprofessional team. Pain is the most common manifestation of SCD in adults, and the sequelae of end-organ damage—such as the need for hemodialysis secondary to kidney failure—present challenges for patient, family, and provider.

Persons with SCD should be fully immunized with all recommended vaccines, including an annual influenza vaccine and the pneumococcal vaccine as per schedule. Fever management and assessment for serious infections are primary in infants and young children (NHLBI, 2002). In adolescents, issues related to transition and transfer to adult care must be addressed by the patient and health-care provider (McPherson, Thaniel, & Minniti, 2009; Newland, 2008). In the adult, management focuses on the multiple chronic manifestations of SCD.

### Medications

All persons with SCD should understand the causes of pain, pain prevention, self-management at home, emergency treatment, and inpatient treatment in a hospital. The individual learns what best controls his or her pain over time. Parents must be taught to recognize the signs and symptoms of pain in an infant or young child, such as fussiness and crying, refusal to move, swelling in joints, and fever. Parents or patients must learn to distinguish between acute sickle cell pain caused by blocked blood flow, acute pain from another cause (e.g., menstrual cramps), chronic pain from sickle cell bone damage, chronic pain from other causes (e.g., slipped disk), and chronic nerve pain from damage to nerves (e.g., SCD or diabetes). Their assessment of pain according to location, associated symptoms, character, aggravating and alleviating things, timing, environment and effect, and severity will decide the most effective treatment (Platt & Sacerdote, 2002). Over-the-counter medications (acetominophen and ibuprofen) should be tried first when pain starts; narcotic analgesics (morphine and codeine) are needed for more severe pain. Other classes of medications can be added for better pain control if needed.

Hydroxurea is a medication given to persons with SCD to stimulate the production of hemoglobin F or fetal hemoglobin. Everyone is born with a percentage of hemoglobin F making up all hemoglobin, but almost all F is replaced by the increased production of hemoglobin A by the age of four to six months. Hemoglobin F is beneficial in persons with SCD, because it helps prevent RBCs from sickling and improves anemia. Individuals with persistent high concentrations of hemoglobin F have less pain, require fewer transfusions, and have fewer hospital visits related to their SCD (NHLBI, 2002; NIH, 2011). Hydroxyurea can reduce the number of white blood cells in the body, predisposing the individual to infection; therefore, persons taking hydroxyurea must be monitored closely for this and other side effects of the medication. It is safe even in very young children (Wang et al., 2011).

Assessment and management of pain is predominant in adults (Smith et al., 2008). The study found that a major problem in treating pain was that the definition of and severity of pain was different between patients with SCD and health-care providers. But consistently, patients who reported more frequent pain experienced more intense pain and used more opiates; adequate pain relief should not be withheld for episodes of acute pain or for home management pain regimens.

### Nonmedical

Complementary and alternative medicine (CAM) therapies are used by persons with SCD to control distressing signs and symptoms of the disease and particularly pain. The emotional response to pain is very powerful. Techniques such as massage, therapeutic touch, imagery, relaxation, Asian practices, and journaling have been helpful in reducing severity of pain and duration of pain episode (Tanabe et al., 2010). Sibinga, Shindell, Casella, Duggan, & Wilson (2006) found that families of children with SCD also used prayer, spiritual and energy healing, exercise and diet, herbal medicines, megavitamins, and other fold remedies. CAM can be helpful when integrated with traditional Western medicine.

### Cure

Only one treatment has resulted in a cure for SCD—bone marrow transplantation. A very small number of patients have been able to benefit from this new therapy, because it is not widely accessible, expensive, has very restrictive criteria for qualifying as a candidate, and comes with significant risks. A close match, usually a healthy genetically compatible sibling without SCD, is necessary. The bone marrow of the person with SCD is replaced with healthy blood and stem cells from the donor in the hopes that all the new cells produced are likewise free of the sickle gene. Research is ongoing to develop ways to make this procedure safer and more widely available.

### Prevention

As a general rule, throughout the life span and depending on age, Platt and Sacerdote (2002, p. 45) suggest following different aspects of an acronym for prevention of problems with SCD—FARMS:

F—Fluids and fever
A—Air
R—Rest
M—Medication
S—Situations

Adequate hydration can delay the sickling process. Drink plenty of water and manage fever. By breathing as clear air as possible, more oxygen enters the lungs and RBCs, which means more circulating hemoglobin to nourish body organs. Avoid high altitudes and smoking, including inhaling second-hand smoke. Get plenty of sleep, do not overdo physical activity, and take breaks whenever needed. Exercising too strenuously can trigger vaso-occlusive episodes and compromise circulation and tissue health. Prophylactic medications have significantly reduced morbidity and decreased mortality from SCD. Take daily penicillin for children under six, vitamin folate to make new RBC, and hydrea for pain prevention in older children and adults. Avoid temperature extremes, alcohol, and illegal drugs. Living with SCD does not have to include a world of restrictions; being informed and following recommendations for self management can make it possible for the person with SCD to enjoy common activities such as sports participation and air travel.

Eating a healthy diet consisting of a variety of foods that contain essential nutrients and adequate calories is very important for individuals with SCD. Mothers should be encouraged to breastfeed infants or give iron-fortified formula. Once graduated from infant feeding, the diet should include lean meats, poultry, fish, beans, and fat-free or low-fat milk and be low in saturated fat, *trans* fat, cholesterol, salt, and added sugar. Traditional folk ways promoted the consumption of African yams, omega fatty acids, magnesium, zinc, antioxidants, and certain herbs (Ujamaa, 1995); researchers now study these ideas. Learning healthy eating habits early helps a child grow well and avoid illness. Healthy eating can also decrease the risks for heart disease, cancer, stroke, and diabetes in later years.

## Education

Education about SCD is an ongoing component of management no matter what the age of the affected individual. The education must occur over time with frequent reinforcement. Initially, the parent(s) will receive the information, but gradually a shift is made to giving information directly to the child as he or she grows and is able to understand. Parents need to instructed about the type of SCD, manifestations and complications, how to perform physical assessment of child (particularly feeling the spleen for enlargement), measures to prevent vaso-occlusive episodes, how to administer medications appropriately, meaning of test results, and advocacy to navigate the health-care system and utilize community and other resources.

Educational materials were not always available or used by providers, culturally sensitive, or at the appropriate reading level for the caregiver (Hill, 1994). In evaluating a written educational guide on SCD for children with SCD and their families, Mahat, Scoloveno, and Donnelly (2007) reported that the confidence of the caregivers in the study was positively correlated with the caregivers' perception that the information in the guide was helpful and easy to understand.

## Psychosocial Support

Families who have a member affected with SCD need special and continuous emotional support from the health-care team and the larger community. A child with SCD places much stress on the family system from birth—testing physical, emotional, and financial strength. Facilities that care for patients with SCD may have on staff a social worker, psychologist or psychiatrist, a religion associate, and others who are there mainly to help families with these challenges. Families need professionals they can trust and talk to whenever they are worried or upset, or happy. In the typical family, the mother is the primary caregiver for a child with special needs; she has the most responsibility to make sure the child receives the appropriate care through the health-care system and at home. The child, however, must be nurtured to have a positive attitude and be as independent as possible. Many organizations offer summer camps and other enrichment experiences for children with SCD.

Support groups for the individual and the family are also helpful to let them know their feelings are normal and they are not alone. Being involved in advocacy for SCD is therapeutic for the individual and family. There is power in having a voice (sicklecellwarriors.com).

Assessing quality of life for these individuals is important. Issues related to work or lack of work, feelings of social isolation, disruptions in relationships, and social activities can be addressed through support mechanisms (Mann-Jiles & Morris, 2009). SCD should not control the person or their world; the individual and family must learn ways to cope with the reality and the uncertainty of living with SCD.

## WOMEN WITH SCD

### General Health

The female with SCD usually exhibits delayed growth and development characteristic of children with SCD. During adolescence, issues about body image and self-esteem may surface. Girls may feel different from everyone else, because puberty and sexual maturation and the onset of menarche occur later than in nonaffected girls: at 13.9 years compared to 12.2 years in normal Black controls in Washington, D.C. and at 16.1 years compared to 13.1 years in normal Jamaican controls (Serjeant & Serjeant, 2001). But females often have normal fertility potential by age 20 years (Rodgers, 1997; Serjeant & Serjeant, 2001). Menstruation for the woman with SCD may bring about increased fatigue related to the state of chronic anemia and the average loss of 30 to 60 mL of blood every month during reproductive years. Other concerns may be dysmenorrheal or pain with menstrual bleeding (not to be confused with the pain from a vaso-occlusive episode) irregular cycles, and heavy bleeding. Generally, women should follow the acronym FARMS to prevent complications of SCD, keep regular appointments for medical evaluation and laboratory or other tests, keep all immunizations current, eat a healthy and balanced diet, be physically active, and find ways to relieve stress. Any common complication of SCD will be treated as per the standard management recommendations.

### Reproductive Concerns

#### Contraception

There are no absolute contraindications to the use of contraception in women with SCD; they can safely use barrier methods, oral contraceptives, and contraceptive injections. Insertion of an intrauterine device (IUD), however, should be avoided (although not contraindicated) because of the increased risks of uterine bleeding and infection (NHLBI, 2002). Many women experience chronic pelvic pain after IUD placement and malpositioning over time (Benacerraf, Shipp, & Bromley, 2009; Cicchiello, Hamper, & Scoutt, 2011). SCD does not involve blood-clotting abnormalities, but women should have a thorough personal and family history to identify any risk factors for a thromboembolic event, such as family history of clot formation, smoking, hypertension, and obesity. Sterilization is also an option for contraception. The benefits of contraception outweigh the risks associated with pregnancy. Contraception does not protect against sexually transmitted infections, so women should be counseling on avoiding infection.

### Conception

Preconception planning is very important for the women with SCD, to be as healthy and prepared as possible at the time of conception. The woman should receive information about SCD, genetic transmission, prenatal diagnosis, and risks associated with pregnancy. Some women may be advised to take extra folic acid during the preconception time. She should know her options before becoming pregnant. Genetic testing of the (future) father of the child provides information that will inform decisions about preimplantation genetic diagnosis (expensive and not readily available) and in utero prenatal diagnosis (more common). Hydroxyurea has demonstrated teratogenicity in animal models and thus assumed to be dangerous to the human fetus. Three to six months before she is planning a pregnancy, she must discontinue hydroxyurea, and if the intended father has SCD, he too must stop the hydroxyurea (Halsey & Roberts, 2003; NHLBI, 2002).

### Genetic Counseling

The purpose of genetic counseling is to learn information that will help guide a woman in making decisions about a planned or actual pregnancy. Genetic counselors are specially trained professionals who are able to assess the risks of two people producing a child with an inherited disorder based on their genetic makeup or genotype. Testing of the sexual partner is necessary for a complete assessment. Every woman should know her sickle cell status. If she has sickle cell trait or SCD, it is important to have the partner tested. Once informed, the woman (and partner) can choose from several options: to avoid pregnancy completely, request preimplantation genetic diagnosis, to have the baby only after prenatal testing of the fetus reveals a healthy baby, or to terminate a pregnancy if the fetus is affected with the condition. Probabilities of transmitting SCD or sickle cell trait to a child are presented in Table 2.1.

Other factors that must be considered are a woman's religious, ethical, and moral beliefs and cultural background in introducing the topic of genetic counseling and providing information. Two studies published 16 years apart (Gustafson, Gettig, Watt-Morse, & Krishnamurti, 2007 and Rowley, Loader, Sutera, Walden, & Kozyra, 1991) looked at the health beliefs of women regarding genetic testing and counseling for SCD. The samples included African American women. Both research groups used the health belief model as a framework, which looks at beliefs or perceptions of risk and benefit—knowledge of condition (SCD), perceived risk to self and severity, likelihood of benefit, and barriers. Using surveys, both studies found similar results. In Gustafson et al. (2007), African American women had a relatively high belief of the severity of SCD and benefits of genetic counseling but did not believe they were at risk of having a child with the SCD. Rowley et al. (1991) found that the predictors for a patient's intent to have a partner tested among the Black participants of sickle trait carrier status were postcounseling knowledge of disease, lesser perceived burden of intervention, and belief that partner was also a carrier. More effective strategies for conducting counseling and education are needed.

### Pregnancy

Women generally are more symptomatic with blood disorders than men, because they have physiologic and pathologic changes in blood that affect hemostasis during menstruation, pregnancy, and childbirth. During a normal pregnancy, blood volume increases by 50 percent and red cell mass by 25 percent. These mechanisms are meant to provide more oxygen circulating through the system and reaching the fetus (Ebrahim, Kulkarni, Parker, & Atrash, 2009). This results in a net decrease in hemoglobin concentration. Women with SCD already have low counts, so adequate iron is needed to support the red cell mass and placental and fetal growth. These women should be monitored collaboratively during pregnancy by primary care, hematology, and a high-risk obstetrician. Delivery should be in a hospital equipped to deal with high-risk mothers and babies.

During pregnancy, women with SCD may have to take supplemental folic acid. They are also at higher risk of delivering babies that are small in weight for term, so good nutrition during pregnancy is important. Women with sickle cell trait, although not considered high risk, may be advised to take folic acid. Complications during pregnancy among women with SCD include tissue hypoxia leading to acute pain episodes, severe anemia, infections, hypertension and preeclampsia, preterm loss by spontaneous abortion or stillbirth, and maternal mortality. Prenatal care follows standard care except for added vigilance for complications of SCD. More frequent visits to a health-care provider might be warranted. Many women experience more frequent urinary tract infections and episodes of acute chest syndrome.

Most women are able to deliver vaginally. They must be observed closely for postpartum fever, indicative of possible endometritis or wound infection. With proper care before and during pregnancy, women with SCD can have a normal pregnancy and deliver a healthy baby.

## FUTURE RESEARCH IN SCD

Researchers continue to investigate new and promising therapies in the search for a cure that would benefit a majority of individuals with SCD. If gene therapy can ever be applied with SCD, a normal gene would be placed in the bone marrow of a person with SCD and thus cause the body to make normal RBCs. An alternative would be to discover whether they can turn off the sickle cell gene or turn on a gene that makes normal RBCs. Scientists are also working on developing other medications that would increase the production of hemoglobin F, new medications to treat iron overload associated with blood transfusions, and new treatments for pain. Investigators are also seeking to learn more about complications of sickle cell trait (NIH, 2011).

Individuals with SCD are often burdened with requests to participate in numerous research studies simultaneously or consecutively. Many cooperate in hopes that a cure will be found to benefit them directly; this is rarely the case in research. It takes years of investigation and then clinical trials before new medications or therapies become available to the general affected population. Memories of Tuskegee syphilis experiments and the abuse of African American participants as a consequence still might provoke mistrust of researchers and their intentions. Individuals with SCD and families should be encouraged to continue to participate in studies to remain informed about the direction of health care for SCD and to hopefully be a part of finding a cure for everyone.

## REFERENCES

Ballas, S. K., Lieff, S., Benjamin, L. J., Dampier, C. D., Heeney, M. M., Hoppe, C., Johnson, C. S., Rogers, Z. R., Smith-Whitley, K., Wang, W. C., & Telen, M. J. (2010). Definitions of the phenotypic manifestations of sickle cell disease. *American Journal of Hematology, 85*(1), 6–13.

Bediako, S. M., Lavender, A. R., & Yasin, Z. (2007). Racial centrality and health care use among African American adults with sickle cell disease. *Journal of Black Psychology, 33*(4), 422–438.

Benacerraf, B. R., Shipp, T. D., & Bromley, B. (2009). Three-dimensional ultrasound detection of abnormally located intrauterine contraceptive devices which are a source of pelvic pain and abnormal bleeding. *Ultrasound in Obstetrics and Gynecology, 34*(1), 110–115.

Bloom, M. (1995). *Understanding sickle cell disease.* Jackson, MS: University Press of Mississippi.

Bonham, V. L., Dover, G. J., Brody, L. C. (2010). Screening student athletes for sickle cell trait: A social and clinical experiment. *New England Journal of Medicine, 363*(11), 997–999.

Children's Hospital of Philadelphia. (2006). *Sickle cell center: What tests are used to diagnose sickle cell disease?* Retrieved from http://www.chop.edu/service/hema tology/our-programs/sickle-cell-center/diagnosing-and-treating-sickle-cell-disease.html#what_tests

Cicchiello, L. A., Hamper, U. M., & Scoutt, L. M. (2011). Ultrasound evaluation of gynecologic causes of pelvic pain. *Obstetrics and Gynecology Clinics of North America, 38*(1), 85–114.

Day, S., & Chismark, E. (2006). The cognitive and academic impact of sickle cell disease. *The Journal of School Nursing, 22*(6), 330–335.

Diggs, L. W. (1973). Anatomic lesions in sickle cell disease. In H. Abramson, J. F. Bertles, & D. L. Wethers (Eds.), *Sickle cell disease: diagnosis, management, education, and research* (pp. 189–229). St. Louis, MO: C. V. Mosby.

Ebrahim, S. H., Kulkarni, R., Parker, C., & Atrash, H. K. (2010). Blood disorders among women: Implications for preconception care. *American Journal of Preventive Medicine, 38*(4), S459–S467.

Edelstein, S. J. (1986). *The sickled cell: From myths to molecules.* Cambridge, MA: Harvard University Press.

Erikson, E. H. (1985). *Childhood and society.* New York: W. W. Norton & Company, Inc.

Gustafson, S. L., Gettig, E. A., Watt-Morse, M., & Krishnamurti, L. (2007). Health beliefs among African American women regarding genetic testing and counseling for sickle cell disease. *Genetics in Medicine, 9*(5), 303–310.

Halsey, C., & Roberts, I. A. G. (2003). The role of hydroxyurea in sickle cell disease. *British Journal of Haematology, 120*(2), 177–186.

Harris, K. M., Haas, T. S., Eichner, E. R., & Maron, B. J. (2012). Sickle cell trait associated with sudden death in competitive athletes. *The American Journal of Cardiology, 110*(8), 1185–1188.

Hassell, K. L. (2010). Population estimates of sickle cell disease in the U.S. *American Journal of Preventive Medicine, 38*(4), S512–S521.

Herrick, J. B. (1910). Peculiar elongated and sickle-shaped red blood corpuscles in a case of severe anemia. *Archives of Internal Medicine, 6*(5), 517–521.

Hill, S. A. (1994). *Managing sickle cell disease in low-income families.* Philadelphia, PA: Temple University Press.

Hudson, K. L., Holohan, M. K., & Collins, F. S. (2008). Keeping pace with the times: The Genetic Information Nondiscrimination Act of 2008." *New England Journal of Medicine, 358*(25): 2661–2663.

Lebby, R. (1846). Case of absence of the spleen. *Southern Journal of Medicine and Pharmacy, 1*, 481–483.

Lessin, L. S., & Jensen, W. N. (1974). Sickle cell anemia 1910–1973: An overview. *Archives of Internal Medicine, 133*(4), 529–532.

Mahat, G., Scoloveno, M. A., & Donnelly, C. B. (2007). Written educational materials for families of chronically ill children. *Journal of the American Academy of Nurse Practitioners, 19*(9): 471–476.

Mankad, V. N. (1995). Sickle cell disease and other disorders of abnormal hemoglobin. In D. R. Miller, R. L. Baehner, & C. H. Smith (Eds.), *Blood Diseases of Infancy and Childhood: In the Tradition of Carl H. Smith* (pp. 415–459). St. Louis, MO: C. V. Mosby.

Mann-Jiles, V., & Morris, D. L. (2009). Quality of life of adult patients with sickle cell disease. *Journal of the American Academy of Nurse Practitioners, 21*(6), 340–349.

McPherson, M., Thaniel, L., & Minniti, C. P. (2009). Transition of patients with sickle cell disease from pediatric to adult care: Assessing patient readiness. *Pediatric Blood & Cancer, 52*(7), 838–841.

Merriam-Webster. (2012). *Sickle.* Retrieved from http://www.merriam-webster.com/dictionary/sickle

New Jersey Department of Health and Senior Services. (2005). *Newborn screening and genetic services: Sickle cell disorders.* Retrieved from www.state.nj.us/health/fhs/nbs/documents/hemo_prof.pdf

Newland, J. A. (2008). Factors influencing independence in adolescents with sickle cell disease. *Journal of Child and Adolescent Psychiatric Nursing, 21*(3), 177–185.

Newland, J. A., & Dobson, C. (2006). Understanding sickle cell disease in African American women. In C. F. Collins (Ed.), *African American women's health and social issues* (2nd ed., pp. 46–64). Westport, CT: Praeger.

NHLBI. (2002). *The management of sickle cell disease* (4th ed.). NIH Publication No. 02-2117. Bethesda, MD: U.S. Department of Health and Human Services.

NHLBI. (2009). *Health topics: Sickle cell anemia.* Bethesda, MD: U.S. Department of Health and Human Services. Retrieved from http://www.nhlbi.nih.gov/health/health-topics/topics/sca/

NHLBI. (2011). *HHS announces sickle cell disease initiative.* Bethesda, MD: U.S. Department of Health and Human Services. Retrieved from http://www.nhlbi.nih.gov/about/directorscorner/previousdirectors/shurin/2011-messages/hhs-announces-sickle-cell-disease-initiative/index.html

NHLBI. (2012). *Sickle cell disease guidelines.* Bethesda, MD: U.S. Department of Health and Human Services. Retrieved from http://www.nhlbi.nih.gov/guidelines/scd/index.htm

NIH. (2011). Sickle cell disease: Symptoms, diagnosis, treatment and recent developments. *NIH Medline Plus, 5*(4), 18. Retrieved from http://www.nlm.nih.gov/medlineplus/magazine/issues/winter11/articles/winter11pg18.html

NNSGRC. (2012). *National newborn screening status report—updated 07/30/2012.* San Antonio, TX: University of Texas Health Science Center. Retrieved from http://genes-r-us.uthscsa.edu/sites/genes-r-us/files/nbsdisorders.pdf

Norman, B. J., & Miller, S. D. (2011). Human genome project and sickle cell disease. *Social Work in Public Health, 26*(4), 405–416.

Pass, K. A., Lane, P. A., Fernhoff, P. M., Hinton, C. F., Panny, S. R., Parks, J. S., Pelias, M. Z., Rhead, W. J., Ross, S. I., Wethers, D. L., & Elsas II, L. J. (2000). U.S. newborn screening system guidelines II: Follow-up of children, diagnosis, management, and evaluation. Statement of the Council of Regional Networks for Genetic Services (CORN). *Journal of Pediatrics, 137*(4), S1–S46.

Pauling, L., Itano, H. A., Singer, S. J., & Wells, I. C. (1949). Sickle cell anemia, a molecular disease. *Science, 110*(2865), 543–548.

Platt, A. F., & Sacerdote, A. (2002). *Hope and destiny: The patient's and parent's guide to sickle cell disease and sickle cell trait.* Roscoe, IL: Hilton Publishing Company.

Platt, O. S., Rosenstock, W., & Espeland, M. A. (1984). Influence of sickle hemoglobinopathies on growth and development. *The New England Journal of Medicine, 311*(1), 7–12.

Platt, O. S., Brambilla, D. J., Rosse, W. F., Milner, P. F., Castro, O., Steinberg, M. H., & Klug, P. P. (1994). Mortality in sickle cell disease: life expectancy and risk factors for early death. *The New England Journal of Medicine, 330*(23), 1639–1644.

Quinn, C. T., Rogers, Z. R., McCavit, T. L., & Buchanan, G. R. (2010). Improved survival of children and adolescents with sickle cell disease. *Blood, 115*(17), 3447–3452.

Roberts, D. J., & Williams, T. N. (2003). Haemoglobinopathies and resistance to malaria. *Redox Report, 8*(5), 304–310.

Rodgers, G. P. (1997). Overview of pathophysiology and rationale for treatment of sickle cell anemia. *Seminars in Hematology, 34*(Suppl. 3), 2–7.

Rowley, P. T., Loader, S., Sutera, C. J., Walden, M., & Kozyra, A. (1991). Prenatal screening for hemoglobinopathies. III. Applicability of the health belief model. *American Journal of Human Genetics, 48*(3), 452–459.

SCDAA. (2012). *Legislative issues.* Baltimore, MD: Sickle Cell Disease Association of America, Inc. Retrieved from http://www.sicklecelldisease.org/index. cfm?page=legislative-initiatives

SCDAI. (2012). *Understanding sickle cell: Frequent ask questions.* Chicago, IL: Sickle Cell Disease Association of Illinois. Retrieved from http://sicklecelldisea se-illinois.org/understanding-sickle-cell/frequent-ask-questions/

Serjeant, G. R., & Serjeant, B. E. (2001). *Sickle cell disease* (3rd ed.). New York: Oxford University Press.

Sibinga, E. M., Shindell, D. L., Casella, J. F., Duggan, A. K., & Wilson, M. H. (2006). Pediatric patients with sickle cell disease: use of complementary and alternative therapies. *Journal of Alternative and Complementary Medicine, 12*(3), 291–298.

Smith, W. R., Penberthy, L. T., Bovbjerg, V. E., McClish, D. K., Roberts, J. D., Dahman, B., Aisiku, I. P., Levenson, J. L., Roseff, S. D. (2008). Daily assessment of pain in adults with sickle cell disease. *Annals of Internal Medicine, 148*(2), 94–102.

Tanabe, P., Porter, J., Creary, M., Kirkwood, E., Miller, S., Ahmed-Williams, E., & Hassell, K. (2010). A qualitative analysis of best self-management practices: sickle cell disease. *Journal of the National Medical Association, 102*(11), 1033–1041.

Therrell, B. L., Johnson, A., & Williams, D. (2006). Status of newborn screening programs in the United States. *Pediatrics, 117*(5 Pt 2), S212–S252.

Treadwell, M. J., & Gil, K. M. (1994). Psychosocial aspects. In S. H. Embury, R. P. Hebble, N. Mohandas, & M. H. Steinberg (Eds.), *Sickle cell disease: Basic principles and clinical practice* (pp. 517–529). New York: Raven Press.

Ujamaa, D. (1995). *Back to our roots: Cooking for control of sickle cell anemia and cancer prevention.* Atlanta, GA: Al Mai Dah Publishers.

USPSTF. (2007). *Screening for sickle cell disease in newborns: U.S. preventive services task force recommendation statement.* Rockville, MD: Agency for Healthcare Research and Quality.

Wailoo, K. (1991). "A Disease *Sui Generi*": The origins of sickle cell anemia and the emergence of modern clinical research, 1904–1924." *Bulletin of the History of Medicine, 65*(2), 185–204.

Wailoo, K. (1997). *Drawing blood: Technology and disease identity in twentieth century America.* Baltimore, MD: Johns Hopkins University Press.

Wailoo, K., & Pemberton, S. G. (2006). *The troubled dream of genetic medicine: Ethnicity and innovation in Tay-Sachs, cystic fibrosis, and sickle cell disease.* Baltimore, MD: Johns Hopkins University Press.

Wang, W. C., Ware, R., Miller, S. T., et al. (2011). Hydroxycarbamide in very young children with sickle-cell anaemia: A multicentre, randomized, controlled trial (BABY HUG). *Lancet, 377*(9778), 1663–1672.

Washington State Department of Health. (n.d.). *Genetic services policy project: Sickle cell disease.* Retrieved from depts.washington.edu/genpol/docs/SCD1pg.pdf

Wethers, D. L. (2000a). Sickle cell disease in childhood: Part I. Laboratory diagnosis, pathophysiology and health maintenance. *American Family Physician, 62*(5), 1013–1020.

Wethers, D. L. (2000b). Sickle cell disease in childhood: Part II. Diagnosis and treatment of major complications and recent advances in treatment. *American Family Physician, 62*(6), 1309–1314.

Wojciechowski, E. A., Hurtig, A., Dorn, L. 2002. A natural history study of adolescents and young adults with sickle cell disease as they transfer to adult care: A need for case management services. *Journal of Pediatric Nursing, 17*(1), 18–27.

Wong, W.-Y., Powars, D. R., & Overturf, G. D. (1995). Infections in children with sickle cell anemia. *Infectious Medicine, 12*(7), 331–338.

**3**

---

# Promoting Cervical Cancer Prevention among African American Women

## *Denise M. Linton*

### CERVICAL CANCER

Cervical cancer is preventable but it remains a problem in the United States, especially among African Americans. The American Cancer Society (ACS, 2011a) estimated that approximately 12,710 women in the United States would be diagnosed with cervical cancer and approximately 4,290 would die from the disease in 2011. It was estimated that approximately 2,170 African Americans in the United States would be diagnosed with invasive cervical cancer and another 860 women would die from cervical cancer in 2011 (ACS, 2011b). Cervical cancer incidence and mortality rates for the period 2003–2007 were higher among African Americans than their Caucasian counterparts (ACS, 2011b). And, Table 3.1 demonstrates that between 2004 and 2008, African American women had the second highest cervical cancer incidence rates but the highest mortality rates compared to women of other minority groups (ACS, 2012). African Americans remain almost twice as likely to die from cervical cancer as Caucasians (ACS, 2011b).

Cervical cancer tends to occur more commonly among women who are not screened regularly; approximately 80 percent of cervical cancer in the United States occurs in women who are not screened regularly with the Pap test or who have never had a Pap test (ACS, 2004). Cervical cancer is more common in women who are 50 years of age and is slightly less commonly diagnosed at an early age among African Americans compared to Caucasians—42 percent compared to 49 percent (ACS, 2012).

More than 90 percent of all cases of cervical cancer are caused by the human papillomavirus (HPV), which is primarily transmitted through

Table 3.1

Cervical Cancer Incidence and Mortality Rates per 100,000 by Race in the United States, 2004–2008

| Race | Incidence | Mortality |
| --- | --- | --- |
| African American | 10.6 | 4.3 |
| American Indian or Alaska Native | 9.8 | 3.4 |
| Asian American or Pacific Islander | 7.4 | 2.1 |
| Hispanic/Latino | 12.2 | 3.1 |
| White | 7.7 | 2.2 |

*Source:* Adapted from ACS (2012), *Cancer fact and figures 2012*, Atlanta, GA: ACS. Retrieved from http://www.cancer.org/acs/groups/content/@epidemiologysurveilance/documents/document/acspc-031941.pdf

sexual activity. The HPV attacks cells in the cervical area and over a period of more than 10 years, these cells develop into cervical cancer if the abnormality is not detected and treated. Other risk factors for cervical cancer include early age of first sexual activity, multiple sex partners, multiparity, smoking, history of sexually transmitted infections (STIs), and long-term oral contraception use (ACS, 2011a). Therefore, African Americans can reduce their risk for cervical cancer by delaying the age of their first sexual encounter, limiting the number of sex partners, quitting smoking, practicing safe sex in order to prevent STIs (chlamydia, gonorrhea, syphilis, trichomonas, and herpes), and avoiding long-term use of oral contraception.

A family history of cervical cancer is not a risk factor for cervical cancer. However, there is new evidence that women with HPV can infect their newborns with the HPV and females who have never had sex and are HPV positive had mothers who were HPV positive (Porterfield, 2011). Cervical cancer is asymptomatic in its early stages, but as it progresses, women may experience abnormal menstruation, bleeding after sex, menopause, examination of the pelvis, and/or douching (ACS, 2012). As the cancer spreads or metastasizes outside the cervical area and the pelvis, women may complain of fatigue (a symptom of anemia that is subsequent to excessive bleeding), vaginal discharge, and lower abdominal pain.

## CERVICAL CANCER SCREENING: THE PAP TEST

The Pap test has been credited with the significant reduction of cervical cancer, because abnormal cells can be identified and treated before they progress to cervical cancer. Initially, Pap testing was solely performed using the conventional method; after the introduction of a vaginal speculum to facilitate visualization of the cervix, two specimens are collected by placing (1) the longer end of a "spatula" in the cervical os and rotating it in a clockwise direction in order to obtain cells from the ectocervix (external cervical area) and (2) a small "brush" in the cervical os and rotating it clockwise in order to obtain cells from the endocervix (internal cervical area). Each specimen is placed on the designated area on a slide, fixed with a specific agent, and sent to the laboratory for cytology testing. However, LBC tests (Thin-Prep® and Surepath®) were approved by the Federal Drug Administration in the early 2000. In this method, specimens are collected in a similar manner as the conventional method except that both cervical areas can be sampled with a special "brush," placed in a liquid medium, and sent to the laboratory for cytology testing. HPV DNA testing may be performed with or without Pap testing among women who are 30 years of age or older. Although the LBC tests are more expensive than the conventional Pap test, they have the advantage of being more sensitive (true positive test result). The conventional Pap test has a sensitivity of 51 percent (Reust, 2001). The sensitivity of the Pap test is 52–90 percent, HPV testing 71–100 percent, and increases to 90–100 percent when the Pap test and HPV DNA testing are combined (Mariani, 2004). Therefore, more and more health-care delivery systems are using LBC tests.

Women who are on their menses should not obtain Pap testing; instead, they should wait for approximately a week after their menses. If the Pap test is performed while a woman is having minimal vaginal bleeding, the pathologist may not be able to evaluate the cervical cells and the result may read "bloody smear." This is especially true of the conventional method in which the specimen is fixed on a slide.

### Barriers and Facilitators of Pap Testing

One can surmise that the high cervical cancer mortality rates among African Americans can in part be attributed to low Pap test utilization. African Americans may not be obtaining Pap testing because of low socioeconomic status, the physical and psychological consequences of Pap testing, misconceptions, and providers do not recommend Pap testing.

Selvin and Brett (2003) found that African Americans with a usual source of care were more likely to be up to date with Pap testing than those who were poor, had low educational levels, and were uninsured. African Americans need to be informed of where they can receive free or low-cost Pap testing. Women of childbearing age who are uninsured can receive Pap testing free of cost from their local health units. Women can receive Pap testing through their states' Breast and Cervical Cancer Prevention Program. The National Breast and Cervical Cancer Early Detection Program (NBCCEDP) was developed in response to the Breast and Cervical Cancer Mortality Prevention Act of 1990 (CDC, 2011) because of the low screening rates among women who belong to minority groups, are underinsured or without insurance, and have low income. Through this program, women who meet eligibility criteria receive mammograms and Pap tests free or at a low cost. Eligibility criteria for Pap testing include (1) underinsured or uninsured, (2) 250 percent at or below the federal poverty level, and (3) 18 and 64 years of age. According to Tangka et al. (2010), in 2005, more than 34 percent of NBCCEDP-eligible women (3.1 million women) did not receive recommended Pap tests from either NBCCEDP or other sources. More information can be obtained from local programs.

Hoyo et al. (2005) found that middle-aged African Americans did not adhere to Pap testing because of pain, which is a physical consequence of Pap testing and can be reduced by developing rapport with women and having a caring attitude, which helps to reduce anxiety and relaxes the muscles of the body including those in the vaginal area. Additionally, pain can be reduced by (1) informing women of exactly what will be done and what is being done, (2) using the smallest size vaginal speculum, (3) warming and moistening the speculum with water or water-based lubricant, (4) encouraging women to take slow deep breathes, (5) using distraction during speculum insertion into the vagina, and/or (6) medicating postmenopausal women who have atrophic vaginitis with estrogen vaginal cream (if there are no contraindications). Additionally, it is especially important to prepare women who are obtaining their first Pap test, because a negative first experience can prevent adherence with future testing.

Women can contribute to pain reduction during Pap testing by not douching. Women should not douche unless prescribed by their providers and should definitely not douche prior to obtaining a Pap test. Douching dries the vaginal and cervical areas, thus making the Pap test and pelvic examination painful. Additionally, it reduces the normal flora of the vagina and makes women more prone to vaginal infections. If a woman douches and the provider proceeds with the Pap test, the interpretation on the result of the Pap test may read "scant cellularity" and in some cases "reactive cellular changes;" both require repeat testing, which may be difficult for women to comply with because of various personal reasons such as child care, no insurance, time constraints, and work schedule.

Ackerson (2010) conducted a qualitative study among 24 U.S. born African American women who were between19 and 60 years of age; they were recruited from a health department, domestic assault center, emergency shelter, and churches in Michigan. The objective of the research study was "to explore personal influencing factors that contribute to Papanicolaou (Pap smear) testing in African American women who do (routine-use group) and do not (non-routine-use group) obtain routine testing" (Ackerson, 2010, p. 136). The researcher found that

> Routine-use group was socially influenced to value preventive health care while the non-routine-use group was not. Previous health care experiences with having a Pap smear and pelvic exam were positive for routine-use group and negative for non-routine-use group. Cognitively, both groups believed Pap smears tested for cancer and sexually transmitted diseases. Vulnerability to cervical cancer was thought to run in families; participants believed they were either safe from risk or hoped that the odds were in their favor. In addition, there was a link between avoiding routine preventive care and a trauma history (sexual, physical, medical), eliciting negative perceptions towards Pap smears and pelvic exams. (Ackerson, 2010, p. 136)

A history of trauma can provide clues regarding why African Americans are not obtaining regular Pap testing. The degree of physical and psychological consequences of the Pap testing is often directly related to trauma. Therefore, it is important to enquire about a history of trauma from sexual abuse, including incest, rape, and domestic violence among African Americans. The following quotes depict the psychological and physical consequences of Pap testing among African American women who have a history of trauma. Firstly,

> One participant who reported a history of sexual abuse (Monica, age 36), stated: I am generally traumatized by the experience of laying on the table and it is so gross . . . I don't really know why, I mean, I have a sexual abuse thing from my childhood, but I am more or less over that, I think I kind of moved on. But that Pap smear just feels like a violation every single time. It's horrible, absolutely horrible. (Ackerson, 2010, p. 141)

Second, a woman with a history of domestic violence (Bonnie, age 19) said:

> I do feel uncomfortable every time I get it, the Pap. I really don't enjoy them at all. If there's a different method that I could choose to help to figure out if I was having an infection, I think I would choose that over a Pap, because it makes me feel uncomfortable for a complete stranger to come and check you out. . . . I would prefer a woman than a man . . . I've been physically abused by males and I don't like, I really don't agree with males like that. (Ackerson, 2010, p. 141)

Finally, a history of incest contributes to not adhering to Pap testing as is evidenced by, "I've had a traumatic experience in my life through incest therefore, just the fear of anybody trying to put some instrument up me is scary (Rose, age 49)" (Ackerson, 2010, p. 141). It is possible that women who have a history of trauma are more likely to obtain Pap testing if they have a female provider and if they are distracted during the examination and testing using, for example, imagery.

Misconceptions about the Pap test need to be dispelled among African Americans. The Pap test does not test for other types of cancers such as ovarian cancer, benign lesions such as fibroids, fertility status, HPV strains that do not cause cervical cancer, or STIs. However, the Pap test result may include STIs such as herpes, trichomonas, and other infections that include candida vaginitis and bacterial vaginosis (presence of white blood cells and clue cells). If women are not informed of the real reason for Pap testing, they may not obtain Pap testing because they believe that they are not at risk for cervical cancer.

African American women may not obtain a Pap test because their providers do not recommend testing and/or discuss it with them or their provider is male. It is possible that providers do not recommend Pap testing because they are not knowledgeable about screening guidelines, they have time constraints that prevent them from performing screening tests, and/or they do not believe that African Americans are interested in disease prevention. However, personal knowledge regarding when to obtain a Pap test and the frequency of Pap testing can empower African American women and their advocates who can then request Pap testing and adhere to the frequency of testing.

It is important to know that organizations (American Cancer Society [ACS], American College of Obstetricians and Gynecologists [ACOG], and U.S. Preventive Services Task Force [USPSTF]) vary regarding when to start and stop Pap testing and the frequency of testing. But, generally, African Americans, and all females, should have their first Pap test at 21 years of age and their last Pap test between 65 and 70 years of age if they have had adequate screening or more than three normal results and no abnormal results in the preceding 10 years, or if they have had their cervix removed for benign reasons (ACS, 2012; ACOG, 2009; AHRQ, 2010). Any African American who is 65 years or older and has a new sex partner should resume Pap testing because of the possibility of HPV infection by the new partner. Women who have had a hysterectomy with removal of their cervix because of cervical cancer should continue screening. The author has knowledge of African American women who have had abnormal cells and cancer of the vaginal cuff after they have had a hysterectomy secondary to benign reasons and cervical cancer. The frequency of Pap testing varies according to organization, the method of testing, and personal history but should occur approximately every two to three years (ACS, 2012; ACOG, 2009; AHRQ, 2010).

Knowing other individuals who influence the decision to obtain a Pap test is very important. African American mothers are as influential as health-care providers in their daughters' decision to obtain Pap testing; this is evident in the following quote:

> "She [mother] influenced me by seeing her life as being healthy . . . she takes care of herself, her body, and it's a beautiful thing to me (Carmon, age 50)." . . . "They[doctors] talked to me about it, how . . . important it is because if you can go ahead of time . . . before it spreads or gets worse . . . is really good." Some participants also perceived that providers showed concern about their health when they inquired specifically about the Pap smear test. (Ackerson, 2010, p. 139)

### Pap Test Results

Pap test result may be reported as normal or abnormal. African Americans who receive a normal Pap test result have cervical cells that are without abnormalities and are HPV negative (if older than 30 years of age) and should follow up for repeat testing according to screening guidelines discussed above. An abnormal test result may be subsequent to cervical cell changes that vary from mild to severe, which are usually caused by infection with the HPV. It is important that African Americans who have abnormal Pap test result follow up with their providers, because it is only then that one can see the effectiveness of Pap testing, which is intended to identify and treat abnormal cervical cells while they are still asymptomatic.

It is important to follow up for the result of an abnormal Pap test despite feelings of fear and anxiety, because precancerous lesions can be treated and the prognosis is better for early stage cancer when compared to advanced stage cancer. Women who are diagnosed with disease that is localized have a five-year survival rate of 91 percent, while those who are diagnosed with cervical cancer have a one-year relative survival rate of 87 percent and a five-year relative survival rate of only 69 percent (ACS, 2012). African Americans may be informed that they have an abnormal Pap test result and they need to return for follow-up without an explanation regarding what is wrong and what follow-up entails; they should be educated in order to allow them to make informed decisions and be active participants in their health care.

The types of abnormal Pap test results vary considerable and their management is very complex and individualized. The management or treatment of cervical cell abnormality is usually based on the American Society for Colposcopy and Cervical Pathology's guidelines; the woman's age and pregnancy status are considered. A repeat Pap test is performed if the Pap test result is atypical squamous cells of undetermined significance (ASCUS) or lower, while colposcopy with or without endocervical curettage (ECC) or endocervical sampling (ECS) is performed in women whose result is higher than ASCUS (Feltmate & Friedman, 2010).

The types of abnormal cervical cells are generally identified by colposcopy examination, ECC, and ECS during a pelvic examination in the clinic setting. It is important that women refrain from douching prior to these tests and they should not be having their menses; douching results in drying of the vagina and cervix and can cause the procedure to be painful, while the blood from the menses limits visualization of the cervix. The last menstrual period is important because ECC and ECS are not performed during pregnancy as the gestational sac may be punctured and excessive bleeding may occur. The colposcopy is not usually a painful procedure, but the author found that women who are not psychologically prepared may be anxious and experience pain. Therefore, women need to be informed of what to expect before and during each procedure and receive premedication with an analgesic or an antianxiety agent as needed.

The colposcopy is indicated for women with (1) persistent ASCUS, (2) ASCUS with positive high risk HPV, (3) atypical squamous cells cannot exclude a high-grade squamous intraepithelial lesion (ASC-H), (4) atypical glandular cells (AGC), (5) low-grade intraepithelial lesion (LSIL), (6) high-grade intraepithelial lesion (HSIL), (7) invasive cancer that is suspicious, and (8) the presence of malignant cells (Feltmate & Feldman, 2010). During colposcopy, the cervix is visualized with a colposcope after the application of acetic acid; the acetic acid causes a burning sensation. Visualized abnormal cervical cells are biopsied; some providers' biopsy specific areas of the cervix if no abnormal cells are visualized, while others apply diluted Lugol's or Schiller's solution. Lugol's solution should not be used in women who are allergic to iodine, because it comprises iodine and potassium iodide. Lugol's solution is also used if there is excessive bleeding after colposcopy, ECC, or ECS.

ECC and ECS are indicated for women with (1) ASCUS, (2) LSIL, (3) HSIL, (4) AGC, and adenocarcinoma in situ (Feltmate & Feldman, 2010). ECC and ECS entail sampling endocervical tissue with a curette; because if the endometrium is involved, women tend to experience a cramping pain. The following quote depicts some of the physical and psychological consequences of the diagnostic tests and the likelihood that women may not return to their health-care provider for follow-up.:

> Two of the non-routine-use participants had experiences with cervical biopsies (Ladon, age 23 and Anna, age 47) and reported that the biopsies were painful: . . . sticking this metal thing in your vagina to open it up and that's very uncomfortable to me . . . depending upon what they're scraping . . . they might scrape something off . . . that's abnormal, that's kind of painful . . . it scared me and I don't want to go back and get another test. (Ackerson, 2010, p. 141)

The result of the diagnostic test(s) varies from HPV positive and precancerous lesions to cervical cancer. Women who have HPV positive results will have repeat Pap test with or without colposcopy, while those with precancerous lesions (abnormal areas that are localized to the cervix) will have treatment procedures that include cryosurgery or cauterization, Laser procedure, and loop excision. Women in whom the abnormal cells are localized to the cervical area usually have the affected area(s) "burnt" (cauterization) or "frozen" (cryosurgery).

Women with more extensive precancerous cervical lesions usually have the affected area(s) removed using a wire loop during loop-excision procedure. Conization of the cervix is indicated for women whose abnormality is severe or cancer in situ, while women with cancer are referred to gynecology cancer specialists for treatment. Follow up after treatment is individualized and varies from repeat Pap testing with or without colposcopy every 4 to 12 months for 1 to 2 years. Generally, routine Pap testing is performed when repeat tests are normal.

Women who cannot afford to follow up their abnormal Pap test results may be eligible for assistance through the Breast and Cervical Cancer Prevention Program. In 2000, the program was modified to include women who are diagnosed with cervical cancer. Since the inception of this program in 1990, it has expanded from 8 to 50 states, but the administration of this program varies from state to state. Through this program, African Americans in the 50 states and the District of Columbia who are diagnosed with precancerous lesions and cervical cancer and meet eligibility criteria can be treated through Medicaid (CDC, 2011).

## ADOLESCENTS AND YOUNG ADULTS

Cervical cancer is not common among African American college-aged students, but the high rate of HPV infection among young adults may serve as a proxy measure for future disease developments. Increasing health awareness and promoting preventive health behaviors, particularity among populations with an excess burden of HPV-associated disease, can prove beneficial in promoting healthy lifestyles throughout life (Bynum, Brandt, Friedman, Annang, & Tanner, 2011, p. 301).

Pap testing should begin at 21 years of age and adolescents who have abnormal Pap test results should be managed conservatively in order to preserve fertility and cervical competence. Infertility can occur if the cervical os becomes scarred and stenosed from treatment procedures. On the other hand, cervical incompetence may occur subsequent to excision procedures.

Additionally, the HPV tend to "clear" without treatment in this age group. The treatment of abnormal Pap test result is individualized. For example, a woman with the result of less than HSIL usually has a repeat Pap test in 12 months and if the repeat Pap test is negative, routine screening is resumed.

In addition to Pap testing, this age group and their parents need to be educated about the cervical cancer vaccines. Bynum et al. (2011) conducted a cross-sectional research study among African American college students at three historically Black colleges and universities in southeast United States. The researchers wanted "to assess gender differences in HPV knowledge, vaccine acceptance, HPV-related health beliefs and behaviors, and health information preferences" (Bynum et al., 2011, p. 297). The "overall knowledge of HPV was low among this sample of college students . . . and a majority thought that HPV vaccines protect against all HPV infections" (Bynum et al., 2011, p. 300). The researchers also found that the females would rather receive information from their health-care providers and pamphlets. Therefore, African American adolescents and young adults can be educated about HPV by their providers and pamphlets from providers and possibly at community and campus health fairs/events.

## CERVICAL CANCER VACCINES

Since the HPV is the primary cause of cervical cancer, two drug companies, Merck & Company, Inc. and SmithKline Pharmaceuticals, developed cervical cancer vaccines—Gardasil® and Cervarix®, respectively. Gardasil® was FDA approved in 2006 for use among females between 9 and 26 years of age to prevent cervical cancer caused by HPV types 16 and 18 in addition to preventing genital warts caused by HPV types 6 and 11 (Merck, 2011; MPR, 2011b). It was approved for use in males in 2009. Cervarix® was FDA approved in 2010 for use only among females between 10 and 25 years of age to prevent cervical cancer caused by HPV types 16 and 18 (MPR, 2011a). Both vaccines are efficacious against HPV types 31, 33, 45, 52, and 58 that are related to HPV type 16 and HPV type 45 that is related to HPV 18. These HPV types are the etiologic agents in approximately 20 percent of all cases of cervical cancer. The vaccines are more efficacious among women who have never had sex and are therefore recommended with childhood immunizations. This recommendation has led to much controversy and parental concerns regarding the HPV vaccines. Both vaccines are administered intramuscularly as a series of three shots at zero, two, and six months for Gardasil® and zero, one, and six months for Cervarix®. Women who are allergic to yeast should not receive Gardasil®, while women who are allergic to latex should not be given Cervarix®, and neither vaccine should be taken by pregnant women since vaccine effects on the fetus is not known (MPR, 2011a, b). Women who receive either vaccine and discover that they are pregnant should inform their providers who should report it to pregnancy registries that monitor the effects of medications on the fetus and newborn.

During postlicensure surveillance among individuals who received Gardasil® between June 1, 2006 and December 31, 2008, more than 12,000 adverse events occurred (Merck, 2011). Less than 10 percent of the adverse events were serious and most adverse reactions were similar to those of other vaccines (Merck, 2011). The adverse effects of the cervical cancer vaccines include fatigue, headache, myalgia, gastrointestinal upset, and local reaction. Women who receive Gardasil® should be observed for at least 15 minutes after receiving the vaccine, because they may have syncope, falls, and injure themselves (Merck, 2011). Additionally, women who are on oral contraception pills (OCPs) or who have a family history of clotting disorders may have thromboembolic events (Merck, 2011). Therefore, providers need to inquire about OCP use and a family history of clotting disorders. Women with these risk factors who decide to obtain the vaccine should be educated about the signs and symptoms of thromboembolic diseases and the importance of going to the emergency department immediately if they occur.

There are some insurance companies that pay for the series of three vaccines, which cost an average of $300–$400. Those without insurance can qualify through company-sponsored program if they meet eligibility criteria, which include annual income, being uninsured, and are 18–26 years of age. Despite the availability of the cervical cancer vaccines, women still need to obtain Pap testing, which screens for cervical cancer; the vaccines are (1) not used for the treatment of active diseases such as genital, anal, vulvar, vaginal, or cervical lesions and dysplasia, (2) do not protect all individuals who receive them, and (3) their effectiveness has not been demonstrated in women who are more than 26 years old (Castle, Cox, & Palefsky, 2010).

## CONCLUSION

African Americans are dying from cervical cancer although there are risk reduction activities and effective prevention strategies. The prevention strategies include Pap testing, the follow-up of abnormal Pap test results, and cervical cancer vaccines. Unfortunately, there are many barriers to accessing these strategies; there are instances when "the people perish because of lack of knowledge." Therefore, the author hopes that the information regarding the cervical cancer prevention strategies will empower us to conquer cervical cancer, a preventable cancer that is taking the life of too many of our women.

## REFERENCES

Ackerson, K. (2010). Personal influences that affect motivation in pap smear testing among African American women. *Journal of Obstetric and Neonatal Nurses*, *39*(2), 136–146.

ACOG. (2009). ACOG Practice Bulletin No. 109. Cervical cytology screening. Retrieved from http://journals.lww.com/greenjournal/documents/pb109_cervical_cytology_screening.pdf

ACS. (2004). *Can cervical cancer be found early?* Atlanta, GA: ACS. Retrieved from http://www.cancer.org/docroot/CRI/content/CRI_2_4_3X_Can_cervical_cancer_be found

ACS. (2011a). *Cancer facts and figures 2011*. Atlanta, GA: ACS. Retrieved from http://www.cancer.org/acs/groups/content/@epidemiologysurveilance/documents/document/acspc-029771.pdf

ACS. (2011b). *Cancer facts and figures for African Americans 2011–2012*. Atlanta, GA: ACS. Retrieved from http://www.cancer.org/acs/groups/content/@epidemiologysurveilance/documents/document/acspc-027765.pdf

ACS. (2012). *Cancer fact and figures 2012*. Atlanta, GA: ACS. Retrieved from http://www.cancer.org/acs/groups/content/@epidemiologysurveilance/documents/document/acspc-031941.pdf

AHRQ. (2010). *The guide to clinical preventive services 2010–2011: Recommendations of the U.S. preventive services task force*. AHQR Publication No. 10-05145. Rockville, MD: U.S. Health and Human Services. Retrieved from http://www.ahrq.gov/clinic/pocketgd1011/pocketgd1011.pdf

Bynum, S. A., Brandt, H. M., Friedman, D. B., Annang, L., & Tanner, A. (2011). Knowledge, beliefs, and behaviors: Examining human papillomavirus-related differences among African American college students. *Journal of American College Health*, *59*(4), 296–302.

Castle, P. E., Cox, J. T., & Palefsky, J. M. (2010). Recommendations for the use of human papillomavirus vaccines. *UpToDate*. Retrieved from http:www.uptodate.com/contents/recommendations-for-the-use-of-human-papillomavirus-vaccine?view=print

CDC. (2011). *National breast and cervical cancer early detection program: 20 years of screening women and saving lives*. Atlanta, GA: CDC. Retrieved from http://www.cdc.gov/Features/CancerScreeningWomen/

Feltmate, C. M., & Feldman, S. (2010). Colposcopy. *UpToDate*. Retrieved from http://www.uptodate.com/contents/colposcopy?source=search_result&search=colposcopy&selectedTitle=1%7E60

Hoyo, C., Yarnall, K. S. H., Skinner, C. S., Moorman, P. G., Sellers, D., & Reid, L. (2005). Pain predicts non-adherence to Pap smear screening among middle-aged African American women. *Preventive Medicine*, *41*(2), 439–445.

Mariani, S. M. (2004). Conference report—Early cancer diagnosis: Beating the odds. *Medscape General Medicine*, *6*(3), 18. Retrieved from http://www.medscape.com/viewprogram/3254_pnt

Merck. (2011). *Gardasil*. Whitehouse Station, NJ: Merck & Co., Inc.

MPR. (2011a). *Cervarix*. Retrieved from http://www.empr.com/cervarix/immunization/drug/7722

MPR. (2011b). *Gardasil.* Retrieved from http://www.empr.com/gardasil/immunization/drug/5305

Porterfield, S. P. (2011). Vertical transmission of the human papillomavirus from mother to fetus: Literature review. *The Journal of Nurse Practitioners, 7*(8), 665–670.

Reust, C. E. (2001). Does the increased sensitivity of the new papanicolaou (Pap) tests improve the cost-effectiveness for cervical cancer? *The Journal of Family Practice, 50*(2), 175.

Selvin, E., & Brett, K. M. (2003). Breast and cervical cancer screening: Sociodemographic predictors among white, black, and Hispanic women. *American Journal of Public Health, 93*(4), 618–623.

Tangka, F. K. L., O'Hara, B., Gardner, J. G., Turner, J., Royalty, J., Shaw, K., Sabatino, S., Hall, I. J., & Coates, R. J. (2010). Meeting the cervical cancer screening needs of underserved women: The National Breast and Cervical Cancer Early Detection Program, 2004–2006. *Cancer Causes Control, 21*(7), 1081–1090. Retrieved from http://www.ncbi.nlm.nih.gov/pubmed/20361353

# 4

# African American Women and Breast Cancer Issues

## *Patricia K. Bradley*

My grandmother was diagnosed with breast cancer in the 1970s. No one in my family knows how long she suffered with this disease. What were her initial symptoms? At what point did she seek help for them? Growing up, I remember Mom-Mom as a strong, kind woman who greeted the seven of us on our Sunday visits with a smile, a hug, and unconditional acceptance of our faults. She listened patiently to our complaints about our siblings and encouraged us to be kind to one another. Mom-Mom quietly took care of my toddler daughter during the week as I struggled with teenage motherhood and finishing high school. She had a very close relationship with her four sisters. The "Atwell girls" would travel together to participate in the milestone events (birthdays, graduations, holidays) for my siblings and me. And no one knew.

My mother became aware of my grandmother's problems when Mom-Mom called her from the hospital after her radical mastectomy, to say, she had "just had a little surgery" and wanted my mother to know where she was. During the next five years before her death, she had surgeries to remove her estrogen producing organs (ovaries and adrenal glands), radiation, and chemotherapy, the extent of which we really are not sure. We do know that Mom-Mom was given pain medication by her doctors, because we found the many unopened bottles in her home after her death. My grandmother mostly did not take the meds because she did not want to "die an addict" as her sister always cautioned family members about using pain meds. The way my grandmother handled her breast cancer I suspect was the way she handled most of her life problems: being strong and being silent so as not to burden her family. This chapter is written in memory of my grandmother and the many other strong Black women with stories to tell about their breast cancer journey.

## WHAT MY GRANDMOTHER DIDN'T KNOW ABOUT BREAST CANCER

Knowing what breast cancer is and how it affects African American women is essential to our understanding of how to help African American women survive this disease. Cancer is a disease of abnormal growth and spread of cells in the form of a tumor in the body. Much remains unknown about the disease including where it comes from and how to prevent it. What we do know is that African Americans have the highest death rate and shortest survival of any racial and ethnic group in the United States for most cancers (American Cancer Society [ACS], 2011). One in three women in the United States is at risk for developing cancer in her lifetime and cancer is the second leading cause of death for women after cardiovascular disease (ACS, 2012a). Cancers affecting primarily women include breast, uterine, ovarian, and cervical cancer. Other cancers of concern include lung and colorectal cancers. This chapter will focus on breast cancer, the most commonly diagnosed cancer among African American women.

Breast cancer is the second leading cause of cancer death (after lung cancer) for African American women. Breast cancer can occur in men; however, it most commonly occurs in women. African American women are at high risk for both a greater mortality rate and a presentation for cancer treatment at a later stage of disease. Although the incidence rate of breast cancer is about 16 percent lower in African American women than in White women, the death rate is 39 percent higher (ACS, 2011). The overall five-year relative survival after breast cancer is 77 percent for African American women and 90 percent for Caucasians (ACS, 2011). This survival differential has been attributed to multiple variables, including not having access to early detection services, treatment differences, a lack of insurance, low socioeconomic status (SES), and aggressive tumor and clinical characteristics (Dunn, Agurs-Collins, Browne, Lubet, & Johnson, 2010; Vona-Davis & Rose, 2009). Furthermore, the difference in death rates has remained despite increased efforts to improve survival through the development of effective detection techniques and an increase in the number of possible treatment options.

Breast cancers diagnosed in African American women are more likely to have factors associated with advanced stage and poor prognosis, such as higher grade (cells grow rapidly and spread faster), distal stage, and negative hormone receptor status (Dunn et al., 2010). In fact, only about half (51%) of breast cancers diagnosed among African American women are at a local stage, compared to 61 percent among White women.

Later stage at diagnosis among African American women has been largely attributed to the low frequency of mammograms and the lack of timely follow-up of suspicious results (ACS, 2011). There is also evidence that aggressive tumor characteristics such as triple-negative cancers are more common in African American than White women, particularly younger women under age 40 (Ray & Polite, 2010).

## FINANCIAL STATUS AND SURVIVAL DISPARITIES: WHAT'S BEING POOR GOT TO DO WITH IT?

Socioeconomic status is highly correlated with cancer risk and outcomes across the cancer continuum from prevention to palliative care. Persons with lower SES are more likely to engage in behaviors that increase cancer risk, such as tobacco use and physical inactivity. In addition, groups with lower SES are often the focus of marketing campaigns promoting these unhealthy behaviors in poorer communities. Community and environmental concerns for these populations include fewer opportunities for physical activity, unsafe conditions for low-cost physical activity such as walking, and unhealthy food environments such as food deserts where people have less access to fresh fruits and vegetables (Baskin et al., 2011; Walker, Keane, & Burke, 2010).

Financial, structural, and personal barriers to quality health care, including lack of or inadequate health insurance, reduced access to recommended preventive care and treatment services, and lower literacy levels are influenced by lower SES. Individuals with no health insurance and those with Medicaid insurance are more likely to delay seeking treatment and to be diagnosed with advanced cancer. For many, lack of insurance or inadequate insurance leads to missed, delayed, or fewer treatment opportunities (Darby, Davis, Likes, & Bell, 2009). These factors disproportionately impact African Americans, because compared with 9 percent of Whites, 25 percent of African Americans live below the federal poverty threshold. In addition, 19 percent of African Americans are uninsured, while only 11 percent of Whites lack health insurance (ACS, 2011).

## UNDERSTANDING OVERWEIGHT AND OBESITY: BLACK WOMEN SEE ONLY CURVES

Another factor contributing to survival disparity may be obesity. Obesity is a major health problem in the United States, and according to the American Cancer Society, more than 50 percent of African American women are overweight or obese (ACS, 2011). In my growing up years, I remember praying that I would inherit my "Atwell" characteristics. I longed to fill out my blouses and grow some "meat on my bones" to coincide with wide-hips, a legacy of my ancestors. To have an "Atwell" was not considered fat in my family; it was considered having the coveted curves that are valued by people in my culture. Little did we know that these curves could one day be detrimental to our health. In addition to diabetes, heart disease, and stroke, obesity increases the risk of many cancers, including cancers of the breast (in postmenopausal women), colon, endometrium, and kidney. Being overweight also increases the risk of cancer recurrence, decreases the likelihood of survival for many cancers, and increases the risk of developing other illnesses following a cancer diagnosis (ACS, 2012a). Additionally, breast cancer survivors are at risk for added weight from weight gain, a common side effect of breast cancer treatment (Halbert et al., 2008).

With African American women being at risk for obesity, treatment influenced weight gain, and poor outcomes related to breast cancer diagnoses, it is important to help African American survivors to become aware of and change their dietary and physical activity behaviors. Stolley, Sharp, Wells, Simon, and Schiffer (2006) collected quantitative and qualitative data on the attitudes, beliefs, barriers, and facilitators of health behavior changes in 27 overweight/obese African American breast-cancer survivors. Focus groups were used to collect information on the barriers and facilitators for behavior change. Facilitators identified included the use of culturally congruent interventions that took into consideration the needs of African American women such as child-care support and access to safe places to exercise, fresh fruits, and vegetables. Most study participants reported making dietary changes after their diagnosis, and some increased their physical activity. As Stolley et al. (2006) points out so well, their study results underscore the need for culturally competent health-behavior interventions to help African American women to make the necessary dietary and physical activity changes.

## AFRICAN AMERICAN WOMEN UNDER FORTY: AM I TOO YOUNG TO HAVE BREAST CANCER?

Breast cancer has been considered a disease of age with higher risk for diagnosis attributed to older-aged women. In various focus groups that I have conducted with African American breast cancer survivors, I have heard stories being relayed from women under 40 who were told by a doctor not to worry about a symptom (such as a lump or thickening) in their breast because they were "too young to have breast cancer" (Bradley, Scharf, & Ahlum Hanson, 2011). More recently, scientists have begun to investigate the effect of breast cancer on younger women.

As a vulnerable population, young African American women experience the greatest breast cancer burden in the United States, experience the highest incidence, and have the poorest outcomes from breast cancer (ACS, 2012a). Although African American women have an overall lower incidence of breast cancer, African American women younger than 35 years of age are more likely than Caucasian women of all ages and postmenopausal

African American women to be diagnosed with breast cancer and exhibit tumor characteristics associated with poorer survival. The lifestyle factors that may also contribute to the risk of aggressive, premenopausal breast cancer in African Americans include earlier age at menarche and first birth, having more children, and lower rates of breastfeeding (Dunn et al., 2010; Ray & Polite, 2010).

## WHAT DOES IT MEAN TO BE TRIPLE NEGATIVE?

Premenopausal African American women appear to be most at risk for basal-like breast cancer, a subtype of breast cancer associated with shorter survival due to its aggressiveness and difficulty in treating. These tumors are referred to as "triple negative" because they do not express estrogen receptor, progesterone receptor, or Her2/neu proteins. African American and Hispanic women have a higher risk of triple-negative breast cancer among younger women, with African American women facing worse prognosis than other ethnic groups (Anders & Carey, 2009). The persistence overtime of the incidence and survival disparity has been attributed to differences in risk factors and SES, lack of and delays in treatment, and inadequate treatment for African American women (Amirikia, Mills, Bush, & Newman, 2011; Dunn et al., 2010; Ray & Polite, 2010).

A hopeful finding that Anders and Carey (2009) highlighted is the fact that triple-negative breast cancers are generally very susceptible to chemotherapy. This is an important finding given the fact that African Americans are in a high-risk group to receive suboptimal doses of chemotherapy (Magai, Consedine, Adjei, Hershman, & Neugut, 2008). Women need to be informed of the usefulness of a full regimen of chemotherapy and encouraged to follow through with the treatment protocol.

## BREAST CANCER SCREENING: AM I "BORROWING TROUBLE"?

There are several myths about breast cancer that hinder women from getting the appropriate screening exams. High on the list of myths is "If a mammogram finds something it is too late" (Bradley, Scharf, & Ahlum Hanson, 2011). Women who hold this belief often do not want to know if they have cancer, especially if they have no symptoms. Having a mammogram to look for symptoms of breast cancer is considered "borrowing trouble" and is often discouraged. Unfortunately, no established preventive measures currently exist for breast cancer. Early detection methods such as mammography and prompt follow-up treatment are the next best method for reducing breast cancer mortality and improving breast cancer survival (ACS, 2012c).

The primary purpose of a screening test is to detect cancers at stages when they are still highly curable. In fact, for cancers of the cervix and colon, early detection tests can lead to the prevention of the disease through the identification and removal of precancerous lesions. Detecting cancer at an earlier stage can reduce the extent of treatment needed, improve the chances of cure, extend life, and thereby improve the quality of life for cancer survivors.

Screening for breast cancer before symptoms appear increases the chance that the cancer will be detected at an early stage providing diagnosed women with the greatest probability of survival. The detection of breast cancer involves medical interventions including mammography screening and diagnosis, monitoring, and follow-up of uncertain or suspicious findings with a breast biopsy. The American Cancer Society recommends that average-risk women aged 40 and older get annual mammograms as well as regular clinical breast exams (CBEs) by a health-care provider. For women at high risk for breast cancer, the American Cancer Society recommends annual screening using magnetic resonance imaging (MRI) in addition to mammograms beginning at age 30 (ACS, 2012b). Women are also encouraged to be familiar with the appearance and feel of their breasts to note for any changes that may need follow-up by a health professional.

The failure of African American women to participate in breast cancer screening programs is attributed to many factors, including cultural attitudes and beliefs, lack of access to health care, lower SES, and prior negative experiences, which are often classified as barriers in the literature (Conway-Phillips & Underwood, 2009). Perceptions of low risk for breast cancer has been identified as a major factor in low screening rates of African American women (Halbert et al., 2006; Underwood, Richards, Bradley, & Robertson, 2008).

## BARRIERS TO BREAST CANCER SCREENING

Barriers to cancer screening have often been divided into three categories: patient, provider, and system-related factors, with most investigations focusing on patient-related barriers (Wujcik & Fair, 2008). Patients experience intrapersonal barriers and are less likely to get appropriate screening when they perceive mammograms as painful and uncomfortable, distrust the medical system and providers, have a fear of finding cancer, hold fatalistic beliefs about cancer, and embrace the misconception that screening is unnecessary or even harmful. Interpersonal barriers occur when the provider fails to communicate to the patient the importance of mammography or to provide patient education necessary to understand screening and follow-up diagnostic tests. System-related barriers such as lack of access, high cost, lack of health insurance, facilities, and providers and institutional racism are structures that impede screening (Young, Schwartz, & Booza, 2011).

Despite generally similar screening rates, breast cancer is detected at an advanced stage more often in African American than in White women. The one factor most often associated with African American women's advanced stage is delay in seeking treatment (Gullatte, Phillips, & Gibson, 2006; Maly et al., 2011; Wujcik et al., 2009). Many women delay the completion of recommended testing for weeks to months. When delay occurs through incomplete screening and delayed follow-up, the potential benefits of identifying breast cancer at the earliest, most treatable stage are diminished. Delay may occur at any point in the progression of testing and may be because of patient, provider, or system influences. The usual follow-up after an incomplete or abnormal mammogram screening includes diagnostic procedures such as additional mammography views (compression or magnification) and breast ultrasonography, sometimes followed by biopsy (core or excisional). The sequence of tests and procedures continues until a diagnosis of cancer is confirmed or ruled out (Wujcik & Fair, 2008).

## IS IT DELAY IN SEEKING TREATMENT OR SELF-CARE FOR BREAST CANCER SYMPTOMS?

Just as in barriers to screening, delay in seeking treatment for breast cancer symptoms is most often viewed as being patient-initiated. African Americans' fatalistic attitudes and distrust of the health-care system are two patient-related characteristics most often linked to delay in seeking treatment (Powe & Finnie, 2003); however, not all African American women are impacted by these cultural beliefs. In a study of African American women's psychosocial responses to breast cancer symptoms, Bradley (2005) found that the women who were least likely to delay seeking diagnosis and treatment for breast cancer symptoms had particular financial and support characteristics that matched those of White women who do not delay. Those who did not delay reported having a regular source of medical care providing them access to treatment and a relationship with a health provider. Participants also reported having a source of support from participation in organizations such as attendance at church and knowledge about cancer and detection procedures. Additionally, contrary to other studies reporting fatalistic beliefs of African Americans about cancer (Phillips, Cohen, & Moses, 1999; Powe, Hamilton, & Brooks, 2006; Spurlock & Cullins, 2006), the majority of participants believed that their symptom was something that could be taken care of (Bradley, 2005).

Some individuals try to take care of their symptoms themselves before seeking professional help. Most African Americans seek help from extended family members, very close family friends, ministers, and church leaders (Bailey, 1987). Quite often, only after exhausting available inner, familial, and spiritual resources, does the person seek medical advice. This cultural model of care-seeking, as identified by Bailey (1987), has been characterized as a form of delay; however, it is also a self-care model that can be considered when planning intervention projects.

In a pilot study developing methods of preparing African American women for a breast biopsy, Bradley, Kash, Piccoli, and Myers (2005) developed and implemented an educational counseling session describing breast biopsy procedures and addressing emotional concerns. African American women in the study were receptive to the breast biopsy education and relayed that they felt that they did benefit from receiving this service. Furthermore, they reported interest in participating in research in the future if asked to do so.

The significance of findings from these studies is that when African American women are given adequate information and appropriate resources, they are more likely to identify breast cancer symptoms and to get prompt treatment for them. Increased participation in routine mammography screening—with subsequent detection through biopsies and other tests, and treatment of the disease at an early stage—offers the best opportunity for decreasing mortality and improving survival. To benefit from early detection, African American women must have access to using these methods.

## ACCESS TO CARE AND CLINICAL STUDIES

The American Cancer Society's Cancer Action Network (ACS CAN) has championed the passing of legislation to assist individuals and families affected by cancer to combat a serious system-related financial barrier. The passage of the Patient Protection and Affordable Care Act in 2010 has brought hope to those facing a cancer diagnosis (ACS CAN, 2012). The law improves the affordability of insurance coverage by increasing insurance subsidies and eliminating arbitrary annual and lifetime caps on coverage for all insurance plans. Implementation of the Affordable Care Act should go a long way to decreasing barriers to screening and treatment for African American women.

Health-care providers play an important role in connecting African American women to screening, treatment, support, and breast cancer education. Negative health encounters are significant practitioner-related barriers to African American women seeking prompt treatment and follow-up care. Behavioral interventions directed toward health providers and African American women must include education to increase knowledge of the efficacy and availability of early detection activities as well as addressing personal emotions (Bradley, 2006).

Racism is a significant system-related barrier resulting in delayed seeking of treatment. For African Americans, perceived or actual differences in treatment contribute to the perception of racism in the health-care system. Almost 20 years ago, Outlaw (1993) examined the influence of racism on the cognitive processing of African Americans and suggested that racism be included as a stressor variable for African Americans in Lazarus and Folkman's (1984) stress and coping model. The challenge for researchers, clinicians, and educators is to understand the historically based realities and the impact of events for the individual that underlie African Americans' sentiments of distrust of the health-care system, health providers, and research (Gamble, 1993). When asked about reasons for not participating in clinical studies, many African American women have reported their primary reason as not being asked or informed by their physicians (Durant, Legedza, Marcantino, Freeman, & Landon, 2011; Freedman, 1998; Linden et al., 2007; Outlaw, Bourjolly, & Barg, 2000).

Acknowledging African American women's experience with racism and discrimination and understanding the influence racism has on perceptions of health and illness are crucial steps for health providers in developing trustworthy relationships and providing culturally appropriate interventions (Outlaw, 1993; Campesino, Saenz, Choi, & Krouse, 2012). In the case of breast cancer and African Americans, perceived racism may play a factor in underutilization of screening activities influencing African American women's delayed seeking of care and subsequent negative health outcomes.

## STRENGTH AND SILENCE: WAS MY GRANDMOTHER A "SUPERWOMAN"?

Beauboeuf-Lafontant (2007) and Woods-Giscombé (2012) have described a phenomenon in the African American community of the strong Black woman being considered a "Superwoman." This cultural imperative in which women are understood to be strong during adversity yet silent about abuses has been transferred from generation to generation as a survival strategy (Outlaw, 2006). My grandmother was indeed strong and silent, but was she a "Superwoman"? Did she possess the positive characteristics of showing strength such as goal-directness and assertiveness? I don't believe we ever saw Mom-Mom as an assertive person due to her soft-spoken quiet manner with her overbearing husband and among her outspoken sisters. Beauboeuf-Lafontant (2007) also notes that for a majority of the women (like my grandmother), being silently strong contributes to levels of selflessness, powerlessness, and self-silencing that contribute to psychological distress and a heightened risk for depression. Furthermore, Woods-Giscombé (2012) suggests that the cultural and psychosocial factors of the Superwoman role, such as focusing on the needs of others and making personal health a secondary or tertiary priority, might explain delays in health-seeking behaviors, the limited adherence to recommendations made by health-care professionals, and the lower rates of screening procedures for conditions that are treatable if caught in the early stages such as breast cancer screening and colonoscopies. Wow . . . I have to say again, we really didn't know what my grandmother was thinking or feeling. My best guess now is that she did not want to bother us with her fears and burdens.

How does someone get support when they are being strong and silent? In a project using focus groups to uncover how African Americans live beyond breast cancer (Bradley, Scharf, & Ahlum Hanson, 2011), a young survivor relayed how she realized much after her diagnosis that her attempt to be strong and silent so as not to burden her family only served to "block the blessings" coming her way from her family and friends. She described that only now, two years later, was she able to be more open, to discuss her issues, and to accept help from others.

## GETTING CONNECTED AND OTHER WAYS TO SURVIVE BREAST CANCER

Silence is often used by survivors as a protection for others, but sometimes it is a mode of self-protection to guard against the negative views of others. Hamilton, Moore, Powe, Agarwal, and Martin (2010) investigated the perceptions of support among older African American cancer survivors and found support from family, friends, and fellow church members to have positive outcomes among older African American cancer survivors. At the same time, misconceptions, fears, and negative cultural beliefs within the African American community negatively influenced the social support available to this group of respondents. Survivors reported feeling ostracized and feeling hurt, alone, and socially isolated when completely abandoned by friends. This led to withdrawal and subsequent silence as a self-protection strategy.

Hamilton and Sandelowski (2004) sought to determine the types of social support that African Americans use to cope with the experience of cancer. In addition to traditional sources of support, the study participants described using types of social support not currently emphasized in the literature. The emotional support of "presence of others" was reported most frequently. Other forms of emotional support involved encouraging words, distracting activities, and protecting and monitoring. In addition to the traditional instrumental support such as transportation, financial, and household tasks assistance, other intangible forms of support included family members, friends, and fellow church members offering to pray for them, assistance to continue religious practices, to remain in their homes when ill, and to maintain social roles in their family, workplace, or church. Informational support included what to expect, how to manage symptoms and interpret information, and served to validate the information received. This culturally informed understanding of social support among African Americans as identified by

Hamilton and Sandelowski (2004) has similar components of community connection identified by Heiney and colleagues (2011).

The theory of community connection (Heiney et al., 2011) has been described as close relationships with women and men who are members of a neighborhood, a church, a work group, or an organization. Connection is particularly relevant for African American women with breast cancer because of the emotional, social, and practical support that comes from identifying with and being involved in a caring community environment (Hamilton et al., 2010; Henderson & Fogel, 2003).

In a project to develop breast cancer educational materials for African American women (Bradley, Scharf, & Living Beyond Breast Cancer, 1999), connection was the core theme that emerged as a way to live beyond a cancer diagnosis. Focus groups were used to explore African American women's thoughts and concerns about surviving and living beyond a breast cancer diagnosis. African American women expressed that positive coping happens through "Getting Connected" to five areas: self, God or nature, family and friends, other survivors, and the health-care treatment team. The process used to make this connection involves surviving the impact of hearing the diagnosis, making decisions about treatment, relating to others for support, and living beyond breast cancer through follow-up with health providers. Strategies for living beyond a breast cancer diagnosis included the use of spirituality, informed decision-making, developing and maintaining positive connections, and reaching out to others for support and with encouragement.

In 2011, a second edition of the "Getting Connected" educational booklet was produced after focus groups revealed that the content was still relevant and useful to African American women going through a breast cancer diagnosis and beyond. African American women relayed having a high quality of life and positive family functioning following diagnosis. Major factors enabling this coping were the positive connections; expression of emotions with family, friends, and providers; and the use of spirituality.

## PSYCHOSOCIAL CONCERNS OF YOUNG AFRICAN AMERICAN WOMEN

Researchers have only recently begun to write about issues of young survivors (Camp-Sorrell, 2009; Peate, Meiser, Hickey, & Friedlander, 2009) and African American breast cancer survivors specifically (Johnson Farmer, 2009; Lewis, Sheng, Rhodes, Jackson, & Schover, 2012; Phillips & Cohen, 2011). For example, Phillips and Cohen (2011) explored the meaning of breast cancer risk for African American women age 40 and under. They found that young women at high risk for breast cancer have unique emotional and support needs that are shaped by their stage in life and relationships with significant others, their faith, and their interactions with the health-care delivery system.

Lewis et al. (2012) investigated psychosocial concerns of younger Africa American breast cancer survivors diagnosed before the age 50. Of greatest concern for these survivors were problems with their relationships, feelings of distress about infertility issues, the lack of information about sexual dysfunction, and feelings of isolation. These problems appeared to be more prevalent and more severe than for White women of the same age and older (Lewis et al., 2012). Similar to other studies of African American women (Germino et al., 2011; Masi & Gehlert, 2008), participants described a general distrust of the health system and a feeling of alienation. Their strong sense of spirituality did not seem to fully combat the impact of their stressful environments leading to physical, psychological, social, functional, and spiritual quality of life issues similar to those described by Ashing-Giwa and Lim (2009).

Johnson Farmer's (2009) quality of life work with young African American women revealed that quality of life for young African American breast cancer survivors although challenging, as they struggled with their day-to-day life issues, a life threatening disease (breast cancer), and unstable relationships, was also filled with hopes, dreams, and visions of a positive future. This is useful information for clinicians attempting to provide support and balance to young women in their breast cancer journey.

## I'VE BEEN THROUGH SOMETHING: BREAST CANCER SURVIVORSHIP

The world of survivors is continuing to grow (ACS, 2012b). Research exploring issues of survivorship especially quality of life have begun to include more African American women as less is known about this population of women and stage of illness (Barton-Burke et al., 2006; Russell, Ah, Giesler, Storniolo, & Haase, 2008). Bradley, Barsevick, and colleagues (2012) conducted focus groups to evaluate the cultural relevance and completeness of a stress and coping model of cancer survivorship in describing quality of life for African American breast cancer survivors. Perceived racism, fatalism, and medical mistrust were hypothesized to be stressors in the stress and coping model. Cancer fatalism is a belief that death is inevitable when cancer is present and has been identified as a barrier to cancer screening, detection, and treatment (Powe & Finnie, 2003). This phenomenon is particularly prevalent among African Americans (Phillips, Cohen, & Moses, 1999; Powe, Hamilton, & Brooks, 2006; Spurlock & Cullins, 2006).

We interviewed 60 African American women one to five years after the treatment of breast cancer. Problems and coping resources regarding the physical, emotional, financial, and spiritual toll of cancer treatment were uncovered pertaining to in-treatment issues. Few participants mentioned discrimination and medical mistrust in relation to survivorship, and no participants were recorded as having taken a fatalistic attitude toward their survivorship. When a fatalistic attitude was observed, it involved resolving financial issues or "giving problems to God"—a spiritual coping skill. No respondents took a fatalistic attitude toward health or finding appropriate resources for problems. We suspect that this lack of discussion of racism, discrimination, or cancer fatalism is connected to the survivor's view of the medical provider as a supportive resource as well as the use of spirituality as a coping resource.

## WE'VE COME THIS FAR BY FAITH: SPIRITUALITY AS A WAY OF COPING

African Americans have been using spirituality and religion for generations as effective resources for coping with both illness and adversity (Gallia & Pines, 2009; Gibson & Hendricks, 2006; Newlin, Knafl, & Melkus, 2002; Outlaw, 1993; Tate, 2011). Studies examining explanatory models for health beliefs in general and cancer specifically among African Americans have uncovered salient themes of spirituality as a way of coping with illness (Fatone, Moadel, Foley, Fleming, & Jandorf, 2007; Hamilton, Powe, Pollard, Lee, & Felton, 2007; Phillips & Cohen, 2011; Roff, Simon, Nelson-Gardell, & Pleasants, 2009).

Black spirituality, as analyzed by Newlin, Knafl, and Melkus (2002), is viewed as a multidimensional concept that includes components of joy, fulfillment, and celebration; fear and abandonment; and personal and religious identity. They suggest that belief in God allows Black women to achieve trust and to accept outcomes. This belief also offers meaning, strength, comfort, and social support that allows Black women to endure their cancer through active religious coping strategies. Women involved in these activities report lower levels of depressive symptomatology, greater psychological well-being, and a sense of inner peace and acceptance of their disease.

Hamilton and colleagues (2007) examined the use of spirituality for African Americans with cancer and found that during their cancer trajectory, participants felt that God was there with them, healing, protecting, and in control of their lives. They also believed that God provided types of support not available from family members or friends. In return, these participants dedicated their lives to God through service in their churches or through helping others. Many African Americans perceive their survival from cancer as a gift from God. Therefore, for them, finding a way to give back is an important component of their spirituality. Women with these beliefs are often motivated through their experiences with breast cancer to reach out to others in what Wilmoth and Sanders (2001) have termed "health activism." Participants in their study sought to help other women to be more aware of their risk and of breast cancer screening methods.

Morgan, Tyler, and Fogel (2008) revisited the concept of fatalism as noted in the literature and concluded that although concerned about their health, African American women want the best for their health and want to be educated about ways to prevent, screen, and treat health conditions such as cancer; and in fact, African Americans are finding hope in a cancer diagnosis rather than despair and thoughts of death. Morgan, Tyler, and Fogel's (2008) perception of cancer activism is that it is a phenomenon that has evolved from efforts of health-care providers and community lay health advisors to reduce the fear and fatalistic attitudes held in the African American community about cancer. Although nearly impossible to totally eradicate the notion of cancer fatalism in the African American community, fatalism and fatalistic attitudes are potentially modifiable. Morgan and colleagues suggest that using culturally targeted faith-based interventions has and will continue to play a major role in this transformation from cancer fatalism to cancer activism among African Americans.

## SUCCESSFUL STRATEGIES OF ENGAGING AFRICAN AMERICAN WOMEN

Using culturally relevant recruitment strategies for research studies and breast cancer awareness outreach activities may be an important resource in reducing racial disparities in breast cancer mortality. Portrayal of positive coping in the media and use of culturally sensitive approaches have also been identified as key strategies to connect women to care and to decrease cancer fatalism. Kelley (2011) found that nurses can be important partners in using collaborative work between different agencies within rural communities to reach underserved minority populations in their own communities.

Using African American women from the community to serve as leaders, advocates, peer breast health educators, and lay health advisors and Train-the-Trainer formats has been successful in engaging high-risk women and survivors. Other successful strategies identified in the literature include storytelling, witnessing and positive testimonies, providing social support, social networking, and developing social support networks (Gibson, 2008). Effective methods in delivering multifaceted programs that include culturally specific breast health information have incorporated photographs, prose, narratives, poetry, and quotations (Bradley, Berry, Lang, & Myers, 2006; Crump et al., 2008; Gibson, 2008; King et al., 2010; Kooken, Haase, & Russell, 2007; Robertson, Franklin, Flores, Wherry, & Buford, 2006; Rosenzweig et al., 2011).

## CONCLUSION

There are many unknowns about breast cancer. What is known is that finding breast cancer at an early stage and doing something about it right away offers the best chance of a positive outcome for women diagnosed with breast cancer. What is also known about breast cancer is that women who have supportive services including access and referrals to screenings, adequate treatment resources, and positive relationships with health-care providers are more likely to seek care promptly than those without.

A woman's best overall preventive health strategy is to reduce her known risk factors as much as possible by avoiding weight gain and obesity (for postmenopausal breast cancer), engaging in regular physical activity, and minimizing alcohol intake. Women should consider the increased risk of breast cancer associated with combined estrogen and progestin menopausal hormone therapy use when evaluating treatment options for menopausal symptoms (ACS, 2011).

To increase the survival rate of African American women diagnosed with breast cancer, it is imperative that health professionals become more involved in assuring access to early detection methods. It is important to explore our setting for structures that foster prejudice and discrimination, identifying and eliminating access and availability of services barriers, and advocating policy changes. Increasing the number of positive health-care encounters and the sensitivity and cultural appropriateness in outreach programs and treatment environments may increase the likelihood of African American women seeking treatment earlier, the probability of survival, and the improvement of the quality of care.

Currently, interventions with African American women are primarily designed to address individual behavioral barriers to care. To remain at this level of intervention without addressing social policy and provider issues puts the sole responsibility for change on the individual. Individual, provider, and social policy levels of intervention must be addressed to impact the health delivery system and to increase access for African Americans. We must identify the barriers to access and to advocate change on the health policy and health provider levels directed toward assuring access to quality care for all individuals.

Health-care providers' culturally sensitive and trustworthy interactions are needed to help in addressing the barriers of discrimination and racism present in the existing system. Getting all health-care providers to recommend mammography, to perform clinical breast exams, and to encourage women to be familiar with their breast and any changes is essential to increasing African American women's screening behaviors.

Survivors can be assisted in positive coping through supportive networks that include connectedness and openness to spirituality. Research and program development tailored to African American women must also take into consideration additional burdens and institutional and health policy barriers. Findings from studies testing the effectiveness of culturally appropriate recruitment and culturally relevant interventions need to be disseminated widely and supported and implemented by health-care and community systems.

## REFERENCES

ACS. (2011). *Cancer facts and figures for African Americans 2011–2012.* Atlanta GA: ACS.

ACS. (2012a). *Cancer facts and figures 2012.* Atlanta GA: ACS.

ACS. (2012b). *Cancer prevention & early detection facts and figures 2012.* Atlanta GA: ACS.

ACS. (2012c). *Cancer treatment and survivorship facts and figures 2012–2013.* Atlanta GA: ACS.

ACS CAN. (2012). *Patient Protection and Affordable Care Act (PPACA).* Retrieved from http://www.acscan.org/healthcare

Amirikia, K. C., Mills, P., Bush, J., & Newman, L. A. (2011). Higher population-based incidence rates of triple-negative breast cancer among young African American women: Implications for breast cancer screening recommendations. *Cancer, 117*(12), 2747–2753.

Anders, C., & Carey, L. A. (2009). Biology, metastatic patterns, and treatment of patients with triple-negative breast cancer. *Clinical Breast Cancer, 9*(2), S73–S81.

Ashing-Giwa, K. T., & Lim, J.-W. (2009). Examining the impact of socioeconomic status and socioecologic stress on physical and mental health quality of life among breast cancer survivors. *Oncology Nursing Forum, 36*(1), 79–88.

Bailey, E. J. (1987). Sociocultural factors and health care-seeking behavior among black Americans. *Journal of the National Medical Association, 79*(4), 389–392.

Barton-Burke, M., Cavaretta, J. A., Nkimbeng, M. J., Nowacka, J. E., Proctor, C., Shi, J., Webb, J., & Worchester, A. (2006). Black women and breast cancer: A review of the literature. *Journal of Multicultural Nursing & Health, 12*(2), 11–20.

Baskin, M. L., Gary, L. C., Hardy, C. M., Yu-Mei, S., Scarinci, I., Fouad, M. N., & Partridge, E. E. (2011). Predictors of retention of African American women in a walking program. *American Journal of Health Behavior, 35*(1), 40–50.

Beauboeuf-Lafontant, T. (2007). You have to show strength: An exploration of gender, race, and depression. *Gender & Society, 21*(1), 28–51.

Bradley, P. K. (2005). The delay and worry experience of African American women with breast cancer. *Oncology Nursing Forum, 32*(2), 243–249.

Bradley, P. K. (2006). Breast cancer in African American women. In C. F. Fisher (Ed.), *African American Women's Health and Social Issues* (2nd ed., pp. 36–45). Westport, CT: Praeger.

Bradley, P. K., Scharf, M. N., & Living Beyond Breast Cancer. (1999). *Getting connected: African Americans Living Beyond Breast Cancer.* Ardmore, PA: Living Beyond Breast Cancer.

Bradley, P. K., Kash, K. M., Piccoli, C. W., & Myers, R. E. (2005). Breast biopsy education: Preparing African American women for breast biopsy. *Cancer Control: Journal of Moffitt Cancer Center, Cancer Culture and Literacy Supplement, 12*(2), 100–102.

Bradley, P. K., Berry, A., Lang, C., & Myers, R. E. (2006). Getting ready: Developing an educational intervention to prepare African American women for breast biopsy. *Association of Black Nursing Faculty Journal, 17*(1), 15–19.

Bradley, P. K., Scharf, M. N., & Ahlum Hanson, A. (2011). *Getting connected: African Americans Living Beyond Breast Cancer* (2nd ed.). Haverford, PA: Living Beyond Breast Cancer.

Bradley, P. K., Barsevick, A. M., Donnelly, T. A., & Micco, E. S. (2012). Post-treatment problems and coping resources of African American breast cancer survivors. Poster session presented at *Cancer survivorship research: Translating science to care*. Arlington, VA.

Camp-Sorrell, D. 2009. Cancer and its treatment effect on young breast cancer survivors. *Seminars in Oncology Nursing, 25*(4), 251–258.

Campesino, M., Saenz, D. S., Choi, M., & Krouse, R. S. (2012). Perceived discrimination and ethnic identity among breast cancer survivors. *Oncology Nursing Forum, 39*(2), E91–E100.

Conway-Phillips, R., & Millon-Underwood, S. (2009). Breast cancer screening behaviors of African American women: A comprehensive review, analysis, and critique of nursing research. *Association of Black Nursing Faculty Journal, 20*(4), 97–101.

Crump, S. R., Shipp, M. P.-L., McCray, G. G., Morris, S. J., Okoli, J. A., Caplan, L. S., Thorne, S. L., & Blumenthal, D. S. (2008). Abnormal mammogram follow-up: Do community lay health advocates make a difference? *Health Promotion Practice, 9*(2), 140–148.

Darby, K., Davis, C., Likes, W., & Bell, J. (2009). Exploring the financial impact of breast cancer for African American medically underserved women: A qualitative study. *Journal of Health Care for the Poor & Underserved, 20*(3): 721–728.

Dunn, B. K., Agurs-Collins, T., Browne, D., Lubet, R., & Johnson, K. A. (2010). Health disparities in breast cancer: Biology meets socioeconomic status. *Breast Cancer Research and Treatment, 121*(2), 281–292.

Durant, R. W., Legedza, A. T., Marcantonio, E. R., Freeman, M. B., & Landon, B. E. (2011, Spring). Willingness to participate in clinical trials among African Americans and whites previously exposed to clinical research. *Journal of Cultural Diversity, 18*(1), 8–19.

Fatone, A. M., Moadel, A. B., Foley, F. W., Fleming, M., & Jandorf, L. (2007). Urban voices: The quality-of-life experience among women of color with breast cancer. *Palliative & Supportive Care, 5*(2), 115–125.

Freedman, T. G. (1998). Why don't they come to pike street and ask us? Black women's health concerns. *Social Science & Medicine, 47*(7), 941–947.

Gallia, K. S., & Pines, E. W. (2009). Narrative identity and spirituality of African American churchwomen surviving breast cancer survivors. *Journal of Cultural Diversity, 16*(2), 50–55.

Gamble, V. N. (1993). A legacy of distrust: African Americans and medical research. *American Journal of Preventive Medicine, 9*(6), 35–38.

Germino, B. B., Mishel, M. H., Alexander, G. R., Jenerette, C., Blyler, D., Baker, C., Vines, A. I., Green, M., & Long, D. G. (2011). Engaging African American breast cancer survivors in an intervention trial: Culture responsiveness and community. *Journal of Cancer Survivorship, 5*(1), 82–91.

Gibson, L. M. (2008). Teaching strategies to facilitate breast cancer screening by African-American women. *Journal of National Black Nurses Association, 19*(2), 42–49.

Gibson, L. M., & Hendricks, C. S. (2006). Integrative review of spirituality in African American breast cancer survivors. *Association of Black Nursing Faculty Journal, 17*(2), 67–72.

Gullatte, M. M., Phillips, J. M., & Gibson, L. M. (2006). Factors associated with delays in screening of self-detected breast changes in African-American women. *Journal of National Black Nurses Association, 17*(1), 45–50.

Halbert, C. H., Kessler L., Wileyto, E. P., Weathers, B., Stopfer, J., Domchek, S., Collier, A., & Brewster, K. (2006). Breast cancer screening behaviors among African American women with a strong family history of breast cancer. *Preventive Medicine, 43*(5), 385–388.

Halbert, C. H., Weathers, B., Esteve, R., Audrain-McGovern, J., Kumanyika, S., DeMichele, A., & Barg, F. (2008). Experiences with weight change in African-American breast cancer survivors. *Breast Journal, 14*(2), 182–187.

Hamilton, J. B., & Sandelowski, M. (2004). Types of social support in African Americans with cancer. *Oncology Nursing Forum, 31*(4), 792–800.

Hamilton, J. B., Powe, B. D., Pollard, A. B., Lee, K. J., & Felton, A. M. (2007). Spirituality among African American cancer survivors: Having a personal relationship with God. *Cancer Nursing, 30*(4), 309–316.

Hamilton, J. B., Moore C. E., Powe, B. D., Agarwal, M., & Martin, P. (2010). Perceptions of support among older African American cancer survivors. *Oncology Nursing Forum, 37*(4), 484–493.

Heiney, S. P., Hazlett, L. J., Weinrich, S. P., Wells, L. M., Adams, S. A., Underwood, S. M., & Parrish, R. S. (2011). Antecedents and mediators of community connection in African American women with breast cancer. *Research & Theory for Nursing Practice, 25*(4), 252–270.

Henderson, P. D., & Fogel, J. (2003). Support networks used by African American breast cancer support group participants. *Association of Black Nursing Faculty Journal, 14*(5), 95–98.

Johnson Farmer, B. (2009). *Quality of life: The humanbecoming perspective. A descriptive exploratory study* (PhD dissertation). Marquette University, Milwaukee, WI.

Kelley, M. A. (2011). Recruitment of African American women for research on breast cancer early detection: Using culturally appropriate interventions. *Southern Online Journal of Nursing Research, 11*(1).

King, D. W., Duello, T. M., Miranda, P. Y., Hodges, K. P., Shelton, A. J., Chukelu, P., & Jones, L. A. (2010). Strategies for recruitment of healthy premenopausal women into the African American nutrition for life (A NULIFE) study. *Journal of Women's Health, 19*(5), 855–862.

Kooken, W. C., Haase, J. E., & Russell, K. M. (2007). "I've Been through Something": Poetic explorations of African American women's cancer survivorship. *Western Journal of Nursing Research, 29*(7), 896–919.

Lazarus, R. S., & Folkman, S. (1984). *Stress, appraisal, and coping.* New York: Springer.

Lewis, P. E., Sheng, M., Rhodes, M. M., Jackson, K. E., & Schover, L. R. (2012). Psychosocial concerns of young African American breast cancer survivors. *Journal of Psychosocial Oncology, 30*(2), 168–184.

Linden, H. M., Reisch, L. M., Hart, A., Harrington, M. A., Nakano, C., Jackson, J. C., & Elmore, J. G. (2007). Attitudes toward participation in breast cancer randomized clinical trials in the African American community: A focus group study. *Cancer Nursing, 30*(4), 261–269.

Magai, C., Consedine, N., Adjei, B., Hershman, D., & Neugut, A. (2008). Psychosocial influences on suboptimal adjuvant breast cancer treatment adherence among African American women: Implications for education and intervention. *Health Education & Behavior, 35*(6), 835–854.

Maly, R. C., Leake, B., Mojica, C. M., Liu, Y., Diamant, A. L., & Thind, A. (2011). What influences diagnostic delay in low-income women with breast cancer? *Journal of Women's Health, 20*(7), 1017–1023.

Masi, C. M., & Gehlert, S. (2008). Perceptions of breast cancer treatment among African American women and men: Implications for interventions. *Journal of General Internal Medicine, 24*(3), 408–414.

Morgan, P. D., Tyler, I. D., & Fogel, J. (2008). Fatalism revisited. *Seminars in Oncology Nursing, 24*(4), 237–245.

Newlin, K., Knafl, K., & Melkus, G. D. (2002). African-American spirituality: Concept analysis. *Advances in Nursing Science, 25*(2), 57–70.

Outlaw, F. H. (1993). Stress and coping: The influence of racism on the cognitive appraisal processing of African American. *Issues in Mental Health Nursing, 14*(4), 399–409.

Outlaw, F. H. (2006). African American women and depression. In C. F. Collins (Ed.), *African American women's health and social issues* (2nd ed., pp. 142–157). Westport, CT: Praeger.

Outlaw, F. H., Bourjolly, J. N., & Barg, F. K. (2000). A study of recruitment of black Americans into clinical trials through a cultural competence lens. *Cancer Nursing, 23*(6), 444–451.

Peate, M., Meiser, B., Hickey, M., & Friedlander, M. (2009). The fertility-related concerns, needs, and preferences of younger women with breast cancer: A systematic review. *Breast Cancer Research and Treatment, 116*(2), 215–223.

Phillips, J. M., & Cohen, M. Z. (2011). The meaning of breast cancer risk for African American women. *Journal of Nursing Scholarship, 43*(3), 239–247.

Phillips, J. M., Cohen, M. Z., & Moses, G. (1999). Breast cancer screening and African American women: Fear, fatalism, and silence. *Oncology Nursing Forum, 26*(3), 561–571.

Powe, B. D., & Finnie, R. (2003). Cancer fatalism: The state of the science. *Cancer Nursing, 26*(6): 454–465.

Powe, B. D., Hamilton, J., & Brooks, P. (2006). Perceptions of cancer fatalism and cancer knowledge: A comparison of older and younger African American women. *Journal of Psychosocial Oncology, 24*(4), 1–13.

Ray, M., & Polite, B. N. (2010). Triple-negative breast cancers: A view from 10,000 feet. *Cancer Journal, 16*(1), 17–22.

Robertson, E. M., Franklin, A. W., Flores, A., Wherry, S., & Buford, J. (2006). African American community breast health education: A pilot project. *Association of Black Nursing Faculty Journal, 17*(1), 48–51.

Roff, L., Simon, C., Nelson-Gardell, D., & Pleasants, H. (2009). Spiritual support and African American breast cancer survivors. *Affilia, 24*(3), 285–299.

Rosenzweig, M., Brufsky, A., Rastogi, P., Puhalla, S., Simon, J., & Underwood, S. (2011). The attitudes, communication, treatment, and support intervention to reduce breast cancer treatment disparity. *Oncology Nursing Forum, 38*(1), 85–89.

Russell, K., Ah, D. V., Giesler, R. B., Storniolo, A. M., & Haase, J. E. (2008). Quality of life of African American breast cancer survivors: How much do we know?" *Cancer Nursing, 31*(6), E36–E45.

Spurlock, W. R., & Cullins, L. S. (2006). Cancer fatalism and breast cancer screenings in African American women. *Association of Black Nursing Faculty Journal, 17*(1), 38–43.

Stolley, M. R., Sharp, L. K., Wells, A. M., Simon, N., & Schiffer, L. (2006). Health behaviors and breast cancer: Experiences of urban African American women. *Health Education & Behavior, 33*(5), 604–624.

Tate, J. D. (2011). The role of spirituality in the breast cancer experiences of African American women. *Journal of Holistic Nursing, 29*: 249–255.

Underwood, S. M., Richards, K., Bradley, P. K., & Robertson, E. (2008). Pilot study of the breast cancer experiences of African American women with a family history of breast cancer: Implications for nursing practice. *Association of Black Nursing Faculty Journal, 19*(3), 107–113.

Vona-Davis, L., & Rose, D. P. (2009). The influence of socioeconomic disparities on breast cancer tumor biology and prognosis: A review. *Journal of Women's Health, 18*(6), 883–893.

Walker, R. E., Keane, C. R., & Burke, J. G. (2010). Disparities and access to healthy food in the United States: A review of food deserts literature. *Health & Place, 16*(5), 876–884.

Wilmoth, M. C., & Sanders, L. D. (2001). Accept me for myself: African American women's issues after breast cancer. *Oncology Nursing Forum, 28*(5), 875–879.

Woods-Giscombé, C. L. (2010). Superwoman schema: African American women's views on stress, strength, and health. *Qualitative Health Research, 20*(5), 668–683.

Wujcik, D., & Fair, A. M. (2008). Barriers to diagnostic resolution after abnormal mammography: A review of the literature. *Cancer Nursing, 31*(5), E16–E30.

Wujcik, D., Shyr, Y., Li, M., Clayton, M. F., Ellington, L., Menon, U., & Mooney, K. (2009). Delay in diagnostic testing after abnormal mammography in low-income women. *Oncology Nursing Forum, 36*(6), 709–715.

Young, R. F., Schwartz, K., & Booza, J. (2011). Medical barriers to mammography screening of African American women in a high cancer mortality area: Implications for cancer educators and health providers. *Journal of Cancer Education, 26*(2), 262–269.

# 5

# The Skinny on Fat and Exercise: Truth about Obesity among Black Women

## *Portia Johnson and Yvonne Wesley*

## INTRODUCTION

According to the U.S. Department of Health and Human Services, more than one-third of American adults were obese in 2009–2010 (Ogden, Carroll, Kit, & Flegal, 2012). These authors make the point that persons with obesity are at greater risk of hypertension and diabetes mellitus, while others link obesity to cardiovascular disease (Bozorgmanesh, Hadaegh, & Azizi, 2010) and certain cancers (Reynolds, Donohoe, & Doyle, 2011). As shown in Figure 5.1, U.S. national survey data suggests that income does not always have a linear relationship to the prevalence of obesity among adults aged 20 and over. When looking at total poverty income ratio levels—high ($\geq 350\%$), medium (130%–350%), and low ($\leq 130\%$)—then separating males from females, medium income males appear to have the highest prevalence of obesity. The highest prevalence of obesity for females were found among the low-income group.

Furthermore, looking at obesity prevalence by race/ethnicity appears to change the picture. For example, among the Non-Hispanic Black males, the highest prevalence of obesity was within this high-income subgroup of males; whereas for Non-Hispanic White males, the highest prevalence of obesity was among the medium-income males. Among the females, the lowest prevalence of obesity was in the highest-income subgroup, although this was least marked among Non-Hispanic Black females. Figure 5.1 demonstrates that Non-Hispanic Black females have the highest prevalence of obesity within all three income subgroups.

**Figure 5.1**

Prevalence of Obesity among Adults Aged 20 years and Over, by Poverty Income Ratio (PIR), Gender, and Race/Ethnicity in United States for 2005–2008

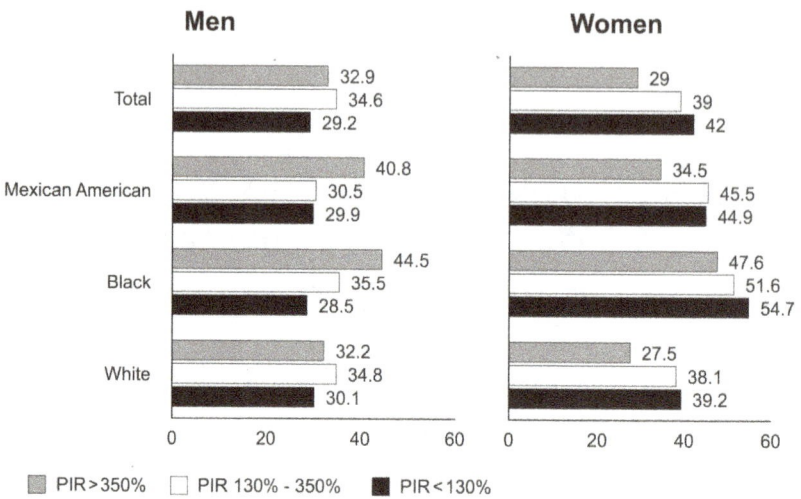

*Note:* Persons of other race/ethnicities are included in total.

*Source:* CDC/NCHS (n.d.), *National health and nutrition examination survey, 2005–2008.* Hyattsville, MD: National Center for Health Statistics.

Specific to Black women, Gaston, Porter, and Thomas (2011) report that Black women have a higher prevalence of major risk factors for obesity, such as physical inactivity, poor nutrition, and increased stress. They note that many other less clear and complex contributing factors such as attitude, behaviors, and culture compound the problem of obesity among Black women.

In a study of 351 Black women where 47 percent had a 4-year college degree, Gaston et al. (2011) found that 64 percent were either obese or extremely obese. While less than one-third of the participants were satisfied with their weight, more than half of the women were pleased with their health knowledge, attitudes, and behaviors. Similar to Centers for Disease Control and Prevention National Health and Nutrition Examination Survey (CDC NHANES) data, this sample of mixed-income Black women have a high level of obesity regardless of their socioeconomic status.

As college-educated professionals, nurses have also been shown to be overweight or obese (Naidoo & Coopoo, 2007). Although there is a void in the literature on Black nurses in the United States, in Naidoo and Coopoo's South African study of 107 hospital based nurses, mean age 37, the authors found that only 52 percent reported they were engaged in some form of weight loss activity. However, on average, the nurses were 5.2 feet (1.58 m) tall and weighed 163 lbs (74 kg). Using three measures of obesity—mean body fat, body mass index (BMI), and waist-to-hip ratio (WHR)—Naidoo and Coopoo (2007) found that the nurses were obese or overweight. Despite the focus of the study on the relationship of obesity and lower back pain, their study documents that Black educated professionals also struggle with weight issues.

Found mainly in anecdotal journalism such as blogs and Web postings, there is a general consensus that nurses should practice what they preach. Some argue that taking on a lifestyle change to lose weight may take more effort for nurses compared to those who are not nurses, have stable work hours, and less stressful environments (Durning, 2011). Bloggers ask nurses to be part of the obesity solution instead of the problem. In an article provided on New York University's website, an investigator suggests that nurses have higher overweight and obesity patterns due to workplace psychological stress, which leads to negative behavioral patterns (Englesius, 2007). Bloggers on the *American Journal of Nursing*'s webpage also describe how nurses are teachers and need to "walk the talk." The blogger suggests that nurses need to model the information that they share with patients (McDaniel, 2009). Even in Britain, overweight and obese nurses face challenges with patient confidence in their health tips (Gorgan, 2009). Gorgan (2009) suggests that nurses as well as Black women struggle with obesity. Nevertheless, the solution is multifactorial and is not easily resolved with income and education.

## FAT MEASUREMENTS AND GENETICS

Del Parigi (2010) describes obesity as excess adipose tissue mass. Obesity has been measured by various methods that include (1) the Metropolitan height/weight table, (2) skinfold thickness, (3) body mass index (BMI), (4) bioelectrical impedance, (5) crude weight, (6) densitometry, (7) dual energy X-ray absorptiometry (DEXA), (8) lean body mass (LBM), and (9) waist-to-hip ratio (WHR).

First developed by a life insurance company in the early 1900s, height/weight tables helped insurance companies set premiums based on how long a person was expected to live because of their healthy weight. According to Flegal, Carroll, Kuczmarski, and Johnson (1998), the tables were developed from a convenient sample of people aged 25 to 59, who purchased life insurance. Even though some health-care providers still use this method, this history makes the table inappropriate for use among most of today's Americans.

Skinfold measurement has also gathered attention and has been a popular method to measure body composition in epidemiologic studies. Different from combinations of weight and weight as used in BMI, skin calipers measure skinfold thickness to determine adipose tissue amounts. Providing a direct measure of body fat, this method has been appealing to many. However, the skinfold measure is limited, because not all body fat is accessible to the calipers. The distribution of subcutaneous fat, which can vary significantly over the human body as well as intraabdominal and intramuscular fat, make the skinfold method less valid (Bellisari, Roche, & Siervogel, 1993; Rosenbaum, Leibel, & Hirsch, 1997).

Considered one of the most practical and therefore the most popular method of measuring obesity, Kuczmarski, Carroll, Flegal, & Troiano (1997) suggest the use of BMI, which is a person's weight in kilograms divided by their height in meters squared (kg/m$^2$; Table 5.1). It determines the degree to which a person may be overweight or obese and gives a reasonable assessment of total body fat. Knowing ones BMI is important, because it relates to health conditions like heart disease and Type 2 diabetes. It should be noted that Rush et al. (2007) explain that ethnicity may influence the interpretation of BMI as muscularity and fat mass are different according to race/ethnicity. In a sample of 721 New Zealand and South African Black and White women, Rush et al. (2007) found significant differences in total body fat relative to their BMIs. Moreover, they note that the inconsistency in prior research is due, in part, to race/ethnicity as BMI and waist circumference are poor measures of obesity's relationship with disease risk. The authors suggest that total body fat rather than BMI is a better indicator for disease risk (Rush et al., 2007).

When measuring lean body mass (LBM), the difference between lean tissue and total body mass can be used to determine the amount of adipose tissue. Moyad (2004) explains that the body can be seen as mainly two different types of tissue: (1) lean tissue or (2) adipose tissue. Lean tissue is involved in nutritional metabolic pathways related to overall size, according to Moyad (2004). He explains that lean tissue consists mainly of muscle, bone, extracellular water, nervous tissue, a variety of organs, and all of the cells that are not adipose. By dividing body composition into two parts, lean and adipose tissues, an anthropometric method can be used.

Table 5.1
Classification of Weight by BMI

| Healthy Weight | Overweight | Obesity (Class 1) | Obesity (Class 2) | Severe Obesity (Class 3) |
| --- | --- | --- | --- | --- |
| 18.5–24.9 | 25–29.9 | 30–34.9 | 35–39.9 | 40 or more |

Another method of measuring body fat is to divide the body on the basis of chemical composition, rather than anatomy. Moyad (2004) tells how bioelectric impedance analysis is based on the idea that LBM is a better conductor of electricity than fat. The less lean tissue, the more electrical resistance. Once the total body mass has been established, then the percent of body fat can be calculated. Two to four electrodes are placed on the extremities, while the person is dressed and laying down. A small radio frequency is applied to the electrodes to measure electrical current impedance. In less than a minute, a printout is provided with the percent of body fat. Another simple method of measuring obesity is the WHR. The waist is the largest abdominal circumference between the umbilicus and the crest of the iliac. The hip is just below the iliac crest. A WHR greater than 0.80 in women and 0.90 in men is a fairly accurate predictor of disease risk.

Crude weight, perhaps the simplest method of determining obesity, is simply stepping on a scale and reading the values. Densitometry is based on the notion that adipose tissue does not weigh as much as lean tissue. While sitting on a scale submerged in water, the percentage of total body mass that is made up of fat tissue can be determined when comparing the person's weight from a standard scale. Considered one of the most accurate methods of measuring weight, dual energy x-ray absorptiometry (DEXA) uses an X-ray beam and body scanner. Depending on the professional you are working with, you will find there is still disagreement on the best, cheap, simple, accurate, and reliable measure of obesity. Aside from measuring obesity, genetics as a predisposition to obesity is another topic of discussion.

The literature that examines the interaction between environment and genetics links blood pressure and BMI. Taylor (2009) mentions that markers on chromosome 1 and 8 interact with obesity and hypertension. The association between BMI and hypertension was only noted in obese or overweight Blacks. However, Taylor (2009) indicates that obesity genetic markers are not particularly associated with genetic risks for hypertension among Blacks. The FTO gene is one of the more studied genes for obesity. Adeyemo and colleagues (2010) concluded that a genetic variant within the FTO may be a better method of studying the link between genes and obesity among Blacks. Presently, there are conflicting findings regarding genetics and a predisposition to obesity. Moreover, Adeyemo et al. (2010) explain that the link between the FTO gene and obesity is found most often among people of European descent compared to persons of African descent. Demerath et al. (2011) highlight the point that physical activity may play a role in conflicting findings among Blacks. For example, inactive African American men were found to have a significant positive relationship between the rs9939609 A[1] allele and increased BMI. However, this was not held true for African American women. For now, we cannot fully ascertain to what degree genetics may play in terms of the cause for the high prevalence of obesity among Black women. More research studies are needed.

### Black Women's Perception of Fat Mind-Set toward Obesity

Gaston et al. (2011) found, in a study of 351 African American women, that even though these women were mostly obese or extremely obese, they considered their health knowledge, attitude, and behaviors to be healthy and appropriate. They rated their general health to be "good" or "very good." Gaston et al. (2011) suggest that Black women have ambivalent attitudes and negative feelings toward weight norms and physical activity. Both Black women and men, according to Gaston et al., often perceived overweight women as more attractive and emotionally stronger than appropriate or underweight women. Perhaps, their perceptions were reinforced by popular TV icons such as Mo'Nique and Queen Latifah, thereby reducing stigma or social pressure to change diet and exercise habits. These authors stress the point that Black women do not see their weight as an important issue, nor did the participants see their weight as a limitation stopping them from participating in physical activities such as sex, exercise, or sports. Although Oprah perceived her weight as one to be changed, this TV icon demonstrated the hardship of sustainability of weight loss as a Black woman.

In an essay by Kumanyika (2005), the point is well taken that a catch-22 exists. Denigrating stereotypes such as the role of Mammy in *Gone with the wind* already exist in the American culture and should not be enhanced. Therefore, it is not the intention of this chapter to perpetuate stereotypes that all Black women are disinterested in losing weight. However, findings from Gaston et al.'s (2011) study also revealed that there is not an inverse relationship between obesity and social class among Black women. In other words, whether rich or poor, Black women tend to be overweight and/or obese. Their study also showed that obese or extremely obese women with graduate level education had (1) the highest general health rating, (2) the lowest level of satisfaction with their weight, and (3) believed they had control over their health.

Solovay (1991) and, more recently, Parham and Scarinci (2007) found that African American women believe obesity has an advantage noting that "if you are fat and get sick, you've got some meat stored." Using focus groups of low-income Black men and women living in the Mississippi Delta, the authors revealed the follow themes: (1) overeating, (2) obesity is not a major health concern, and (3) a poor definition of a healthy balance of eating and exercise. Despite this type of mind-set, the participants indicated that social support interventions may be helpful in eliminating obesity.

When thinking about obesity and Black women, the question can be raised: Do Black women perceive that they are as overweight or obese as the Centers for Disease Control and Prevention (CDC) current statistics say they really are? According to the CDC (2011), 50 percent of Black women in the United States are obese. Black women accept themselves and are accepted by their peers, according to Averett and Korenman (1999) and Gaston et al. (2011). They see themselves as "beautiful and healthy." Potentially, this perception may create a safe haven or a support system, thereby making it more difficult to see the dangers of obesity and for weight changes to occur. This perception also has a direct effect on how well one can say that they feel in terms of their health on any given day.

Black women tend to be more pleased with their body weight than White women, according to Ristovski-Slijepcevic, Bell, Chapman, and Beagan (2010). In fact, they contend that Black women develop their own strong paradigm of positive self-evaluation as a result of their stigmatization in the larger society. Forming an "Afrocentric" point of view allows Black women to resist mainstream images and create positive self-definitions (Ristovski-Slijepcevic et al., 2010). The Afrocentric point of view may contribute to the acceptance of obesity in the Black community, which may lead to negative health outcomes.

## BLACK MEN'S PERCEPTION OF FAT

Cachelin, Rebeck, Chung, and Pelayo (2002) note that Black men have a greater affinity for larger women and were less tolerant of very thin figures compared to White men. They found that Black men differed significantly from White women; in that Black men chose the heaviest female figure as attractive ($p = 0.02$), while White women chose the thinnest male figures. These results were found among a sample of 1,229 participants: 801 women and 428 men, in which 288 were Asian, 548 Hispanic, 208 African American, and 185 were White. Ristovski-Slijepcevic et al. (2010) posit an explanation for why Black women are obese or overweight. These authors suggest that Black men prefer women of a larger body type. Compared to their White male counterparts, Black men tend to relate more favorable traits with large women, as acknowledged by Ristovski-Slijepcevic and colleagues (2010).

However, Seo and Torabi (2006) provide conflicting findings that race did not significantly predict attitudes and perceptions about obesity. This was due to the fact that Seo and Torabi (2006) asked questions that both Blacks and Whites agreed upon. For example, both racial groups saw obesity as a problem in the United States. They perceived that obese people could do something about their weight, and that obese people have a higher chance of getting cancer. Seo and Torabi (2006) did not query Black men's attitude toward body size preferences.

## LIFESTYLE PATTERNS: FRIEND OR FOE

When looking at perceptions that Black women have about weight, cultural traditions must be taken into account. In terms of cultural perception of weight and obesity, Bramble, Cornelius, and Simpson (2009) conducted four focus groups of Afro-Caribbean and African American women (age 40 and older) to explore cultural factors related to eating, exercise, and weight. The women did not perceive the BMI as being a good indicator of their body size. Here are direct quotes from the focus groups:

> "Today it means something different than what I did before. Today it means if you have a BMI of 25 or 30 that you're obese. Obesity means to me how I feel my agility, personally, how I feel and how I look in my clothes. If I don't look good in my clothes or don't feel good in my clothes than I feel I am obese."
>
> "To me, what is obesity is not obesity to someone else and they have a blanket format that states what obesity is. So, I weigh 185, and I am 5'2" so for them, I am way over the 20 or 30 pounds over the desired weight for my height so I would be considered obese based on their standards but in my eyes, I am not obese."

However, another participant shared how she viewed herself in terms of body size:

> "O.K. I think I am obese. I never was this big in my life. This is the biggest I have been and I don't like to look at my body because I see the fat hanging around! This is how I see myself!"

Culturally, Black women have food practices (cooking style, food preference, and food portion size) that have been handed down from generation to generation. Some cultural foods are highly processed and cooked with large quantities of fat and sugar (Carlisle 2011). Bramble et al. (2009) findings also suggest that Afro-Caribbean women sense a loss of their culture as they attempt to prepare food according to their traditions while they are in the United States. The women perceived a loss of physical activity while living in the United States as they were not required to walk miles to get food, work in a garden, wash clothes, or clean their homes. In fact, the women agreed that there was a change in their food choices and preparation after moving to the United States. The African American women shared a different view on food preparation and family meals (Bramble et al., 2009). Similar to Afro-Caribbean women, the African American women spoke of traditional food preparation from their grandparents and great-grandparents. However, the African American women acknowledge that their family history of illness and food preparation require a lifestyle change. Bramble et al. conclude that the focus group findings reaffirmed similarities as well as the cultural variations across the African Diaspora that can affect health education interventions.

In a report that describes the results of fitness centers in an urban setting, Choitz et al. (2010) found that urban residents were less likely to participate in leisure time physical activity than nonurban residents. Outlining the barriers to physical activity, Choitz et al. (2010) mentioned the following as excuses:

> Old age, personal health, socio-economic status, geography, social and physical environment, disability, lack of access to facilities, time constraints, roles within the family, stage of change, and cost.

These are frequently cited as barriers to increased physical activity and exercise.

Despite an attrition rate of 50 percent, Choitz and colleagues (2010) were pleased that the typical participant, a 53-year-old Black woman took the initiative to start exercising. By placing fitness centers in the urban setting, the authors were able to eliminate common barriers and more than 800 predominately women ($n = 620$) engaged in physical activity, thereby improving health and wellness. As diet and exercise are important to health, Choitz et al. (2010) recommend the development of strategies that include social marketing, affordable fees, fitness centers in the urban community, and an understanding of motivation, family lifestyle demands, and personal expectations.

Thomas, Moseley, Stalling, Nichols-English, and Wagner's (2008) qualitative data highlights barriers to exercise not mentioned by Choitz et al. (2010). Focus group data revealed that Black women were concerned about sweating and messing-up their hair. Moreover, a woman shared that her husband enjoyed big thighs and stated he did not want her to lose weight.

The husband's comments may have given the woman cause to remain overweight and not exercise.

## TREATMENT AND OBESITY PREVENTION

Burke and Wang (2011) offer three methods for the management of overweight and obesity: (1) lifestyle modification, (2) pharmacotherapy, and

(3) bariatric surgery. Lifestyle modification includes setting goals, self-monitoring food intake, and exercising to prevent or treat obesity. Weight loss medications are appropriate for persons with a BMI of at least 30 kg/m² with one who has no comorbidities or someone with a BMI of at least 27 kg/m² and comorbidities. Common bariatric surgeries to achieve weight loss include the Roux-en-Y gastric bypass, commonly known as the "gastric bypass"; the laparoscopic adjustable gastric banding procedure, commonly known as the "lapband"; vertical-banded gastroplasty; and biliopancreatic diversion and duodenal switch. Regardless of the treatment method, the authors stress the importance of behavioral strategies as lifestyle modification to maintain or lose weight.

## CONCLUSION

In summary, the skinny on fat and exercise among Black women is very complex and not easy to resolve. Black women have greater BMIs and other measures of weight compared to other women. It is also clear that increased weight produces health problems. In addition, the literature suggests that Black men prefer full-figured women. It is also evident that Black women have numerous excuses for a sedentary lifestyle and poor eating patterns. What remains unclear is the role of genes, the environment, and interventions to curb the rising prevalence of obesity among Black women.

This chapter took a closer look at the bio-psycho-social reasons that may explain why there is so much obesity among Black women. Leaving room to question the biological link between race and obesity, the chapter highlighted recent literature regarding the FTO gene and its response activity. However, study findings are conflicting and seem to suggest the relationship between the FTO gene and BMI may not currently exist within Black women. Beyond physiologic reasons for obesity among Black women, the psycho-social-cultural impacts were examined, with special attention given to attitudes among Black men and women. With lifestyle habits of eating and exercise, it appears many Black men and women disagree with social and medical definitions of obesity. In fact, the literature suggests whether U.S. born or not, many Black men and women embrace a more stout body size.

More studies are needed that investigate the impact of Black men's attitudes on Black women's behavior regarding body size. As many women are influenced by their partners' opinions, studies that provide insight on the association between Black men and women are important. Specifically, more investigations are needed that show the impact of attitudes and subjective norms toward a specific behavior that may influence intention.

In addition, research that examines muscularity and the distribution of body fat among Blacks is also needed. Sustainability is also another fertile area for investigation, as the current status of obesity treatment and prevention relies mainly on lifestyle modification; however, there is no one size fits all. What works for one ethnic/racial group may not work for everyone or even for persons within the same ethnic group. After all is said and done, it is also important to look at the role of stress viewed as racism and the coping mechanisms used in the Black population. Also there are an abundance of fast food restaurants primarily located in the poorer Black communities as well as a deficit in those neighborhoods of supermarkets, which often voids the members of the community of fresh fruits and vegetables and less processed foods. Given these issues, the solution to weight loss for African Americans is complex. The political, environmental, and research community will continue to join hands to ascertain a viable option for this chronic disease.

## NOTE

1. All living things have cells. Cell make up tissue and organs. Inside each cell is a nucleus. Inside the nucleus is a thread-like structure called chromosomes. Each chromosome is composed of very long chains of DNA. Building blocks of the DNA are nucleotides. The nucleotide consists of one of four DNA bases: thymine, adenine, guanine, and cytosine. Represented in the letters TAGC, a single strand of DNA can have any sequence of these letters. This four-letter code produces protein that gives

| Gene Name | Master Data Set Name | Alleles |
| --- | --- | --- |
| FTO | rs9939609 | A/T |

living things a structure. Humans have thousands of different proteins that are all coded by the four letters, TAGC. Variation at a base single is called a single nucleotide polymorphism. Sometimes, when the gene is copied, a single base pair gets left out, added, or substituted; the changes are called SNPs. The SNPs account for many of the differences among humans. rs9939609 is a SNP in the fat mass and obesity-associated FTO gene, aka the "fat gene." In other words, the rs9939609 is the change in the FTO gene that has been associated with increased BMI.

## REFERENCES

Adeyemo, A., Chen, G., Zhou, J., Shriner, D., Doumatey, A., Huang, H., & Rotimi, C. (2010). FTO genetic variation and association with obesity in West African and African Americans. *Diabetes, 59*(6), 1549–1554.

Averett, S. L., & Korenman, S. (1999). Black-white differences in social and economic consequences of obesity. *International Journal of Obesity and Related Metabolic Disorders, 23*(2), 166–173.

Bellisari, A., Roche, A. F., & Siervogel, R. M. (1993). Reliability of B-mode ultrasonic measurements of subcutaneous adipose tissue and intra-abdominal depth: Comparisons with skinfold thickness. *International Journal of Obesity Related Metabolic Disorders, 17*(8), 475–480.

Bozorgmanesh, M., Hadaegh, F., & Azizi, F. (2010). Diabetes prediction, lipid accumulation product, and adiposity measures; 6-year follow-up: Tehran lipid and glucose study. *Lipids in Health & Disease, 9*(1), 45. doi:10.1186/1476-511X-9-45

Bramble, J., Cornelius, L. J., & Simpson, G. (2009). Eating as a cultural expression of caring among Afro-Caribbean and African American: Understanding the cultural dimensions of obesity. *Journal of Health Care for the Poor and Underserved, 20*(2), S53–S68.

Burke, L. E., & Wang, J. (2011). Treatment strategies for overweight and obesity. *Journal of Nursing Scholarship, 43*(4), 368–375.

Cachelin, F. M., Rebeck, R. M., Chung, G. H., & Pelayo, E. (2002). Does ethnicity influence body-size preference? A comparison of body image and body size. *Obesity Research, 10*(3), 158–166.

Carlisle, D. (2011). Hard to stomach. *Nursing Standard, 26*(15–17), 20–21.

CDC. (2011). *U.S. obesity trends.* Atlanta, GA: CDC. Retrieved from http://www.cdc.gov/obesity/data/trends.html

Choitz, P., Johnson, M. P., Berhane, Z., Lefever, G., Anderson, J. K., & Eiser, A. R. (2010). Urban fitness centers: Removing barriers to promote exercise in underserved communities. *Journal of Health Care for the Poor and Underserved, 21*(1), 221–228.

Del Parigi, A. (2010). Definition and classification of obesity. *Endotext.* Retrieved from http://www.endotext.org/obesity/obesity1/obesityframe1.htm

Demerath, E. W., Lutsey, P. L., Monda, K. L., Kao, W. H. L., Bressler, J., Pankow, J. S., North, K. E., & Folsom, A. R. (2011). Interaction of FTO and physical activity level on adiposity in African-American and European-American adults: The ARIC study. *Obesity, 19*(9): 1866–1872.

Durning, M. (2011). *Can fat nurses be good nurses?* Retrieved from http://scrubsmag.com/can-fat-nurses-be-good-nurses/

Englesius, E. (2007). *Nurses . . . heal thyself: A multidisciplinary study of obesity in the nursing profession.* Retrieved from http://www.nyu.edu/classes/keefer/EvergreenEnergy/englee.html

Flegal, K. M., Carroll, M. D., Kuczmarski, R. J., & Johnson, C. L. (1998). Overweight and obesity in the United States: Prevalence and trends, 1960–1994. *International Journal of Obesity, 22*(1), 39–47.

Gaston, M. H., Porter, G. K., & Thomas, V. G. (2011). Paradoxes in obesity with mid-life African American women. *Journal of the National Medical Association, 103*(1), 17–25.

Gorgan, E. 2009. *Overweight and obese nurses, a constant in the NHS.* Retrieved from http://news.softpedia.com/news/Overweight-and-Obese-Nurses-a-Constant-in-the-NHS-107580.shtml

Kuczmarski, R. J., Carroll, M. D., Flegal, K. M., & Troiano, R. P. (1997). Varying body mass index cutoff points to describe overweight prevalence among U.S. adults: NHANES III (1988 to 1994). *Obesity Research, 5*(6), 542–548.

Kumanyika, S. (2005). Obesity, health disparities, and prevention paradigms: Hard questions and hard choices. *Preventing Chronic Disease, Public Health Research, Practice, and Policy, 2*(4), 1–9.

McDaniel, P. (2009). *Obesity and advice: Should nurses practice what they teach?* Retrieved from http://ajnoffthecharts.com/2009/08/24/obesity-and-advice-should-nurses-practice-what-they-teach/

Moyad, M. A. (2004). Fad diets and obesity—Part I: Measuring weight in a clinical setting. *Urologic Nursing, 24*(2), 114–119.

Naidoo, R., & Coopoo, Y. (2007). The health and fitness profiles of nurses in KwaZulu-Natal. *Curationis, 30*(2), 66–73.

Ogden, C. L., Lamb, M. M., Carroll, M. D., & Flegal, K. M. (2010). *Obesity and socioeconomic status in adults: United States 1988–1994 and 2005–2008.* NCHS Data Brief No. 50. Hyattsville, MD: National Center for Health Statistics.

Ogden, C. L., Carroll, M. D., Kit, B. K., & Flegal, K. M. (2012). *Prevalence of obesity in the United States, 2009–2012.* NCHS Data Brief No. 82. Hyattsville, MD: National Center for Health Statistics.

Parham, G. P., & Scarinci, I. C. (2007). Strategies for achieving healthy energy balance among African Americans in the Mississippi Delta. *Preventing Chronic Disease, 4*(4), A97.

Reynolds, J. V., Donohoe, C. L., & Doyle, S. L. (2011). Diet, obesity and cancer. *Irish Journal of Medical Science, 180*(2), 521–527.

Ristovski-Slijepcevic, S., Bell, K., Chapman, G. E., & Beagan, B. L. (2010). Being "Thick" indicates you are eating, you are healthy and you have an attractive body shape: Perspectives on fatness and food choice amongst black and white men and women in Canada. *Health Sociology Review, 19*(3), 317–329.

Rosenbaum, M., Leibel, R. L., & Hirsch, J. (1997). Obesity. *New England Journal of Medicine, 337*(6), 396–407.

Rush, E. C., Goedecke, J. H., Jennings, C. L., Micklesfield, L. K., Dugas, L. R., Lambert, E. V., & Plank, L. D. (2007). BMI, fat and muscle differences in urban woman of five ethnicities from two countries. *International Journal of Obesity, 31*(8), 1232–1239.

Seo, D.-C., & Torabi, M. R. (2006). Racial/ethnic differences in body mass index, morbidity and attitudes toward obesity among U.S. adults. *Journal of the National Medical Association, 98*(8), 1300–1308.

Solovay, J. (1991). Obesity and socioeconomic status: A framework for examining relationships between physical and social variable. *Medical Anthropology, 13*(3), 231–247.

Taylor, J. Y. (2009). Genetic influences on disparities in hypertension and obesity in late life. *Annual Review of Gerontology and Geriatrics, 29*(1), 99–112.

Thomas, A. M., Moseley, G., Stalling, R., Nichols-English, G., & Wagner, P. J. (2008). Perception of obesity: Black and white differences. *Journal of Cultural Diversity, 15*(4), 174–180.

# SECTION II

# MENTAL HEALTH

# 6

# Super Sisters: Daring to Say It . . . Depression

## *Shuana K. Tucker and Lisa M. Loury-Lomas*

### WOMEN AND DEPRESSION

Many women in America suffer from depression, and more than half of them actually realize it or seek some form of treatment. Approximately 7 million women between ages 25 and 40 are diagnosed with depression on an annual basis. On average, women make 3 million visits to mental health professionals yearly and tend to be at a greater risk for major depression onset when compared to males (Kessler, 1995). Women have a higher risk than men of first onset episodes of depression, which can occur at anytime during a woman's life span (McGrath, Keita, Strickland, & Russo, 2001).

The World Health Organization produced a report titled "The Global Burden of Disease" (Murray & Lopez, 1996), which uncovered the fact that depression is the greatest disease burden for women when combined with all other diseases and that woman of color tend to be affected in disproportionate numbers. Despite 40 plus years of research targeting the treatment of depression, it still remains as one of the major public health challenges we face in the United States today (Blackburn, Eunson, & Bishop, 1986; Greenhouse, Stangl, Kupfer, & Prien, 1991; Hollon & Beck, 2004; Kovacs, Rush, Beck, & Hollon, 1981; Thase et al., 1997).

### AFRICAN AMERICAN WOMEN AND DEPRESSION

According to the U.S. Census Bureau, by the year 2050, it is estimated that half of the U.S. population will be comprised of ethnic and racially diverse people. With this rapid change in the landscape of the population, it will be imperative for researchers, clinicians, and the general public to understand that Eurocentric values specific to Whites may not be relevant or useful when addressing the mental health needs among African Americans and other racially diverse groups (USDHHS, 1999).

This poses major concern as clinical depression in African Americans seeking services from primary care facilities reveal that African Americans are showing greater signs and symptoms of depression than any other group (Dwight-Johnson, Unutzer, Sherbourne, Tang, & Wells, 2001). In a report compiled by the U.S. Surgeon General, African Americans reportedly have reduced access to no access to both mental health and health service facilities (USDHHS, 2001). Also, at times, when they are given access, they are less likely to receive the assistance they need, including antidepressant medications to help treat their depression (Melfi, Croghan, Hanna, & Robinson, 2000) and despite willingness to participate in mental health counseling (Blazer, Hybels, Simonsick, & Hanlon, 2000).

African American women's mental health needs have historically been misdiagnosed, underdiagnosed, and undertreated in investigations of psychiatric disorders (Brooks, 1997; Snowden & Pingitore, 2001). Psychiatric diagnoses are a key factor in treatment decision-making for persons seeking mental health services, especially African American women. The immediate and long-term effects of misdiagnoses and underdiagnoses of depression in African American women can have implications for increased incidence and prevalence of both psychiatric and medical disorders (Giles, Perlis, Reynolds, & Kupfer, 1998; Pickering, 2000).

Researchers and clinicians must be mindful of cultural influences when assessing depression in African American women. They must possess cultural competencies that are essential for accurate diagnoses and treatment plan.

African American people in general have a very unique history in the United States as most were introduced to this country via slavery (Billingsley, 1968; Blassingame, 1972; Clark, Anderson, Clark, & Williams, 1999). Some researchers refer to this as "double jeopardy" because women as a whole in our society are confronted with sexism and African American women also are confronted with racism, thus the double affect (Beal, 1969).

African American women are socialized to put the needs of others before their own; are consciously aware of their roles as spouse, mother, professional, caretaker, etc.; and feel guilty when engaging in activities to promote self-development (Carrington, 1980, 2002; Warren, 1994). When compared to their White counterparts, African American women's depression rates have been double (Kessler, 1995). The conflicting role of taking care of personal needs as opposed to family survival needs can leave an African American woman feeling guilty and depressed (Warren, 1994). To accompany this conflict, we must also address other factors that influence an African American woman's life such as discrimination, prejudices, racism, and a legacy of slavery, which impact the social and economic standing of a woman in the 21st century. These factors place African American women at the bottom rung of the hierarchical ladder in terms of economic, social, and political standing (USD-HHS, 1999); yet, African American women exhibit great strength and pride in overcoming adversity and maintain their mental health (Gray-Little & Hafdahl, 2000; USDHHS, 2001).

For many years, African American women have been recognized for their extraordinary individual and collective talents by utilizing their resources, mutual networks, and strong ties to the Black church. By doing so, it has given them the tradition and belief to enhance their survival by relying on each other and sharing experiences for survival (Broman, 1997).

## STIGMA

In today's society, there is an expectation regarding preventative medicine. The idea that good physical health has positive influence on life happiness is an underlying factor of this position. This expectation of using preventive medicine as a means of managing health is seen in the increased frequency of annual wellness visits, increased screening tools used by physicians, and insurance coverage for these medical visits by insurance companies. Additionally, there is an increased awareness of food choice, need for exercise, work life balance, and its affect on an individual's physical health. Along with recommendations from medical professionals, there is marketing of these ideas through commercials, print ads, public service announcements, and casual conversation among friends. It is almost unheard of for one to not participate in some course of regiment of preventive medicine for the purpose of increasing life expectancy and healthy living. With the increased focus on remaining physically healthy, it is surprising that there is not also an increased focus on maintaining one's mental health. Shockingly, there is more than simply a lack of focus in this area. There is a stigma attached to even the discussion of mental health, particularly as it pertains to African American women. Considering the focus on preventive medicine, it is surprising that a preventive approach to wellness in every area is not prevalent. However, the stigma of mental health issues in the African American community is real, continues, and is quite prevalent.

The stigma of having a mental health issue is one that must be addressed in the African American community. To be one of physical well-being, but not mental well-being is to create a false sense of well-being and healthy living. As the mind and body are interconnected where one directly influences the other, it is imperative that both entities receive proactive preventive attention, be professionally examined, and treated if necessary. For there to be an approach of prevention in any area, or even an attempt at remedy for that matter, there must first be an acknowledgement of the potential for disorder. In the African American community, acknowledgement of mental health issues of any kind is taboo (Conner et al., 2010). This refusal is directly related to the stigma associated with mental health. Understanding the stigma is necessary to remove it, because it is a barrier to good women's health.

In many instances, African American women refuse to acknowledge feelings of sadness and depression, because depression has a stigma and is viewed as weakness (Amankwaa, 2003; Waite & Killian, 2008). To risk being viewed as weak is a luxury that African American do not feel they have. In fact, acknowledging any behavior less than strength and courage is a position of fantasy and fairy tale. It is believed to be a stance that simply cannot exist if one is expected to survive. This of course is not true; however, African American often see themselves as warriors who can handle any difficulty life throws their way. To admit feeling depressed is to admit a weakness and to imply that one is unable to handle life. This is not a position African American will allow.

In the African American woman's reality, there is often a position of leadership in the family that is placed upon her. This position is taken because of necessity, not desire. Throughout history, African American women have been the caregivers in their families (Waite & Killian, 2008). Taking on the emotional, physical, and financial responsibility of one's self, siblings, elders, children, and sometimes husbands is a tremendous burden that creates stress and depression. However, in many cases, African American women carry these burdens of responsibility because there is no one else to step in and assist. Often, there is a negative view of African American women that includes being bossy and aggressive. These views are a result of ignorance and lack of understanding of the observer. Behaviors observed are often the result of the tremendous amount of stress placed. In addition to family obligations, challenges experienced by African American women also directly contribute to depression. These challenges include but aren't limited to single motherhood, domestic violence, sexual abuse, body image issues, financial difficulties, and being disadvantaged at work and placed at the bottom of the workplace hierarchy (Hunn & Craig, 2009). They have personally experienced burdens, and they have witnessed family members and friends' experiences of similar burdens, crisis, and tragedy. Even in light of these significant life issues, African American women do not acknowledge feelings of depression. To acknowledge depression is to consider oneself crazy in the African American community (Amankwaa, 2003). In many instances, these women are alone and with little help and support other then the support of God through faith. This also places a stigma on acknowledging feelings of depression because to embrace the idea of depression is to not have faith in God (Amankwaa, 2003). Faith in God is what has sustained the Black family over generations dating back to slavery. To question this faith creates an anxiety and depression that one will not want to acknowledge because of the associated stigma.

The stigma of depression for African American women is also rooted in the history and survival of racism in this country. The burdens of the Jim Crow Era and blatant and subtle racism directly impact the ability for African American women to trust (Hunn & Craig, 2009). Racism continues to be a part of the African American woman's experience (Brown & Keith, 2003). As a result of this ongoing, daily battle, coping mechanisms are developed for survival. The developed coping mechanisms are a result of a worldview. This view was adopted in large part as a result of having to face and overcome many life obstacles and is influenced by social and cultural experiences and values (Amankwaa, 2003; Waite & Killian, 2008). These mechanisms are necessary for women to function in their daily roles in life. Two examples of coping strategies are paranoia and distrust (Hunn & Craig, 2009). This inability to trust contributes to skepticism pertaining to the etiology of a mental health diagnosis and treatment (Anonymous, 2009). Furthermore, these issues of mistrust have also directly impacted how African American women perceive health-care providers. Medical professionals are often not trusted in the African American community because of such historic events as the Tuskegee syphilis experiment. In more recent years, medical professionals have also been seen as people who will use information against African American women and turn them over to social service agencies if any information is discovered. Hospitals, over the years, have also been seen as the place one goes to die (Amankwaa, 2009), which encourages distrust of doctors and institutions. If one doesn't trust the person making the diagnosis, it is impossible for the diagnosis or its origin to be trusted. This issue of lack of trust is relevant to stigma, because often African Americans are seen as foolish and paranoid by Caucasian Americans for their worldview and resistance. Being perceived in a negative light for beliefs and value systems continues to fan the flames of mistrust in African American women. As previously stated, this worldview of distrust evolved out of the need to cope as well as historic and cultural influences.

Without overcoming the negative stigma associated with the idea of having a mental health issue of any kind, but depression in particular, one is unwilling to seek professional help and take steps in resolving issues (Conner et al., 2010). In the instances where individuals are willing to seek treatment, it is not one of talk therapy or counseling but that of medication. Medication is often a viable option for members of the African American community, because it is relatively anonymous and isolated. Picking up a prescription from a pharmacy is relatively benign, because no one can tell the type of medication and allows for an individual to maintain privacy. Additionally, medication can address symptoms without having to acknowledge a label of depression, which helps to mitigate for the associated stigma. In contrast, going to a counseling session requires having to account for time, location, taking the risk of being seen entering or leaving a session, and admitting to self there is an issue. The potential of discovery and the associated stigma directly impacts an individual's willingness to participate in counseling. This hinders obtaining proper treatment and addressing the presenting problems.

There are many barriers present regarding the stigma of depression for African American women. Beliefs and attitudes that present specific barriers are denial that there is a clinical problem, distrust pertaining to health-care providers, and limited knowledge pertaining to the etiology of the disorder (Anonymous, 2009). The stigma felt by African American women is real, but harmful. This form of self-sabotage grounded in the unwillingness or inability to acknowledge a very real issue will allow for it to grow in the community and remain untreated. This will have a direct impact on physical health, which is seen in high percentage of diabetes, high blood pressure, obesity, and heart disease. The stigma must be removed if forward progress is to be made. This removal of the stigma must first start with awareness, acknowledgement, education, and acceptance.

## I AM A SUPERWOMAN . . . MAYBE NOT!

Life happens and women in general are always juggling the day-to-day experiences they are faced with. The first being family, career, health, children, aging parents, and the list goes on. This list is long and can be challenging as they constantly try to find balance. For many African American women, this list becomes even longer as it includes challenges such as being a single parent trying to be both mom and dad while making ends meet financially, possibly living in not the best neighborhoods and encountering poverty and crime, lack of access to nutritional items and quality health care, possibly being overweight and/or obese, and at times faces discrimination because of their culture.

Despite all these potential challenges, ingrained in their psyche is that they are strong and must cope with what life has placed before them, thus being a superwoman! The belief in societal myths that African American women are invincible and can endure any or anyone's adversity without breaking down is psychologically damaging and dates back to the days of slavery, when they had to ignore their emotional needs to survive (Jones & Ford, 2008).

For many, they manage to juggle the above not realizing the toll that this type of pressure has on them emotionally and physically over time.

Despite what was instilled in them, they must face the fact that they are NOT superwomen (Figure 6.1). They are human beings who also need to be nurtured and cared for. They've got to start putting themselves first and taking care of self in order to cope with life's experiences that are placed before them. They must stop pretending that they are always in control of their life circumstances and the behavior of others, most notably their family members, thus enabling them to recover from psychological stress ( Jones & Ford, 2008).

**Figure 6.1**
Super Sister Syndrome

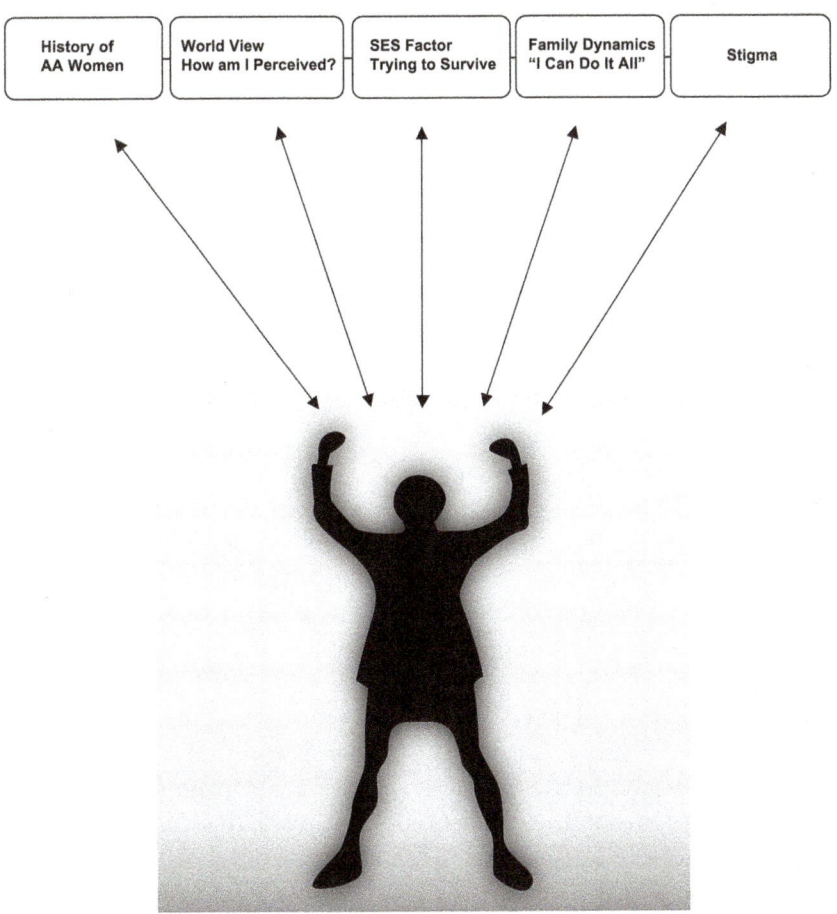

**Super Sister Syndrome**

| History of AA Women | World View How am I Perceived? | SES Factor Trying to Survive | Family Dynamics "I Can Do It All" | Stigma |

*Source:* Tucker-Sims, S., & Loury Lomas, L. (2012). *African American Women's Life Issues Today: Vital Health and Social Matters.*

Several researchers have found that many African American women may become depressed in response to their stressful environments as stated above (Barbee, 1992a; Brown, Brody, & Stoneman, 2000; Geronimus, 1996). Due to the fact that African American women are often juggling multiple roles to survive economically, studies show that physical inactivity, financial strain, low social support, family life burden, violence, and poverty are associated with depressive symptoms (Brown, Parker-Dominguez, & Sorey, 2000; Gibbs & Fuery, 1994; Israel, Farquhar, Schulz, James, & Parker, 2002; Kessler, 2003). These factors intensify the amount of stress in the lives of African American women and can erode self-esteem, self-efficacy, and health (Warren, 1994).

A study was conducted that analyzed neighborhood context, negative life events, and negative affectivity as predictors of the onset of major depression among 720 African American women (Cutrona, Russell, Hessling, Brown, & Murry, 2000). It was discovered that two dimensions of neighborhood context have particular relevance to the well-being of African American women: neighborhood economic disadvantage and neighborhood social disorder (Massey & Shibuya, 1995; Wilson, 1996; Woody, 1992). Neighborhood economic disadvantage addresses the number of residents living below the poverty line, unemployment rates, and single-parent households. Poor neighborhoods are usually characterized by low-quality schools, housing, few recreational activities, and refused services such as credit applications, taxi service, and food delivery (Sooman & Macintyre, 1995; Troutt, 1993). In poverty-stricken neighborhoods, few role models exist of those who have overcome the poverty cycle and become successful, thus resulting in hopefulness and discouragement, which can create vulnerability to depression (Wilson, 1996).

Neighborhood social disorder is the breakdown of structures and processes that maintain order, civility, and safety. Signs of neighborhood social disorder can include poorly maintained and vacant buildings, unsupervised and delinquent youth, and drug use to name a few. If you are not directly victimized from this disorder, it does signal the potential for harm (LaGrange, Ferraro, & Supancic, 1992; Lewis & Salem, 1986). Poorly maintained neighborhoods and unchecked illegal activity are signs that those in power do not care about the neighborhood or its residents, which can lead to feelings of abandonment by mainstream society (Taylor & Hale, 1986). The stress of negotiating daily life in this type of environment may trigger feelings of helplessness and depression (Aneshensel & Sucoff, 1996; Ross, 2000).

Discrimination is another factor that threatens the mental health of African American women. The link between emotional well-being and discrimination may be salient for African American women, because they face the dual effects of both racism and sexism in unique ways (Collins, 2000). Poor African American women face other stressors such as single motherhood and possibly domestic violence (Barbee, 1992b; Cutrona et al., 2000; Jackson, Brooks-Gunn, Huang, & Glassman, 2000; Siefert, Finlayson, Williams, Delva, & Ismail, 2007). Some African American women report negative, racialized exchanges during medical visits, bank transactions, retail shopping experiences, and in other public settings (Lawson, Rodgers-Rose, & Rajaram, 1999). Discrimination and depression vary by African American women's status positions. Education and age are status positions that can shape one's social experiences in complex ways. Research shows that depressive symptoms are more prevalent in younger African American women (Brown & Keith, 2003; Rikert, Wiemann, & Berenson, 2000), although there is evidence that some symptoms increase in extreme old age (George & Lynch, 2003). These findings may reflect on younger women's involvement in balancing the demands of intimate relationships, raising children, establishing stable employment, and advancing in their careers. An active lifestyle may increase younger African Americans' interactions with others, creating spaces where discrimination is encountered (Keith, Lincoln, Taylor, & Jackson, 2010).

Despite the challenges thrust upon African American women during their lifetime, they are considered survivors. However, doing so may create health and emotional issues for them in which they don't seek counseling or some form of assistance to help them cope. Once African American women understand the psychological consequences of racism, sexism, and other societal factors impacting their lives that lead to the denigration and devaluation of African American womanhood, they will not understand what they must change and challenge (Jones & Ford, 2008). Doing so will allow African American women to recognize feelings of depression, accept them, and make better choices to enhance their quality of life.

## COPING

When attempting to cope, one must first acknowledge. Facing stigmas and negative feelings regarding any element of life can make acknowledging to self or others a challenge. However, the only way one will move forward and grow beyond any pain, discomfort, or challenges in life is to acknowledge to oneself and accept the situation. Sometimes, people believe that ignoring a situation will make it go away, but this is not true. Regarding depression, ignoring the feelings, and warning signs can only make it worse. Once acknowledgment occurs, there are many strategies that can be used to assist with managing depression for African American women. These include, but are not limited to, be true to yourself, support, and professional assistance.

Often, depression is the result of attempting to be all things to all people. When this is the case, the focus is on others and not self. This is definitely true for African American women, as previously mentioned. Although this need is understandable, based upon history and many family situations, it is an unhealthy practice as it directly contributes to stress, anxiety, and depression. In attempting to satisfy everyone's needs, great personal sacrifices are made. Time, energy, and finances are used to take care of others; and in many instances, there is little to nothing left for oneself and one's own family. This creates feelings of sadness, hopelessness, and worthlessness. Unfortunately, there is often a great deal of satisfaction that occurs by being a savior to those around you. There can be feelings of satisfaction and accomplishments because you receive positive feedback and validation. This, accompanied by obligation, in many instances contributes to the continued focus on others. The positive feelings are not enough to offset the stress, anxiety, and depression that also accompany these feelings because of time limitations, financial restrictions, and physical exhaustion. In these situations, one must set limits and boundaries of self and others. There is nothing wrong or damaging with helping others. The issue occurs when it comes at the great expensive to physical or mental health. African American women must learn to help to a point where it doesn't create a huge negative impact on one's individual life. Ways to limit are by saying no sometimes even when yes is possible. This will allow for rest and relaxation. In resting, the body and mind are allowed to replenish. Another tactic is taking care of self first and then taking care of others. Often African American women give themselves what's left over after everyone else is deemed fine. If one takes care of self first and then others, there is a greater balance in life and depression is not as great. This is often difficult to do when demands are being placed on an individual, but this is critical. It is only by taking care of self first that one will be able to take care of others effectively. Being true to yourself will allow you to be more effective in your own life and also more effective when choosing to help others.

Creating a community of support is essential for managing depression. Having a supportive community will allow for burdens and responsibilities to be shared. When feeling overwhelmed, you can reach out to someone and ask for help. Often, this is not done because African American women believe they have to do everything themselves. Not only is this untrue, but it is damaging. Asking for help is an indication of having too much to do, not a sign of weakness. Also, everyone needs a safe place to vent problems or concerns, feelings, and brainstorms. Often depression is a result of feeling alone and isolated. Sharing feelings and concerns with the people in life who care about and love you minimizes isolation and reduces depression. Also, sharing with others can allow for validation of feelings regarding a situation and allow for one to not take responsibility for issues and situations unnecessarily. This too will help to reduce depression. Finally, being able to discuss the situation that is contributing to the depressed feelings can help individuals work through negative feelings and let go of them and move beyond. Often, the same situation is replayed repeatedly inside someone's mind. This only causes damage by keeping the focus on the painful issue and having the person stuck in the moment and the situation. In order to heal and manage depression, one must be able to let go and move beyond what caused the initial sadness. This may take the help of a professional.

As discussed earlier, there is great resistance to seeking professional assistance for African American women. In many instances, however, this is essential and necessary. There are times when an individual cannot move beyond a painful situation without the assistance of a professional. As supportive as friends and family can be, there is a lack of objectivity that occurs. With a professional, there is enough personal distance where there is objectivity, which allows for the professional to observe and acknowledge behaviors that might be difficult to address individually. Friends and family love and accept an individual with faults and strengths. They may be reluctant to point out negative behaviors. Also, because these are close personal friends, individuals may not share everything because of feelings of shame and embarrassment. This makes it difficult to discuss certain situations, but a professional creates a safe place with no judgment that allows for difficult discussions that are critical. The professional also has the ability to recognize character traits, behaviors, and solutions and strategies that an untrained person may not.

Finally, adjusting diet can help reduce depression. Caffeine of any kind (i.e., chocolate and coffee) is a stimulant, and although there is a feeling of euphoria in the beginning, the crash that occurs after can often be huge and contributes to depression. Alcohol is another contributor to depression. Alcohol is often used for celebrations and to escape from difficult situations, but alcohol is a depressant. Its purpose is to relax a person. Drinking alcohol when one is already feeling sad is only going to make the sadness worse. Sugar is another element that must be managed. Like caffeine, sugar has the ability to create happy positive feelings for a short time, it then creates a crash that contributes to depression. Managing these three areas can help to manage and reduce stress.

## CONCLUSION

There are many factors that contribute to depression in African American women. Only a few of them were discussed in this chapter. Being aware and being able to identify key factors that are prevalent to any one individual is crucial. This awareness may assist African American women in deciding to seek professional assistance and make the necessary, yet difficult, life changes. Understanding history, worldview, socioeconomic factors, and family dynamics is critical for medical and mental health professionals, if professional interventions are to have an impact with African American women. If they choose to participate in counseling, it will not be an easy journey. Facing and combating stigmas and hidden and overt messages received over a lifetime will be challenging. Treatments that have been normed on Caucasian populations will not be as effective because of the major cultural differences, and all involved parties must be aware of these limitations in order to control them and be patient as new more effective methods are developed. Society is evolutionary, and it is critical that professionals also evolve with the changing dynamics. Finding ways to impact individuals and being open to the personal change will not only have positive influence on African American women, but also in all the lives they touch. This impact can be long lasting, far reaching, and influential for many generations to come.

## REFERENCES

Amankwaa, L. C. (2003). Postpartum depression, culture and African-American women. *Journal of Cultural Diversity, 10*(1), 23–29.

Aneshensel, C. S., & Sucoff, C. A. (1996). The neighborhood context of adolescent mental health. *Journal of Health and Social Behavior, 37*(4), 293–310.

Anonymous. (2009). Mental health; research on mental health discussed by scientists at Wayne State University. *Mental Health Weekly Digest*, 121.

Barbee, E. L. (1992a). African American women and depression: A review and critique of the literature. *Archives of Psychiatric Nursing, 6*(5), 257–265.

Barbee, E. L. (1992b). Ethnicity and woman abuse in the United States. In C. M. Sampselle (Ed.), *Violence against women: Nursing research, practice, and educational issues* (pp. 153–166). New York: Hemisphere.

Beal, F. (1969). Double jeopardy: To be black and female. *New Generation, 51*, 23–28.

Billingsley, A. (1968). *Black families in white America*. Englewood Cliffs, NJ: Prentice-Hall.

Blackburn, I. M., Eunson, K. M., & Bishop, S. (1986). A two-year naturalistic follow-up of depressed patients treated with cognitive therapy, pharmacotherapy and a combination of both. *Journal of Affective Disorders, 10*(1), 67–75.

Blassingame, J. W. (1972). *The slave community: Plantation life in the antebellum south*. New York: Oxford University Press.

Blazer, D. G., Hybels, C. F., Simonsick, E., & Hanlon, J. T. (2000). Marked differences in anti-depressant use by race in an elderly community sample: 1986–1996. *American Journal of Psychiatry, 157*(7), 1089–1094.

Broman, C. L. (1997). Coping with personal problems. In H. V. Neighbors & J. S. Jackson (Eds.), *Mental health in black Americans* (pp. 117–129). Thousand Oaks, CA: Sage.

Brooks, T. J. (1997). The political agenda of healthcare for African Americans. *Journal of Health Care for the Poor and Underserved, 8*(3), 377–382.

Brown, A., Brody, G. H., & Stoneman, Z. (2000). Rural black women and depression: A contextual analysis. *Journal of Marriage and Family, 62*(1), 187–198.

Brown, D. R., & Keith, V. M. (2003). The epidemiology of mental disorders and mental health among African American women. In D. R. Brown & V. M. Keith (Eds.), *In and out of our right minds: The mental health of African American women* (pp. 23–59). New York: Columbia University Press.

Brown, K. A. E., Parker-Dominguez, T., & Sorey, M. (2000). Life stress, social support, and well-being among college-educated African American women. *Journal of Ethnic & Cultural Diversity, 9*(1–2), 55–73.

Carrington, C. H. (1980). A theoretical appraisal of depression in black women. In L. A. Rodgers-Rose (Ed.), *The black woman* (pp. 265–271). Newbury Park, CA: Sage.

Carrington, C. H. (2002). Depression in African American women: A complex phenomenon. *International Journal of Integrative Psychiatry, 2*(1), 21–25.

Clark, R., Anderson, N. B., Clark, V. R., & Williams, D. R. (1999). Racism as a stressor for African Americans: A biopsychosocial model. *American Psychologist, 54*(10), 805–816.

Collins, P. H. (2000). *Black feminist thought.* New York: Routledge.

Conner, K. O., Copeland, V. C., Grote, N. K., Koeske, G., Rosen, D., Reynolds, C. F., & Brown, C. (2010). Mental health treatment seeking among older adults with depression: The impact of stigma and race. *The American Journal of Geriatric Psychiatry, 18*(6), 531–543.

Cutrona, C. E., Russell, D. W., Hessling, R. M., Brown, P. A., & Murry, V. (2000). Direct and moderating effects of community context on the psychological well-being of African American women. *Journal of Personality and Social Psychology, 79*(6), 1088–1101.

Dwight-Johnson, M., Unutzer, J., Sherbourne, C., Tang, L., & Wells, K. B. (2001). Can quality improvement programs for depression in primary care address patient preferences for treatment. *Medical Care, 39*(9), 934–944.

George, L. K., & Lynch, S. M. (2003). Race differences in depressive symptoms: A dynamic perspective on stress exposure and vulnerability. *Journal of Health and Social Behavior, 44*(3), 353–369.

Geronimus, A. T. (1996). Black/white differences in the relationship of maternal age to birth weight: A population based test of the weather hypothesis. *Social Science & Medicine, 42*(4), 589–597.

Gibbs, J. T., & Fuery, D. (1994). Mental health and well-being of black women: Toward strategies of empowerment. *American Journal of Community Psychology, 22*(4), 559–582.

Giles, D. E., Perlis, M. L., Reynolds, C. F., & Kupfer, D. J. (1998). EEG sleep in African-American patients with major depression: A historical case control study. *Depression Anxiety, 8*(2), 58–64.

Gray-Little, B., & Hafdahl, A. R. (2000). Factors influencing racial comparisons of self-esteem: A qualitative review. *Psychological Bulletin, 126*(1), 26–54.

Greenhouse, J. B., Stangl, D., Kupfer, D. J., & Prien, R. F. (1991). Methodologic issues in maintenance therapy clinical trials. *Archives of General Psychiatry, 48*(4), 313–318.

Hollon, S. D., & Beck, A. T. (2004). Cognitive and cognitive behavioral therapies. In M. J. Lambert (Ed.), *Garfield and Bergin's Handbook of psychotherapy and behavioral change: An empirical analysis* (5th ed., pp. 447–492). New York: Wiley.

Hunn, V. L., & Craig, C. D. (2009). Depression, sociocultural factors, and African American women. *Journal of Multicultural Counseling and Development, 37*(2), 83–93.

Israel, B. A., Farquhar, S. A., Schulz, A. J., James, S. A., & Parker, E. A. (2002). The relationship between social support, stress, and health among women on Detroit's eastside. *Health Education & Behavior, 29*(3), 342–360.

Jackson, A. P., Brooks-Gunn, J., Huang, C.-C., & Glassman, M. (2000). Single mothers in low-wage jobs: Financial strain, parenting and preschoolers' outcomes. *Child Development, 71*(4), 1409–1423.

Jones, L. V., & Ford, B. (2008). Depression in African American woman: Application of a psychosocial competence practice framework. *Journal of Women and Social Work, 23*(2), 139, 140.

Keith, V. M., Lincoln, K. D., Taylor, R. J., & Jackson, J. S. (2010). Discriminatory experiences and depressive symptoms among African American women: Do skin tone and mastery matter? *Sex Roles, 62*(1), 48–59.

Kessler, R. C. (1995). The national comorbidity survey: Preliminary results and future directions. *International Journal of Methods in Psychiatric Research, 5*(2), 139–151.

Kessler, R. C. (2003). Epidemiology of women and depression. *Journal of Affective Disorders, 74*(1), 5–13.

Kovacs, M., Rush, A. J., Beck, A. T., & Hollon, S. D. (1981). Depressed outpatients treated with cognitive therapy or pharmacotherapy: A one-year follow-up. *Archives of General Psychiatry, 38*(1), 33–39.

LaGrange, R. L., Ferraro, K. F., & Supancic, M. (1992). Perceived risk and fear of crime: Role of social and physical incivilities. *Journal of Research in Crime and Delinquency, 29*(3), 311–334.

Lawson, E. J., Rodgers-Rose, L. F., & Rajaram, S. (1999). The psychosocial context of black women's health. *Health Care for Women International, 20*(3), 279–289.

Lewis, D. A., & Salem, G. (1986). *Fear of crime: Incivility and the production of a social problem.* New Brunswick, NJ: Transaction Books.

Massey, D. S., & Shibuya, K. (1995). Unraveling the tangle of pathology: The effect of spatially concentrated joblessness on the well-being of African Americans. *Social Science Research, 24*(4), 352–366.

McGrath, E. H., Keita, G. P., Strickland, B. R., & Russo, N. F. (Eds.). (2001). *National depression summit.* Washington, D.C.: American Psychological Association.

Melfi, C. A., Croghan, T. W., Hanna, M. P., & Robinson, R. L. (2000). Racial variation in antidepressant treatment in a Medicaid population. *Journal of Clinical Psychiatry, 61*(1), 16–21.

Murray, C. J. L., & Lopez, A. D. (1996). *Global burden of disease: A comprehensive assessment of mortality and disability from diseases, injuries, risk factors in 1990 and projected to 2020.* Cambridge, MA: Harvard University Press.

Pickering, T. G. (2000). Effects of stress and behavioral intervention in hypertension, headache and hypertension: Something old, something new. *Journal of Clinical Hypertension, 2*(5), 345–347.

Rikert, V. I., Wiemann, C. M., & Berenson, A. B. (2000). Ethnic differences in depressive symptomatology among young women. *Obstetrics and Gynecology, 95*(1), 55–60.

Ross, C. E. (2000). Neighborhood disadvantage and adult depression. *Journal of Health and Social Behavior, 41*(2), 177–187.

Siefert, K., Finlayson, T. L., Williams, D. R., Delva, J., & Ismail, A. I. (2007). Modifiable risk and protective factors for depressive symptoms in low-income African American mothers. *American Journal of Orthopsychiatry, 77*(1), 113–123.

Snowden, L. R., & Pingitore, D. (2001). Frequency and scope of mental health delivery to African Americans in primary care. *Mental Health Services Research, 4*(3), 123–130.

Sooman, A., & Macintyre, S. (1995). Health and perceptions of the local environment in socially contrasting neighborhoods in Glasgow. *Health and Place, 1*(1), 15–26.

Taylor, R. B., & Hale, M. M. (1986). Testing alternative models of fear of crime. *Journal of Criminal Law and Criminology, 77*(1), 151–189.

Thase, M. E., Greenhouse, J. B., Frank, E., Reynolds III, C. F., Pilkonis, P. A., Hurley, K., Grochocinsk, V., & Kupfer, D. J. (1997). Treatment of major depression with psychotherapy or psychotherapy-pharmacotherapy combinations. *Archives of General Psychiatry, 54*(11), 1009–1015.

Troutt, D. D. (1993). *The thin red line: How the poor still pay more.* San Francisco, CA: Consumers Union of the United States, Inc.

USDHHS. (1999). *United States census report.* Rockville, MD: USDHHS.

USDHHS. (2001). *Report of the Surgeon General.* Rockville, MD: USDHHS.

Waite, R., & Killian, P. (2008). Health beliefs about depression among African American women. *Perspectives in Psychiatric Care, 44*(3), 185–195.

Warren, B. J. (1994). Depression in African American women. *Journal of Psychosocial Nursing Mental Health Services, 32*(3), 29–33.

Wilson, W. J. (1996). *When work disappears: The world of the new urban poor.* New York: Vintage Books.

Woody, B. (1992). *Black women in the workplace: Impacts of structural change in the economy.* New York: Greenwood Press.

# 7

# Dementia in African American Women

## *Funmi A. Aiyegbo-Ohadike*

This chapter delves into the mind-altering conditions collectively known as dementia, and commonly referred to as Alzheimer's. The goal of this chapter is to inform and invite further discussions, planning, and policy changes to support families living with this tragic disease. Dementia touches many lives and affects the elderly citizens that we have often relied on as pillars of strength in our community. They are our mothers and grandmothers.

The African American matriarch has been characterized as the cornerstone of the family in multiple media portrayals. Women like Hattie McDaniel who played Mammy in *Gone with the wind* and Diahann Carol as *Claudine* show the Black woman as benevolent and self-assured. She is often characterized as a large woman both in personality and stature, and who struggles but is able to bear all that ails her loved ones. She withstands the burdens of her work life, only to arrive home on time to address the socioeconomic concerns of her family and community of origin. After a lifetime of nurturing and supporting family and friends, many African American women need the same love and care that they have provided. They need support to face the diagnosis of dementia.

Dementia is a chronic progressive disorder of global functioning initially presenting as memory loss and cognitive decline. African American women, like others diagnosed with the disorder, can expect that their cognitive and physical health status will deteriorate over time. The symptoms of dementia are not limited to the hallmark loss of short-term memory; rather they span the full range of human functioning. The symptoms may affect mood, speech, knowledge, understanding, appetite, and movement. The debilitated patient is a shadow of their former self. The patient is deprived of their previous vigor. They become increasingly dependent on others for their total care.

The term "dementia" can be confusing to the general public who may not recognize it as being the same as Alzheimer's disease. Alzheimer's disease is a type of dementia, and not a separate disorder, or final stage of all other types of dementia. Dementia is a permanent condition and should not be confused with transient conditions, such as delirium. Delirium is a temporary disturbance in cognition related to an underlying medical condition. Patients with dementia regardless of specific type will have a loss of short-term memory that worsens over time, leading to a significant degeneration in cognitive, social, behavioral, and physical functioning.

## TYPES OF DEMENTIA

According to the "Alzheimer's disease facts and figures 2010 and 2012," Alzheimer's type dementia accounts for between 60% and 80% of the dementias diagnosed in the United States. With Alzheimer's disease, as in all dementias, there is memory loss and a progressive deterioration of other cognitive abilities, leading to the final stages where there is an inability to function independently. Vascular dementia is the second most common cause of dementia. Vascular dementia occurs resultant to cardiovascular diseases such as stroke and atherosclerosis. Alzheimer's disease may occur alone or in combination with vascular dementia. Additionally, there are less common types of dementia such as Lewy bodies, Picks disease, and dementia related to Parkinson's disease. These conditions cause cognitive decline but occur less often than Alzheimer's disease and vascular dementia (McPhee, Papadakis, & Rabow, 2011, pp. 62–65).

## PREVALENCE AND RISK FACTORS

In a discussion of risk factors, we often refer to modifiable and nonmodifiable risk factors. A modifiable risk factor can be changed through targeted interventions. These interventions include alterations in lifestyle, decreasing environmental exposure to harmful substances, drugs, and other therapies. Nonmodifiable risk factors are innate characteristics that cannot be readily altered. Nonmodifiable risks include age, sex, genetic markers, and family history.

Although not a normal part of aging, age remains the greatest single risk factor for the development of dementia. According to data from the Alzheimer's Association (2012), 45 percent of people over the age of 85 have Alzheimer's disease. The increased life expectancy of women over men is consistent with the increased rates of dementia among women. Figure 7.1 depicts the distribution of dementia by age and sex.

**Figure 7.1**
**Distribution of Alzheimer's Disease by Age and Sex**

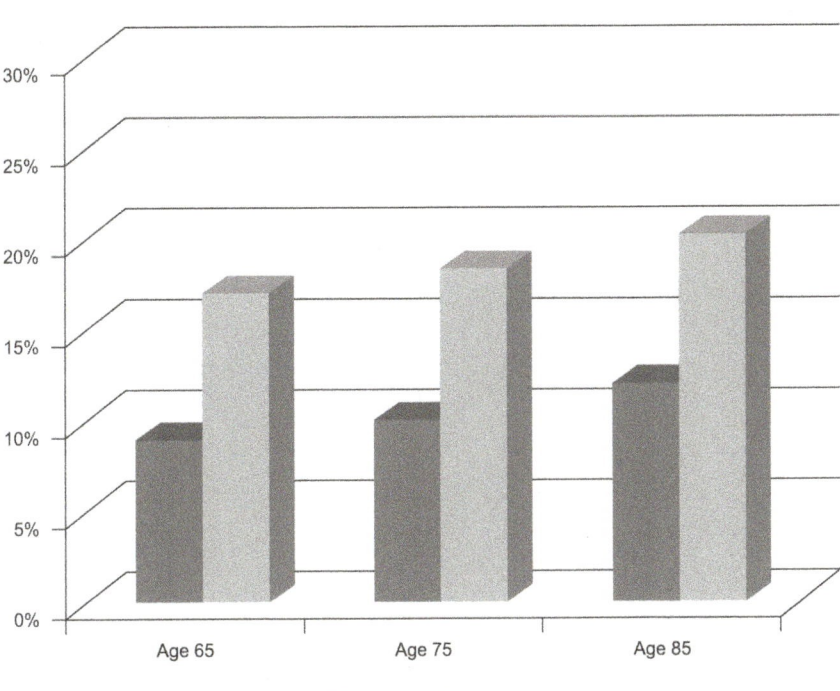

*Source:* Data compiled by Alzheimer's Association from Seshadri, S., Beiser, A., Kelly-Hayes, M., et al. (2006). The lifetime risk of stroke: Estimates from the Framingham Study. *Stroke, 37,* 345–350.

Women account for greater than two-third of the total cases of Alzheimer's disease. Alzheimer's Association (2012) states that in the United States, there are "5.2 million cases of dementia in people over the age of 65, 3.4 million are women and 1.8 million are men" (p. 14). The number of people diagnosed with dementia is expected to increase to a rate that is greater than double the current number of 5.4 million cases—to over 13 million patients by 2050. The most significant factor contributing to this increase is the aging of the population, with a larger segment of the population being over the age of 65.

African Americans have higher rates of Alzheimer's disease prevalence as "estimates are ranging from 14% to almost 100% higher" (Alzheimer's Association, 2012, pp. 15, 16). Figure 7.2 depicts the distribution of Alzheimer's disease by race.

**Figure 7.2**

**Distribution of Alzheimer's Disease by Age and Race**

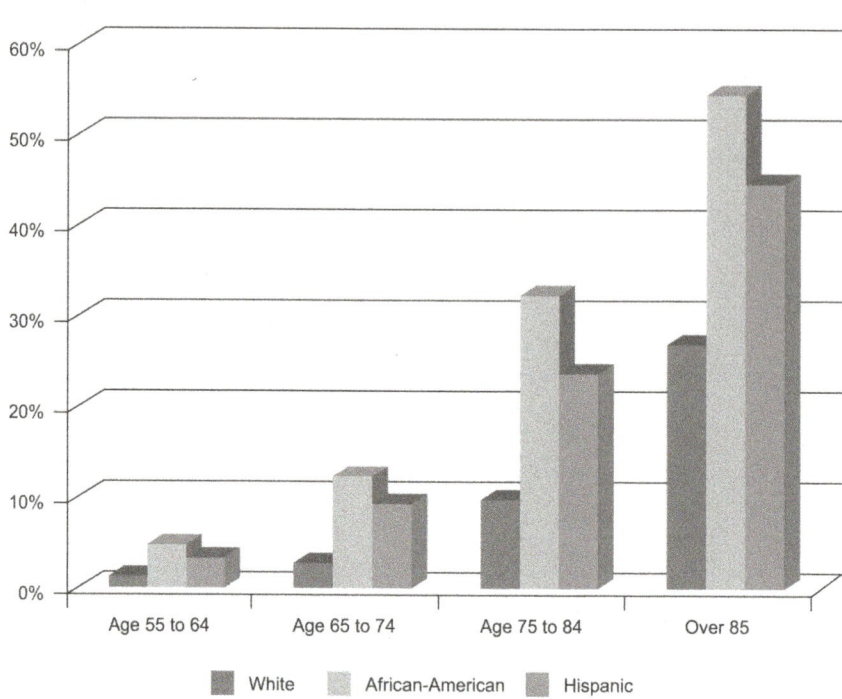

*Source:* Gurland, B. J., Wilder, D. E., Lantigua, R., Stern, Y., Chen, J., Killeffer, E.H.P., et al. (1999). Rates of dementia in three ethnoracial groups. *International Journal of Geriatric Psychiatry, 14*, 481–493.

There are multiple contributing factors to the higher prevalence of Alzheimer's disease in the American community. These factors include higher rates of modifiable risk factors such as hypertension and cardiovascular disease among African Americans in contrast to their White counterparts.

In a 2002 risk analysis spanning 10 years, Green et al. (2002) found evidence of increased genetic and environmental risks for African Americans to develop Alzheimer's disease. First-degree African American relatives of people with Alzheimer's disease had a 43.7 percent risk of developing Alzheimer's disease by age 85, compared to 26.9 percent in Whites. Spouses of African Americans with Alzheimer's disease had an 18.5 percent risk of developing the disease, compared to 10.4 percent of Whites. The researchers found that first-degree African American relatives had overall "a higher cumulative risk of dementia than those of whites with Alzheimer's disease" (Green et al., 2002, p. 329). Although they noted *cumulative* risk was higher, they found that when examined independently, risk factors such as female sex, having a first-degree relative with dementia, and genetic markers for dementia have a similar impact on African Americans as they do on Whites.

To illustrate this point of the interrelationship between genetic and environmental risks, we could use the fictionalized television family, the Cosby's. The family consisted of a mother "Claire," father "Cliff," and their five children: four daughters and one son. In this family, if either Claire or Cliff had Alzheimer's disease, then their children would each have a greater than 40 percent chance of developing the disease themselves by age 85. If Cliff had Alzheimer's, it would increase Claire's chances of developing the disease by 19 percent. Of all of their children, the daughters would be most at risk for developing the disease, as they are female, and more likely to live to age 85, placing them in the higher risk pool. Overall, the family's African American heritage and the associated risks for cardiovascular disease, particularly stroke, would have a significant effect on their likelihood to develop dementia.

## DISEASE PROGRESSION

The National Institute on Aging and the Alzheimer's Association released new guidelines for the diagnosis of Alzheimer's disease in 2011. The new guidelines propose placing Alzheimer's disease into three stages:

1. Preclinical Alzheimer's disease is before symptoms become visible to patients or care providers. In this stage, scientists propose there are changes going on in the patient's brain that may be detected by future testing of biomarkers through imaging and other studies yet to be developed. It is the hope that someday Alzheimer's disease can be diagnosed at the preclinical stage to halt the progression to occult disease. If early identification were possible, with interventions identified to delay onset of the disease, then there would be significant personal, societal, and economic benefits overall. "A hypothetical intervention that delayed the onset of Alzheimer's disease dementia by 5 years would result in a 57% reduction in the number of patients with Alzheimer's disease dementia, and reduce the projected Medicare costs of Alzheimer's disease from $627 to $344 billion dollars" (Sperling et al., 2011, p. 3).

2. Mild cognitive impairment (MCI) is characterized by subtle changes in memory and cognition that cause noticeable changes in a person's functioning, although they remain able to perform most of their usual tasks. At this stage, patients may have deficits that can be detected by cognitive testing with tools such as the Mini-Mental, Mini Cog, and BCRS. There has been controversy regarding cultural bias; it is important at this stage to evaluate the patient for other causes of MCI. If the cognitive impairment occurs suddenly, the patient should be evaluated for delirium—a reversible cause of altered mental status precipitated by an underlying metabolic or infectious process. Conditions such as urinary tract infection, hypothyroidism, elevated serum ammonia levels,

and adverse reactions to medications must be excluded before the diagnosis of dementia is made. A person may remain with MCI for the remainder of their lives or decline in functioning to develop Alzheimer's.

3. A diagnosis of Alzheimer's may be made once a patient has regressed in functioning. At the time of diagnosis, they may require 24-hour care to maintain their safety and provide for all of their physical needs. Their decline may be precipitous or insidious depending on their premorbid health status, their co-morbid conditions, and environmental and psychosocial factors that interact to make their disease trajectory highly individualized. Issues arise for families and caregivers who struggle with progressive changes in three primary domains: cognitive, functional, and behavioral. The changes in cognition are related to memory, thought, and perception. Declines in functioning are manifested as decreased ability to perform activities of daily living (ADL's), such as showering, meal preparation, and medication administration. Behavioral changes may include depression, anxiety, agitation, frustration, and rapidly shifting mood. Over time, the symptoms may worsen to where patients have both receptive and expressive aphasia, difficulty speaking and understanding speech, and dysphagia (difficulty with swallowing). Many ethical issues arise from the loss of cognitive ability. Caretakers are confronted with decisions about further diagnostic testing. Invasive interventions and procedures often do not increase the quality of a patient's life but may extend the length of life for a demented person.

## TREATMENTS

There are pharmacologic and nonpharmacologic treatments for Alzheimer's disease. The Food and Drug Administration (FDA) has approved two classes of medications for the treatment of Alzheimer's disease. The first class developed were the cholinesterase inhibitors—drugs such as Aricept and Exelon. The second class has one drug called an NMDA receptor antagonist—Namenda. The drugs are intended to boost neurotransmitter activity and stimulate brain tissue to function properly. They are most beneficial to people with mild to moderate disease that have not developed the advanced pathology that is associated with late-stage dementia. Some people with advanced disease in studies also demonstrated improvement, although their functional gains were less significant. The drugs claim to slow the progression of disease, delaying the onset of end-stage disease. They are typically well tolerated, although there are reports of gastrointestinal symptoms such as weight loss associated with the use of cholinesterase inhibitors.

There is increasing use of antipsychotic medications—such as Risperdal, Seroquel, and Haldol—to treat the behavioral disturbances associated with dementia. Antipsychotics are FDA-approved medications for the treatment of conditions such as schizophrenia, psychotic depression, and bipolar disorder. The FDA has not approved antipsychotics for the treatment of dementia. The controversy around their use in dementia arises from antipsychotics having a black box warning due to the increased risk of death when used in elderly people.

Antidepressants such as Lexapro, Remeron, and Celexa can be used to treat Alzheimer's disease patients with comorbid depression, poor appetite, and a tearful condition called pseudobulbar affect disorder. Antiseizure medications like Depakote can be used for their mood stabilizing effect. Benzodiazepines drugs such as Ativan, Klonopin, and Ambien are used for their sedative effect—to calm anxiety and aid in sleep.

Patients with Alzheimer's disease may be on none, all, or some combination of these classes of agents. After consulting systematic reviews of evidence performed by various authors in the Cochrane Database, the evidence demonstrates that cognitive enhancers have some efficacy in the treatment of moderate to severe diseases. There was a slight improvement in cognition in those with MCI and no significant benefit noted in those with vascular dementia and Alzheimer's disease. This is worth noting because of the higher rates of vascular dementia in African Americans. The authors reviewed the use of antidepressants (selective seratonin reuptake inhibitors and trazodone) "found that there is some evidence to support the use of certain antidepressants for agitation and psychosis in dementia and further studies are required to determine the effectiveness and safety of SSRIs and trazodone in managing these symptoms" (Seitz et al., 2011).

A review on the evidence to support the use of antipsychotics found "little evidence to support a benefit of haloperidol on manifestations of agitation other than aggression, and that haloperidol should not be used routinely to treat patients with agitated dementia" (Lonergan, Luxenberg, Colford, & Birks, 2002). For the other major class of antipsychotics (atypical), "modest efficacy is evident, but the elevated risk of cerebrovascular adverse events, mortality, upper respiratory infections, [o]edema and extrapyramidal symptoms is a concern, particularly as selective reporting makes interpretation of other potential adverse outcomes impossible" (Ballard, Waite, & Birks, 2006).

There is limited data to support the use of benzodiazepines and anticonvulsants in patients with symptomatic agitation and Alzheimer's disease. Rayner (2007) reports that there have not been reliable, reproducible patient focused studies to support their use to treat the behavioral disturbances associated with Alzheimer's disease. They should be used on an individualized basis with close monitoring for adverse and paroxysmal responses.

## SUPPLEMENTS

Compounds and naturally occurring substances such as vitamin E, vitamin B6, and seleginine as well as herbal remedies like *Ginkgo biloba* have been suggested to have positive benefits on cognition and functioning in patients with Alzheimer's disease. Vitamin E and selegiline acting as antioxidants prevent the formation of toxic free radicals. May et al. (2009) performed a meta-analysis of herbal supplements in the treatment of Alzheimer's disease. They looked at 13 randomized clinical trials (RCTs; n randomized = 1,144) and found a positive effect, although a lack of homogeneity decreased their ability to estimate the effect size, but they were able to recommend further study to explore the full potential of these agents.

## NONPHARMACOLOGIC INTERVENTIONS

Nonpharmacologic interventions can be used at any stage of the Alzheimer's disease process. The interventions include keeping the patient's environment consistent by minimizing frequent changes in caregivers or scheduling. The person with Alzheimer's disease is challenged by their inability to remember. A predictable environment is comforting and reassuring to them. Other nonpharmacologic treatments include reminiscence or memory therapy, where familiar objects from earlier stages of life such as pictures, uniforms, or news reports are used to bring the patient back to a more comfortable time of their lives. Additional modalities include activity therapy where patients, often in groups, sing, dance, or do crafts that engage their senses and distract from some of the anxiety that people with Alzheimer's disease may experience. Aromatherapy and massage therapy have also been used to manage patients with Alzheimer's disease. These modalities have not been demonstrated in RCTs to provide a significant impact on the functioning of patients, but they are a means of providing comfort and caring especially for caregivers in the home setting (Ballard, Waite, & Birks, 2006).

## CAREGIVERS

The caregivers, just like the patients they care for, are mostly female. The Alzheimer's Association (2010) found that 60 percent of caregivers are women, and nearly 50 percent of them are 50 to 64 years old. They are caring for their mothers, aunts, sisters, and friends. In many states, they are providing uncompensated care, which saves the medical system billions of dollars annually. The care that they provide puts them at risk for physical illness and emotional, psychological, and financial stress. Caregivers struggle to understand the needs of their loved ones and meet those needs on a daily basis.

The roles of the caregiver may have evolved slowly with a previously high-functioning elderly person initially requiring assistance with driving or errands. As the patient declines in functioning, the responsibilities of the caregiver increase to include personal care: toileting, bathing, feeding, and continence care. The patient transforms from an independent self-possessed person to a fully dependent and needy ward. For African American women, this may pose particular challenges based upon the patients' pre-Alzheimer's disease health status. If they had diabetes and peripheral vascular disease, they may have already had amputations, requiring assistance with their physical needs before their cognitive status declined. They may have been disabled from an earlier stroke with accompanying paralysis, speech deficits, dysphagia, and continence issues. Their course of illness may be much longer than the typical Alzheimer's disease patient who develops symptoms and declines over five to seven years. Many African American women have premorbid conditions that may cause them to be weakened and debilitated for the years leading up to the onset of their Alzheimer's disease.

Caregivers are faced with providing uncompensated care, because there is no uniform plan to pay for long-term home care for elders. Medicare is the national senior health plan and covers 85 percent of hospitalization costs, doctors' visits, and skilled care. The skilled care benefit refers to covered interventions to aide in the recuperation of a patient after an acute event such as surgery, pneumonia, stroke, pacemaker implant, or feeding tube placement. Skilled care is short term and does not cover a patient for long-term home care to manage chronic conditions like dementia. For example, if a patient living at home with mild to moderate dementia falls and fractures her hip, she would be admitted to the hospital, the surgery would be done, then the patient would likely be referred to a subacute facility for rehabilitation in the hope of returning to baseline level of functioning. Medicare would cover the cost of their hospitalization, the surgery, and subacute rehab. If at the time of discharge she still required skilled care, such as physical therapy, wound care, and management of a new indwelling device, Medicare would cover the cost of home care until the patient achieves a new stable status or returns to their baseline level of functioning.

For wealthy seniors or those who are financially savvy, there are options such as long-term care insurance, estate planning, and reverse mortgages to help preserve the assets that families cherish while still providing the financial resources they need as they age. Poor seniors may qualify for Medicaid—state-sponsored insurance that typically covers the gap in coverage between the 85 percent that Medicare reimburses and the actual cost of care. Medicaid coverage varies by state in terms of scope and depth of services. As more states look to better anticipate the cost of care, they are opting to move their Medicaid beneficiaries over to managed care plans; services such as home care and nursing home care may be covered by Medicaid. Most seniors will not qualify for Medicaid until they have exhausted their savings and their income is limited to their social security payments. They have to have exhausted any other assets available to them. Families may be left with no other option but to sell their homes or sign over assets to nursing homes, if they have not planned ahead for long-term care.

## ADVANCED CARE PLANNING

Advanced care planning (ACP) is the decision-making process that formalizes a patient's values and wishes for end-of-life care. ACP discussions usually lead to establishing a goal for care. Goals of care include comfort, functioning, and longevity. Patients whose goal is comfort desire a palliative approach to care, with avoidance of painful, invasive procedures, which do not add to overall comfort. Choosing a functional goal means a patient desires active treatments to maintain their health status, but as their health declines, they may opt to change to comfort or longevity. A patient that decides to pursue longevity desires life at all costs. They want all tests, treatments, and interventions to keep life going regardless of impact on comfort or dignity.

During the ACP process, the patient, the health-care proxy, other members of the family, and the treatment team including physician, nursing, social worker, and other members of the health-care team are present. The ACP can be made before chronic or acute diseases are diagnosed, although they are often not addressed until a patient's health has declined. According to Raghavan, Smith, and Arnold (2008), African Americans were found

> Less likely to complete advance directives, enroll in hospice, receive appropriate symptom management at the end-of-life, or be satisfied with the quality of end-of-life care and communication. [African Americans were] more likely to receive aggressive treatment at the end-of-life (including artificial nutrition and hospitalization), to stop hospice care to seek life-prolonging treatment, and to die in a hospital. [They continue on to say] over recent decades, while there have been more opportunities for patients to die outside of hospitals, rates of in-hospital deaths have declined for European Americans; a similar decrease has not been observed for African Americans.

During the advance care planning process, if the patient is cognitively intact, they can verbalize their desire for or against life-prolonging care under circumstances where death may be imminent or expected within a reasonably near period of time. They can express whether they want certain interventions, such as cardio pulmonary resuscitation, intubation, placement on life support machine, and blood transfusions to be undertaken. The ACP should allow the patient or their appointed proxy to determine to what extent and under what circumstances they want their life "saved." The cornerstone of the ACP process that should not be omitted is the discussion of trajectory of illness.

Education about the disease process, with realistic prognostication, and anticipatory guidance should be provided in order to help the patient and family to have realistic expectations. When a patient has a chronic degenerative disease, life-prolonging interventions may only prolong suffering and compromise dignity. With Alzheimer's disease, a patient with late-stage disease is at risk for frequent infections, skin breakdown, swallowing difficulties, and pain. Because Alzheimer's disease is a disease that progresses to an end stage where quality of life becomes questionable, individuals and families can be faced with making decisions about initiating artificial nutrition with a percutaneous endoscopic gastrostomy (PEG) tube. PEG tubes are present in nearly one-third of nursing home patients with cognitive deficits. Studies on PEG tube efficacy in prolonging life are inconclusive, although PEGs are presented as a life-saving option for patients who are no longer able to take oral nutrition (Sampson, Candy, & Jones, 2009).

Another issue that may be discussed with the health-care team is diagnostic testing and invasive procedures. The purpose of diagnostic testing for other conditions in patients who already have moderate to severe Alzheimer's disease should be documented and consistent with the ACP goals of the patient. Examples of tests that may be unnecessary would be colonoscopy, imaging tests to identify asymptomatic abnormalities, and biopsies of slow-growing tumors. A test or procedure should only be done if it will change the management of a condition. If the patient is already in a debilitated state, then the treatment team should be questioned regarding the utility of further testing.

## SUMMARY

Alzheimer's disease is the primary type of dementia that affects people over the age of 85. Dementia is not a normal part of aging; it is a devastating disease that consumes the resources of both patients and caregivers. African American women should have a particular awareness of the disease and its management, because they are disproportionately affected by it, as both caregivers and patients. There are opportunities to decrease the prevalence of vascular dementia by treating hypertension and preventing stroke in African Americans who are at significant risk for both conditions. Early identification and acceptance of the diagnosis of dementia allows for comprehensive treatment planning, risk modification, and anticipatory guidance. The progressive nature of dementia means that caregivers need emotional and financial resources to carry them through the entire disease process. The prevalence of dementia will continue to increase as the population ages. Policy makers need to develop comprehensive population-based programs to address gaps in services required to care for elders living with dementia.

## REFERENCES

Alzheimer's Association. (2010). 2010 Alzheimer's disease facts and figures. *Alzheimer's & Dementia, 6*, 1–70. Retrieved from http://www.alz.org/documents_custom/report_alzfactsfigures2010.pdf

Alzheimer's Association. (2012). 2012 Alzheimer's disease facts and figures. *Alzheimer's & Dementia, 8*(2), 1–67. Retrieved from http://www.alz.org/downloads/facts_figures_2012.pdf

Ballard, C. G, Waite, J., & Birks, J. (2006). Atypical antipsychotics for aggression and psychosis in Alzheimer's disease. *Cochrane Database of Systematic Reviews, 1*, CD003476.

Green, R. C., Cupples, L. A., Go, R., et al. (2002). Risk of dementia among white and African American relatives of patients with Alzheimer disease. *Journal of American Medical Association, 287*(3), 329–336.

Lonergan, E., Luxenberg, J., Colford, J. M., & Birks, J. (2002). Haloperidol for agitation in dementia. *Cochrane Database of Systematic Reviews, 2*, CD002852.

May, B. H., Lit, M., Xue, C. C. L., Yang, A. W. H., Zhang, A. L., Owens, M. D., Head, R., Cobiac, L., Li, C. G., Hugel, H., & Story, D. F. (2009). Herbal medicine for dementia: A systematic review. *Phytotherapy Research, 23*(4), 447–459.

McPhee, S. J., Papadakis, M. A., & Rabow, M. W. (2011). *Current medical diagnosis and treatment 2011*. New York: McGraw Hill.

Raghavan, M., Smith, A., & Arnold, R. (2008). *African Americans and end-of-life care: Fast facts and concepts*. Fast Facts Document No. 204. Retrieved from http://www.eperc.mcw.edu/fastfact/ff_204.htm

Rayner, A. (2007). Managing psychotic symptoms in the older patient. *Geriatrics and Aging, 10*(4), 241–245.

Sampson, E. L., Candy, B., & Jones, L. (2009). Enteral tube feeding for older people with advanced dementia. *Cochrane Database of Systematic Reviews, 2*, CD007209.

Seitz, D. P., Adunuri, N., Gill, S. S., Gruneir, A., Herrmann, N., & Rochon, P. (2011). Antidepressants for agitation and psychosis in dementia. *Cochrane Database of Systematic Reviews, 2*, CD008191.

Sperling, R. A., Aisen, P. S., Beckett, L. A., et al. (2011). Toward defining the preclinical stages of Alzheimer's disease: Recommendations from the National Institute on Aging and the Alzheimer's Association workgroups on diagnostic guidelines for Alzheimer's disease. *Alzheimer's & Dementia, 7*(3), 280–292.

# SECTION III

# ENVIRONMENTAL FACTORS

# 8

# African American Women, Intimate Partner Violence, and Community Violence: Health Intersections and Aftereffects

## *Lorraine E. Peeler*

### INTRODUCTION TO DOMESTIC VIOLENCE

The impact of domestic violence is not a mystery. Most people know that women have been seriously harmed through the physical impact of domestic violence that ranges from bodily injury, sexual assault, emotional abuse, to death. There is little information on the complexity of domestic violence in the African American community and the multifaceted outcomes. These outcomes include physical injury and mental illness, which impact women and their children.

I propose in this chapter that the focus on domestic violence in the African American community is too small and needs to be expanded to look at the interactive and aftereffects of living in communities of violence and in homes where violence prevails. I refer to the convergence of violent experiences that occur in and outside of the homes within the African American community as the "vortex of violence." This whirlpool of violent experiences is compounded by being a part of a socially unequal system that oppresses people based on race, class, and gender. Goodman, Smyth, Borges, & Singer (2009) call the intersection of intimate partner violence (IPV), poverty, and mental health a "crisis collision." This is the world of many culturally diverse women specifically Latino, Native American, African American, and immigrant women, although my focus is on African American women.

### Current Definitions

Domestic violence, which is now termed intimate partner violence, is a complicated phenomenon. Because of the complexities of domestic violence, the word went through a metamorphosis. Domestic violence was the buzz-word, and then it emerged into family violence. Family violence broadens the issue to include child abuse, sexual abuse, elder abuse, and sibling abuse, as well as intimate partner violence (which was defined as domestic violence). Although this more inclusive term highlighted the multiple levels of domestic violence, it watered down the specific indicators necessary to understand a major precipitator of violence in the home: violence between intimate partners. Because of the broad sweep in meaning of family violence, what was once called domestic violence is now termed intimate partner violence.

West (2002) identifies the intricacy of violence in the lives of African American women to include childhood sexual abuse, dating violence, intimate partner violence, sexual assault, and sexual harassment. Sullivan, Meese, Swan, Mazure, & Snow (2005) highlight that violence in the lives of women is not an isolated incident of intimate partner violence, but it has precursors, correlates, and outcomes. This not only means that the women are victims, but also that they use violence themselves to meet their needs. For example, research indicates that childhood sexual abuse is a precursor to the acceptance of other forms of violence, especially dating violence and intimate partner violence against women, as well as a precursor to their use of violence. All of these types of violence in the lives of African American women leave their residual effects.

### Statistics and Risk Factors

According to current statistics, over one million people in the United States alone are victims. This includes women across ethnicities, gay/lesbians, and men. The diversification of the family has opened new constellations of intimate partner violence. It is no longer limited to persons who are legally married but any couple that live together intimately. The *National crime victimization survey resource guide* (2012) defines an intimate partner as a current or former spouse, girlfriend, or boyfriend. Violent acts include murder, rape, sexual assault, robbery, aggravated assault, and simple assault. Intimate partner violence is perpetrated in many ways including but not limited to physical, emotional, sexual, psychological, and/or financial. The legal definition of intimate partner violence is "any assault, battery, sexual battery, or any criminal offense resulting in physical injury or death of one intimate partner by another who is residing in the same single dwelling unit" (Brown, 2008).

Intimate partner violence/domestic abuse was declared a major health problem in 1992 by the Surgeon General (Peterman & Dixon, 2003). It has continued to be not only a rapidly growing health concern but also a growing societal concern. Increasingly, during this same period of time, there has been emerging research about the lack of attention given to domestic violence, especially intimate partner violence, against African American women. It is especially notable when the occurrence of intimate partner violence in the African American community is exponential. Bent-Goodley (2001) asserts that the problem of intimate partner violence in the African American community committed against African American women is especially serious. Also, their victimization by their intimate partners is significantly higher than persons of any other race. Intimate partner violence poses an ominous threat to the preservation of the African American family and community.

Chaney (2008a, 2008b) documents that domestic violence hits Black women harder. The Violence Policy Center stated in its 2006 Annual Report that 551 African American women were murdered by males that year (VPC, 2008). When a murder weapon could be identified, 305 of the victims were fatally shot and most during the course of an argument. In addition, there were 1,818 race-identified females murdered by males. And while White women accounted for the largest total of those killed (1,208), African American women were killed at a rate nearly three times higher.

Statistics assert that African American women suffer deadly violence from family members at rates decidedly higher than for other racial groups in the United States (American Bar Association, 2012). The number one killer of African American women aged 15 to 34 is homicide at the hands of a current or former intimate partner. Approximately 40 percent of Black women report coercive contact of a sexual nature by age 18. Only 17 percent of African American sexual assault survivors reported the assault to police (Africana Voices Against Violence, 2002).

Rennison and Welchans (2000) found that African Americans were victimized by intimate partners at significantly higher rates than persons of any other race between 1993 and 1998. African American females experienced intimate partner violence at a rate 35 percent higher than that of White females and about 22 times the rate of women of other races. African American males experienced intimate partner violence at a rate about 62 percent higher than that of White males and about 22 times the rate of men of other races. Comparatively speaking, African American women experience significantly more domestic violence than White women in the age group of 20 to 24 and experience similar levels of intimate partner victimization in all other age categories.

These statistics are clear indicators that intimate partner violence is a much complicated issue for African American women. In addition to the gender issues that are highlighted by the traditional feminist-oriented perspective of intimate partner violence, there are the issues of race, poverty, and substance abuse, which are locked in communities where violence is a chronic condition.

## Race

Research indicates that intimate partner violence (IPV) is evident in all ethnic groups in America, but some groups have significantly higher rates than others. Smith (2005) recognizes that there is a complex interaction between class, race, ethnicity, gender, sexual orientation, religion, and geographic location that inform the lived experience of poverty and the diversity of people who live in poverty. Diversity in this instance is not a warm, fuzzy, and emotional experience but a compounded set of circumstances that limit the life chances of specific groups of people.

Fielding and Caetano (2004) highlight that there are ethnic differences in the prevalence of IPV, and there is a need to assess not only between group differences but also within group dynamics. These ethnic differences include types of violence, socioeconomic status and substance abuse. These ethnic differences are specific risk factors of IPV for each group and need to be assessed separately, because this is rarely done. Consequently, White women and their needs are used as the standard for IPV, and other groups are served comparatively.

Consequently, Fielding and Caetano (2004) outline that there are serious disparities in how African American women and men experience this type of violence in the United States. African American women and men report higher rates of IPV across their lifetimes. They are more likely than Whites and Hispanics to report physical violence in their marital relationships within a year's time and that both spouses were hit or injured.

Another unique factor in IPV against African American women is the prevalence of myths and stereotypes. African American feminist have underscored this perspective over the years that African American women live at an intersection between racism, sexism, and classism (Collins, 2005, 2009; Hooks, 2000). Donovan and Williams (2002) outline some interesting facts about African American women who are rape survivors, which I believe can be generalized to issues of IPV for African American women. They believe that oppressive stereotypical views of African American women, specifically "Jezebel" and the "Matriarch," influence how they are treated in the criminal justice system. Jezebel is sexually promiscuous, lustful, and immoral. The matriarch is superstrong, aggressive, and an emasculator of African American men.

These images are the reasons why African American women are not taken seriously when they report rape. These stereotypes minimize African

American women's long history of sexual exploitation and victimization. The outcome of this minimization is that African American women who are survivors of rape may receive less empathy, consideration, and judicial support than White women (Donovan and Williams, 2002). Trotman Reid (2000) concurs with this view and states:

> There exist at least two myths of African American women: they are either "good" or "bad." The "good" African American woman is strong maternal, hard-working, devoted to family, and quiet. . . . The "bad" African American woman is ugly, lascivious, lazy, negligent, emasculating, and loud. Both views are based on stereotypes born of a need to justify public policies or societal treatment of African American women; they do not come from data or any close investigation of reality. (p. xiii)

I believe these same images and myths can be generalized to African American women who are victims of IPV and leads to similar outcomes. African American women who are victims of IPV are (1) seen as responsible for their assaults, (2) seen as contributors to inner city poverty, (3) seen as responsible for the state of the African male because she does not submit to the traditional view of womanhood in this society, (4) seen as less traumatized because she is strong, and (5) often blamed instead of given empathy. This is evidenced by their failure to report victimization and to utilize available domestic violence resources.

### Substance Abuse

Carrillo and Tello (2008) quote Dr. DiNovo who through her work with women in substance abuse recovery (African American and White) reported being victims of horrific violence. They admit that their partners often beat them when they were high and that their own drinking and drug use contributed to the violence. There is an intimate relationship between substance abuse and IPV. The male partner is usually the supplier of the drugs and the female partner is often used to get the money or substances in exchange for sexual favors. These relationships where substance abuse is central are breeding grounds for violence, sexual abuse, criminality, and degradation. Many of these women were sexually abused as children, and their intoxication is a form of dulling the pain but opens the door to continuous abuse.

This is true across races. But for African American women where substance abuse and poverty is more prevalent in urban areas, women are exposed at earlier ages and more frequently. Substance abuse, especially alcohol, is an important factor that should be accounted for when examining ethnic differences and assessing not only the violence perpetrated on the African

American women but also in the assessment of women as the perpetrated of the violence (Fielding and Caetano, 2004).

### Poverty

Poverty is often ill-defined in research. Definitions range from low socio-economic status, poor, low income, economically disadvantaged, underemployed, and welfare recipients. Researchers of family violence have virtually ignored the connection between IPV and poverty (Goodman et al., 2009). They underscore the intersection between poverty and IPV and found that they co-occur at high rates, produce parallel effects, and in each other's presence, while constraining coping options. Consequently, "both external situational and psychological difficulties are missed when women contending with both poverty and IPV are viewed through the lens of just one or just the other" (Goodman, et al., 2009, p. 306). This research also views poverty and IPV as a reciprocal relationship that has three effects: stress, powerlessness, and social isolation. As a result, there is a direct need for specialized interventions for women who live in poverty.

The U.S. Census Bureau (2006) state that 36.5 million (12.3%) of Americans live in poverty. The majority of these Americans are women; their children and a disproportionate number (over half) are ethnic minorities. In terms of women who are born poor, 11 percent are White, 25 percent African American, and 23 percent Latinas. The percentage of African Americans who are born into poverty and often continue to live the rest of their lives in poverty is staggering. Poverty definitely implicated IPV. Household income is the most significant factor that contributes to IPV, and African American women are disproportionately represented in poverty (Goodman et al., 2009).

The *Women of color health data book: Adolescents to seniors* notes that Black Americans are predominantly an urban population. More than 87 percent of all Blacks in 2003 resided in all 50 states; 54 percent of all Black Americans lived in 13 Southern states where they were concentrated greater than the national average of more than 12 percent of the total population. Consequently, 20 percent of all 2000 census respondents in the South were Black, in contrast to 12 percent in the Northeast, 11 percent in the Midwest, and 6 percent in the West. This is probably true for the 2010 census, because there has been an exodus of northern African Americans returning to South, especially to cities like Atlanta, Charlotte, and Houston.

Subsequently, urban living for African Americans is fraught with economic hardships, which includes chronic unemployment, being members of the working poor, dependent on social services stipends, and the stressors of living in households and neighborhoods with high levels of disorder, disrepair, and unemployment (Stueve & O'Donnell, 2008). There is a direct relationship between low socioeconomic levels and relationship violence. Women living in families with the lowest incomes are seven times more likely to be victimized by an intimate partner (Stueve & O'Donnell, 2008). The other issues in these low-income households are that women and men are both perpetrators of the violence, although men more than women, and that violence are a part of their makeup. It is not just acute but also chronic. This violence that is born from not just their immediate home environment but also a part of their overall living environment exacerbates their physical and mental health and directly impacts every aspect of the family: male, female, and children.

## COMMUNITY VIOLENCE

Race, gender, substance abuse, and socioeconomic status converge in the lives of African American women, unfortunately, at the "vortex of violence." Some see it as a culture of violence that includes the potential of exposure to a continuum of violence that is often expected and normalized on multiple levels—mental/emotional and physical. Stueve and O'Donnell (2008) summarize it as settings where problem solving through aggression is the norm and patterns of violence witnessed in the community may get repeated in domestic relationships and vice versa. Fielding and Caetano (2004) document a positive association between residence in an impoverished area and the occurrence of IPV. They believe this suggests that if you factor out the characteristics of the couple and their use of alcohol or its associated problems, life in poverty-stricken areas influence behavior including IPV (Fielding & Caetano, 2004, p. 311).

This convergence of being marginalized in impoverished areas and being victimized by the violence in the community is actually termed "chronic community violence" (CCV) and exposure to it has an impact on the mental and physical health of its residents. It is a vortex that has a heavy impact on African American women and their families. Unfortunately, the results are overlooked and/or attributed to other issues.

### Chronic Community Violence and Community Violence Exposure

Community is a geographic location often with common laws, culture, and historic roots. In the African American community, in most major cities, it is identified by urban areas with common experiences, especially the incidence of chronic violence. Community violence has been defined in various ways. It is interpersonal violence inflicted on an individual that has the propensity to negatively impact a single person or a community of people. An acquaintance or stranger can commit the violent act. It is a sudden event that comes as a surprise to its victims and can occur in the home, neighborhood parks and recreational areas, school, workplace, and even church. Shahinfar, Fox, and Leavitt (2000) define community violence is the presence of violence and violence-related events within an individual's proximal environment, including home, school, and neighborhood. It may involve direct or threatened harm, be witnessed or experienced, and involve known or unknown perpetrators. It includes physical assault, sexual assault, homicide, mugging, gang violence, unnecessary force by authorities, theft, and family violence in neighborhoods where children and families live, play, and work (Walling, Erikson, Putman, & Foy, 2011, p. 42).

Some define community violence as violence that has been enacted on a member or members of society (Steinbrenner, 2010). It is often seen separately from family or IPV. I believe CCV is not separate from family or IPV but that it is inclusive of any consistent violence that is part of the neighborhood or area in which a person lives, with direct and indirect impact to persons who are exposed to it.

The World Health Organization asserts that community violence is an intentional use of physical force or power that has impact on multiple levels including injury, death, psychological harm, maldevelopment, or deprivation. Violence occurs in all communities, but it is more insidious when it is chronic and families cannot escape its consistent presence in their neighborhoods. Consequently, urban and impoverished neighborhoods are victimized by CCV.

### Community Violence Exposure

CCV is the act and/or the persistence of various forms of violence in a neighborhood. Community violence exposure (CVE) is the aftermath of living under these types of stressful circumstances. It is also defined as the outcomes of constantly witnessing community violence.

Stress theory is the theoretical foundation for understanding the outcomes of a person's chronic exposure (Cooley-Strickland et al., 2009). Current research documents that the exposure to CCV, which is the stressor, has an impact on children, adolescents, and the parents. CVE is a variable that depends on other factors: the age of the population, the urban areas, the specificity of violence exposure (in the home, outside the home, or both), direct victimization, or indirect exposure (Walling et al., 2011).

It is recognized as a major public health problem (Kgur, Dahlberg, Mercy, Zwi, & Lozano, 2002) and an epidemic in the United States, especially in urban centers where minorities and the poor reside. Shahinfar, Fox, and

Leavitt (2000) assert that CCV has been informed by and related to trauma research because of the outcomes to its exposure. The consistent exposure to this type of violence has a major impact on the physical and mental health of its victims. Subsequently, there are direct and indirect victims.

Steinbrenner (2010) states that in his sample, 56 percent of urban adolescent mothers had seen a shooting take place and that the exposure to community violence has a detrimental impact on adolescents. The outcomes include but are not limited to adolescents: mental and physical health impact; emotional, behavioral, and adaptive functioning difficulties; symptoms of posttraumatic stress disorder (PTSD); depression; aggression; decreased scholastic ability; lower levels of success; increased suicidal ideation; and aggressive impulsive behavior (Lambert, Ialonga, Boyd, & Cooley, 2005).

In 2002, Dr. Jenkins wrote a comprehensive article that addressed the impact of community violence on Black women. Her article addressed core issues like exposure to violence, loss of significant others, and impact issues such as psychological distress, loss and grief, parenting, coping strategies, and suggestions for interventions. Stueve and O'Donnell (2008) document a relationship between women who experience discrimination and high levels of CVE and IPV. They found that discrimination and community violence are predictors of physical and emotional IPV.

The emergence of research on African American women and IPV and CVE has highlighted an intersection between the two. There are similarities in the predictors and aftereffects of IPV and CCV. The empirical data leads to the conclusion that they are not separate issues in urban communities but part of a continuum of violence. This indicates that the negative outcomes are similar and compounded when persons are exposed to violence within the home and also in the streets. This grim outlook is exacerbated by the fact that it is not incidental but chronic.

## HEALTH—INTERACTIONS AND AFTEREFFECTS

The literature supports that IPV does not operate in a vacuum. It is in the community and there is a reciprocal relationship between IPV, CVE, and their impact on the family. The study of their interaction (IPV and CVE) has escalated in the last decade and clarity about the consequences is emerging on the physical and mental health consequences of living in a vortex of violence without any relief in sight. Some writers have compared it with persons who are living in a war zone (Steinbrenner, 2010). Not only are there individual-level effects during a time of war, but also societal-level effects: government, law enforcement, schools, and public service agencies experience the brunt of the swirl of violence and chaos.

To begin to address the aftermath of IPV from a physical and mental health perspective, I believe we need to utilize some terms from the medical community: chronic versus acute. When something is chronic, it is marked by a long duration and a frequent recurrence. It is something that is pervasive, always present, and has the propensity to vex, weaken, or trouble the person, community, or society as a whole. On the other hand, when something is acute, it is characterized as being sharp or severe. It has a sudden onset or it is felt, perceived, and experienced intensely. When it is acute, it is seriously demanding urgent attention.

IPV in the African American community is chronic and acute, and therefore complex and compounded by the negative factors of urban living: social inequities, poverty, and substance abuse. When we discuss IPV against African American women, it must be discussed in the context of and as an interaction of the community of which these women are a part. Consequently, there is an interactive effect and an aftereffect that impacts the family on an intergenerational level and on a physical and mental health level.

## PHYSICAL AND MENTAL HEALTH DISPARITIES

The disparity between the health status of African Americans and Whites has been well documented in medical and social science literature. At all stages of life, men, women, and children of African descent experience more health problems and have more negative outcomes than other cultural groups. It appears that existing health promotion programs have not been successful in reducing the rate of disease and illness among African Americans, overall. In addition, very few of these programs factor in the psychosocial and sociocultural issues that may contribute to this health disparity.

IPV by definition includes physical, sexual, and psychological attacks that leave physical injuries and mental stressors. Frequent visits to the hospital for physical injuries and denial or lies about how the injuries occurred are part of the dance of IPV. There is a serious interface even on the health level when you assess African American women and IPV, and it is difficult to talk about them as separate events. Keeshin, Cronholm, and Strawn (2012) identify a direct linkage between exposure to violence and the subsequent development of medical illnesses. Some of the medical illnesses include chronic pain and somatic syndromes (fibromyalgia, chronic fatigue syndrome, and irritable bowel syndrome), respiratory disorders (asthma and chronic obstructive pulmonary disease), obesity, cardiovascular disease, and cancer.

Bent-Goodley (2007) states the physical health issues are compounded by mental health issues and often occur simultaneously with the physical pain. Some recurrent physical conditions include but are not limited to bruises, burns, fractures, and traumatic brain injuries that often result in long-term disabilities (Keeshin et al., 2012). Researchers concur that the longer women stay in these violent environments, mental health problems emerge and are exacerbated. Persistent symptomology include, but are not limited to, increased feelings of fear and anxiety, PTSD, loss of self-efficacy, substance abuse, suicide ideation, and prolonged and complicated grief (Bent-Goodley, 2007; Goodman et al., 2009; Jones, Hughes, & Unterstaller, 2001; Dutton, 2009). For youths, there are similar but additional symptoms: anxiety, depression, aggression, decreased scholastic ability, school disengagement, lower levels of success, criminality, and substance abuse (Steinbrenner, 2010; Cooley-Strickland et al., 2009; Jenkins, 2002; Walling et al., 2011).

Please note that these mental health symptoms are not only experienced by women, but also by their children and complicated by living in neighborhoods where community violence is chronic. This "vortex of violence" against African American women intensifies the development of health issues. Keeshin et al. (2012) concur with this concept of a "vortex of violence" and assert that attempting to isolate just the biological changes that occur when women and children have been exposed to violence is difficult because abuse can be physical, sexual, and emotional; may include interpersonal and community experiences; and vary in the severity, frequency, and duration of the abuse. This as well as other issues complicate scientific study of the interactive repercussions of violence.

Bent-Goodley (2007) believes that culture and society influences health and health disparities among ethnic women survivors of IPV. Bent-Goodley's in-depth look at the intersection of IPV, health, and health disparities yields three levels of barriers that impact the overall health of women of color: individual, institutional, and systemic. On the individual level, there are barriers in terms of health-seeking behaviors, stigmatization, and family secrecy. The barriers in institutions include lack of physician training on IPV, stereotypical views of women of color, inadequate screening tools, lack of cultural competence, and language barriers. Systemic barriers are discriminatory treatment, poverty, and immigration status.

An example of an IPV health issue with a serious interactive effect for African American women is the high incidence of HIV/AIDS among this group. In 2002, HIV was found to be the number one cause of death for African American women aged 25 to 34 (Kaiser, 2006). The number one cause of HIV transmission was through heterosexual relationships. In addition, sexual assault in IPV is clear grounds for the lack of condom use in African American relationships and failure to engage in safe sex. Bent-Goodley (2007) highlights that little research has been done in looking at the connection between health disparities, IPV, and women of color, but it is and continues to be a devastating health problem.

Another interesting finding is the fact that childhood sexual abuse is a precursor to IPV as well as children's exposure to IPV and CCV. Herrenkohl, Sousa, Tajima, Herrenkohl, and Moylan (2008) document an intersection between child abuse and children's exposure to domestic violence and found that the outcomes of these children's lives is extremely negative. Their research not only reviews the intersection of child abuse and domestic violence, but also other risk factors like community violence and related family and environmental stressors.

PTSD, which is often just called trauma, is increasingly identified as a direct consequence of IPV. It is a psychiatric disorder that can occur following the experience of witnessing or being a victim of life-threatening events like violence and abuse. There are clear biological and psychological changes. The symptoms of PTSD fall into three categories: intrusive (e.g., flashbacks and recurrent dreams), avoidance (e.g., feelings of detachment and lack of interest in activities), and arousal (e.g., irritability and outbursts). IPV is not just a physical assault, but also an assault on the mental and emotional health of women and their children.

Jones et al. (2001) reviewed the research to assess the interaction between PTSD and victims of domestic violence. Some of their findings indicate that the compounded factors of the lives of African American women who are victims of IPV make them high risk for PTSD. Multiple victimization experiences, the severity of the experiences, and substance abuse were directly correlated with precursors of past and current abuse. The following demographic characteristics increased the likelihood of the onset of PTSD: younger women, unemployed women, having a large number of children, low income, and low levels of social support. African American women disproportionately display these characteristics along with being victims of IPV.

## CONCLUSION—FUTURE CHALLENGE

This review has established that there are many interactive aftereffects that complicate understanding IPV and the needs of African American women who are its disproportionate victims. Domestic violence as a movement has shaped policy, research, and interventions that have helped women and the society, but there is still significant amounts of work to be done in these same areas for African American women, especially those who are economically disadvantaged.

The major recommendation is that we must begin to see African American women and IPV as the complex issue that is within their communities. It is a part of the "vortex of violence" that is typical of inner-city urban environments. IPV is impacted by CCV fueled by the community in which it exists. The exposure to violence within the home and outside of the home brings on a whirlpool effect that draws families into a space that they often cannot recover from.

This implies that how African American women are served has to go beyond safe houses and an overly feminist counseling perspective to understanding the layers of victimization that is a part of their experience. Once there is a clear comprehension of their plight or as Goodman et al. (2009) asserts, there must be skilled helpers who know how their experiences shape their mental health and coping skills. These interventions should include tools to assist African American women and their families to break the cycle and overcome not just for the short-term but also on a long-term basis.

If African American women are going to be better served in the area of IPV, we must first acknowledge their status as victims and how this status has far-reaching effects. A victim is a person that is injured; sacrificed; destroyed; or subjected to oppression, hardship, or mistreatment under any of various conditions. African American women and their children are victims not only in their homes but also in their communities. The acknowledgement of their victimization should no longer surprise us that trauma, specifically PTSD, is prevalent in the aftermath of these victims of compounded violent experiences.

Victimology is an emerging field of study that attempts to assess why certain people are victims of crime; moreover, how lifestyles affect the chances that a certain person will fall victim to a crime. It is interdisciplinary in its approach and includes the disciplines of sociology, psychology, criminal justice, law, and advocacy. We want to move African American women and the services we provide from a victim focus to a survivor focus. A survivor-focus framework includes an acknowledgement of the need to address the mental health of these women and move away from symptom only and short-term services. We need to (1) accept the serious complexities of their lives (2) address the pervasive influence of poverty, (3) implement immediate and long-term strategies to help them rise above it, (4) encourage a strength-based view and reclaim their power (Goodman et al., 2009). It will take a targeted and comprehensive approach to unravel and intervene in the face of the "crisis collision" (Goodman et al., 2009) and "vortex of violence" in the lives of African American women and their children. This will address the physical and mental health necessary for intergenerational change. This is the challenge!

## REFERENCES

Africana Voices Against Violence. (2002). *Tufts University, statistics, 2002.* Retrieved from www.ase.tufts.edu/womenscenter/peace/africana/newsite/statistics.htm

American Bar Association. (2012). *Domestic violence statistics.* Retrieved from http://www.americanbar.org/groups/domestic_violence/resources/statistics.html

Bent-Goodley, T. B. (2001). Eradicating domestic violence in the African American community: A literature review and action agenda. *Trauma, Violence & Abuse, 2*(4), 316–330.

Bent-Goodley, T. B. (2007). Health disparities and violence against women: Why and how cultural and societal influences matter. *Trauma Violence and Abuse, 8*(2), 90–104.

Brown, C. (2008). Gender-role implications on same-sex intimate partner abuse. *Journal of Family Violence, 23*(8), 9030–9093.

Carrillo, R., & Tello, J. (Eds.). (2008). *Family violence and men of color: Healing the wounded male spirit* (2nd ed.). New York: Springer Publishers.

Chaney, K. (2008a). *Kathy Chaney.* Retrieved from www.chicagodefender.com/article-2110-domestic-violence-hits-black-women-harder.html

Chaney, K. (2008b). Domestic violence hit black women harder. *Chicago Defender.* Retrieved from http://www.highbeam.com/doc/1P3-1584882421.html

Collins, P. H. (2005). *Black sexual politics.* New York: Routledge Press.

Collins, P. H. (2009). *Black feminist thought.* New York: Routledge Press.

Cooley-Strickland, M., Quille, T. J., Griffin, R. S., Stuart, E. A., Bradshaw, C. P., & Furr-Holden, D. (2009). Community violence and youth: Affect, behavior, substance use and academics. *Clinical Child and Family Psychological Review, 12*(2), 127–156.

Donovan, R., & Williams, M. (2002). Living at the intersection: The effects of racism and sexism on black rape survivors. In C. M. West (Ed.), *Violence in the lives of black women: Battered, black, and blue* (pp. 95–105). New York: Haworth Press, Inc.

Dutton, M. A. (2009). Pathways linking intimate partner violence and posttraumatic disorder. *Trauma, Violence & Abuse, 10*(3), 211–224.

Fielding, C. A., & Caetano, R. (2004). Ethnic differences in intimate partner violence in the U.S. general population: The role of alcohol use and socioeconomic status. *Trauma, Violence & Abuse, 5*(4), 303–317.

Goodman, L. A., Smyth, K. F., Borges, A. M., & Singer, R. (2009). When crises collide: How intimate partner violence and poverty intersect to shape women's mental health and coping. *Trauma, Violence & Abuse, 10*(4), 306–329.

Herrenkohl, T. I., Sousa, C., Tajima, E. A., Herrenkohl, R. C., & Moylan, C. A. (2008). Intersection of child abuse and children's exposure to domestic violence. *Trauma, Violence & Abuse, 9*(2), 84–99.

Hooks, B. (2000). *Feminist theory: From margin to center.* Brooklyn, NY: South End Press.

Jenkins, E. J. (2002). Black women and community violence: Trauma, grief, and coping. In C. M. West (Ed.), *Violence in the lives of black women: Battered, black, and blue* (pp. 29–44). New York: Haworth Press, Inc.

Jones, L., Hughes, M., & Unterstaller, U. (2001). Post-traumatic stress disorder (PTSD) in victims of domestic violence: A review of the research. *Trauma, Violence & Abuse, 2*(2), 99–119.

Kaiser, H. J. (2006). *Fact sheet: The HIV/AIDS epidemic in the United States.* Menlo Park, CA: Henry J. Kaiser Family Foundation.

Keeshin, B. R., Cronholm, P. F., & Strawn, J. R. (2012). Physiologic changes associated with violence and abuse exposure: An examination of related medical conditions. *Trauma, Violence & Abuse, 13*(1), 41–56.

Kgur, E. G., Dahlberg, L. L., Mercy, J. A., Zwi, A. B., & Lozano, R. (2002). *World report on violence and health.* Geneva, Switzerland: WHO.

Lambert, S. F., Ialonga, N. S., Boyd, R. C., & Cooley, M. (2005). Risk factors for community violence exposure in adolescence. *American Journal of Community Psychology, 36*(1–2), 29–48.

NCVS. (2012). *The national crime victim survey resource guide.* Washington, D.C.: U.S. Department of Justice. Retrieved from http://www.icpsr.umich.edu/icpsrweb/NACJD/NCVS/

NIH. (2007–2008). *Women of color health data book: Adolescents to seniors.* Bethesda, MD: Office of Research on Women's Health.

Peterman, L. M., & Dixon, C. G. (2003). Domestic violence between same-sex partners: Implications for counseling. *Journal of Counseling and Development, 81*(1), 40–47.

*Post-traumatic stress disorder: Assault on my psyche.* (2007). http://www.blackplanet.com/news/article_comments.html?news_item_id=38577, http://www.blackwomenshealth.com/PTSD.htm

Rennison, C. M., & Welchans, S. (2000). *Intimate partner violence.* NCJ 178247. Washington, D.C.: U.S. Department of Justice. Retrieved from http://bjs.ojp.usdoj.gov/content/pub/pdf/ipv.pdf

Shahinfar, A., Fox, N. A., & Leavitt, L. A. (2000). Preschool children's exposure to violence: Relation of behavior problems to parent and child reports. *American Journal of Orthopsychiatry, 70*(1), 115–125.

Smith, L. (2005). Psychotherapy, classism, and the poor: Conspicuous by their absence. *American Psychologist, 60*(7), 687–696.

Steinbrenner, S. Y. (2010). Concept analysis of community violence: Using adolescent exposure to community violence as an exemplar. *Issues in Mental Health Nursing, 31*(1), 4–7.

Stueve, A., & O'Donnell, L. (2008). Urban young women's experiences of discrimination and community violence and intimate partner violence. *Journal of Urban Health, 85*(3): 386–401.

Sullivan, T. P., Meese, K. J., Swan, S. C., Mazure, C. M., & Snow, D. L. (2005). Precursors and correlates of women's violence: Child abuse traumatization, victimization of women, avoidance coping, and psychological symptoms. *Psychology of Women Quarterly, 29*(3), 290–301.

Trotman Reid, P. (2000). Foreword. In L. C. Jackson and B. Greene (Eds.), *Psychotherapy with African American women: Innovations in psychodynamic perspectives and practice.* New York: Guilford Press, Inc.

U.S. Census Bureau. (2006). www.census.gov/ps.

VPC. (2008). *When men murder women: An analysis of 2006 homicide data.* Washington, D.C.: Violence Policy Center. Retrieved from: http://www.vpc.org/studies/wmmw2008.pdf

Walling, S. M., Erikson, C. B., Putman, K. M., & Foy, D. W. (2011). Community violence exposure, adverse childhood experiences, and posttraumatic distress among urban development workers. *Psychological Trauma: Theory, Research, Practice, and Policy, 3*(1), 42–49.

West, C. M. (2002). Battered, black and blue: An overview of violence in the lives of black women. In C. M. West (Ed.), *Violence in the lives of black women: battered, black, and blue* (pp. 5–27). New York: Haworth Press, Inc.

# 9

## Health-Care Pathways and Issues for African American Women in Prison[1]

### *Catherine Fisher Collins*

African American women in prisons and jails bring to these facilities multiple health complaints and problems. Some of these health problems are rooted in the way in which the African American woman's ancestors were socialized to view the medical profession; how the health system treated them, poverty and a range of other social ills; and their health behavior. In this chapter, I address the historical treatment of African American women's health conditions, their health care issues, and the health problems of the incarcerated African American female.

## HEALTH CARE FOR AFRICAN AMERICAN WOMEN: YEARS OF NEGLECT

In Edward Beardsley's article "Race as a Factor in Health," he describes how Black women were treated in three eras, giving them descriptive names: Denial (1900–1930), Inclusion (1930–1960) and Attempted Restitution (1960–1980) (Beardsley 1990). I included one additional section: "How to Right the Wrong (1980s to present)." Slave, women were viewed as personal property to do with as the slave, master saw fit. For economic reasons, African slaves were brought to America. Women slaves were seen as the suppliers of human resources (babies) to support America's desire for free labor. African American women were encouraged to get pregnant at the age of 15 or younger, and to have anywhere from 10 to 15 babies. Sometimes, the incentives for having this many babies were such choice duties as doing light housework or serving as a nanny for the White master's children. However, once these women and girls came into close quarters with the White slave master, his sons and friends, they might rape them or perform any other perverted sexual act they desired. On one hand, the slave master valued slave women and their babies as a key to keeping the economy moving forward. On the other hand, pregnant slave women and their babies were treated viciously, as demonstrated in the following passage: The contempt felt about African American children and women was never so apparent as when "Mary Turner," pregnant, was hanged, and doused with gasoline as she swung by the neck. As Whites watched this burning woman a man stepped forward with a pocket knife and ripped open the abdomen. . . . Out tumbled the prematurely born child . . . two feeble cries it gave—and received for answer the [boot] heel of a stalwart man, as life was ground out of its tiny form (Day, 1989, p. 245).

It was not uncommon for doctors to participate in the torture and murder of slave girls. Medical practitioners often perfected novel surgical techniques on slave women before performing the procedure on White women, and often without anesthesia. The most notorious practitioner was James Marion Sims, a founder of modern gynecology, who purchased slave women expressly for perfecting gynecological surgery in the 19th century. Sims was primarily a plantation physician who experimented on female slaves suffering from vesicovaginal fistulas. The condition involves tears between the vagina and the bladder or between the bowels and the vagina, and it causes women to continually drip urine from their vagina. The condition often resulted from difficulty in childbirth— remember, girls as young as 12 were raped and impregnated before their bodies were mature enough to sustain a birth. In 1845, owners of the Westcott plantation summoned Sims because a young slave woman named Anarcha had been in labor for three days without delivering. Given the prolonged delivery, Anarcha sustained several fistulas that Sims attempted to correct surgically without anesthesia, even though it had recently become available and Sims used it on Whites undergoing the same surgery. Sims subscribed to the notion that, unlike White women, African women had a psychological tolerance to pain. Sims operated on Anarcha more than 30 times without anesthesia since postoperative infections kept frustrating the surgeries when sutures became infected and the fistula remained open. Sims successfully repaired the fistulas after using silver sutures that resisted infection. Sims operated on at least 10 more slave women over several years, perfecting the surgical technique (Baker, 2007, p. 407). Harriet A. Washington (2006), in her book *Medical Apartheid*, includes a chapter that details other medical atrocities performed by Sims (pp. 227–252). It was this kind of treatment and many others documented in slave oral history that formed the foundation for the distrust of the medical profession by African Americans. "As we reached the era of Denial, White America believed that somehow the descendants of the African slave would disappear because they did not have the ability or fortitude to survive. This notion was the basis for their denial of medical and health services for Black women. By 1914, these Black women, who were once raped and coerced to give birth, were giving birth and dying in childbirth at an alarming rate" (Collins, 1997, p. 81). A few White physicians provided limited care for Black pregnant women, but like most Whites they believed the Black women were "shiftless, of low intelligence, and [loved] carnal pleasure" (Beardsley, 1990, p. 125). In other words, the reasons for withholding health services included shiftlessness (regardless of poor housing and the lack of job opportunities), low intelligence (regardless of their having been educated in segregated schools if at all), and love of carnal pleasure (pregnancy being interpreted as a pleasurable state of being for women).

> With these attitudes and limited health services, Black women were suffering and dying from tuberculosis, venereal diseases (which also claimed the lives of many infants) and childbirth. By the mid-1930s, the Social Security Act began to provide some limited maternal services for mothers and babies. However, hospitals segregated Black women into large, understaffed wards, staffed by prejudiced White nurses and physicians who lacked supplies and other resources for a very sick population. (Collins, 1997, p. 81)

> In the era of Inclusion (1930–1960), there was a glimmer of hope that some of the wrongdoings could be remedied. One of these attempts was once again made by the federal government through the Hill-Burton Act of 1947. This provided resources for the building of hospitals, not especially for Blacks, but more for returning servicemen from World War II. By 1959, there were over 7,000 hospital projects completed or underway. These new hospital projects, however, continued to perpetuate an already segregated hospital system, and there was little change in attitude toward what was now America's sickest segment of the population. With the demands for equality that the Civil Rights and other movements posited, the era of Attempted Restitution found the nation struggling with changing attitudes in the medical, nursing, and health professions. Pressure from the Department of Justice and other governmental interventions found the once segregated medical and nursing schools opening up enrollments and the "colored waiting room" signs being removed. However, by now the harm had been done. African American women had grown to distrust the now open system of health care. Expectant mothers had learned not to depend on White health providers, turning to untrained midwives to deliver their babies. Hospitals were now viewed as a place of last resort, and with this attitude many Blacks began to seek care (often too late) in the last stages of their illness. Lifestyle behaviors that contributed to poor health habits were now embedded for the generations that followed. (Collins, 1997, p. 82)

## HOW TO RIGHT THE WRONG: AFRICAN AMERICAN WOMEN'S HEALTH

As we enter the final era, "How to Right the Wrong," African American women in the nonprison population are still experiencing a high rate of maternal mortality, infant mortality, tuberculosis, cancer, venereal disease, diabetes, hypertension, asthma, hepatitis C, fibroid tumors, pelvic inflammatory disease and now the dreaded acquired immune deficiency syndrome (AIDS) (Collins, 1997, p. 83). African American females who become inmates come to the institutions in most cases in deplorable health from many years of no health-care treatment.

In the general public, there are over 45 million uninsured Americans. Many of these individuals are the working poor, children, homeless people and those living in poverty. When people are poor, they seek medical care late and often in emergency rooms. In 2005, African American women were most likely to be the single head of household (28.5%), while the percentage of White and Asian women heads of household was 16.7 and 17.1, respectively (HRSA, 2007, p. 14). In addition, during this same year, the poverty rate for Black women was 24.2 percent; for Hispanics it was 21.7 percent. The health of these women was reported to also be poor. Diabetes occurred for Black women at a rate of 106.8 per 1,000, compared to 69.1 per 1,000 for White females. The hypertension rate is also very poor. Black women's rate is 353.8 per 1,000; White women, 264.5 per 1,000; and Hispanic women, 200.2 per 1,000 (p. 7). In addition, asthma, a chronic inflammatory disease, affects African Americans at an alarming rate. In 2005, 108.4 per 1,000 Black women suffered from asthma. For White women, that number was 93.8 per 1,000. The lowest number was that of Asian females, at 55.6 per 1,000 (p. 35). Heart disease is the number one killer of women. In 2005, the highest rates of heart disease were among White females (129.7 per 1,000), followed by Black women (107.1 per 1000) (p. 42). These are some of the illnesses that women in the nonincarcerated population are plagued with. If they become incarcerated, they will bring these same health problems to the jail/prison health service, as reported by Maruschak (2006).

## THE HEALTH OF WOMEN PRISONERS

In 2002, there were an estimated 239,000 jailed inmates who reported having existing health problems, including arthritis (13%), hypertension (11%), asthma (10%), and heart disease (6%). It was also reported that 53% of these women upon admission to the jail had health problems. The top nine health problems reported were arthritis (19.4%), asthma (19.4%), hypertension (14.1%), heart problems (9.2%), kidney problems (8.9%), tuberculosis

(4.0%), diabetes (4.1%), hepatitis (5.0%), and stroke (3.3%; Maruschak, 2007, p. 2, Table 2). Also reported among these jailed females were mental impairments (14.9%) and learning impairments (18.0%, Table 5).

The major task of most prison health services is to screen newly committed inmates to detect communicable diseases such as tuberculosis, herpes, hepatitis, HIV/AIDS, and gonorrhea. However, a position statement by the National Commission on Correctional Health Care (2005) points out inadequate screening of female prisoners. Even though prison services may include mental and physical examinations and dental and psychological screenings, some screening is lacking (Collins, 1997; Belnap, 2007, p. 210). "Gynecological exams are not performed upon admission to prison, nor are they routinely provided on an annual basis. . . . As a result, women in prison are at risk for having some diseases, such as breast cancer" and pregnancies (Belnap, 2007, p. 381). Early detection of pregnancies and breast cancer could allow for appropriate interventions that will affect outcome. The rate of pregnancies among women prisoners is estimated to be 5 percent in state prisons and 6 percent in local jails, found when some prisons screen on intake (Greenfield and Snell, 1999). In New York State, "about 10 percent of women inmates are pregnant when they enter prison" (Wynn, 2000, p. 60).

Once women enter state prisons, their need for nutritious foods, prenatal vitamins and follow-up care is essential for their health and that of the baby. Recently, the media reported on the shackling and restraint of pregnant women by prison officials, a procedure that is dangerous and inappropriate. The professional literature is relatively silent on this subject, but Amnesty International (2007) reported "that being restrained or shackled could be harmful to their pregnancy and child. Lack of mobility may hamper a woman's ability to move during contractions to alleviate pain and can be dangerous during transportation due to the risk of falling and an inability to break the fall when restrained" (2006, p. 3). Clearly the use of restraints and removing the newborn infant immediately to a relative or to foster care can cause these mothers to become depressed and angry. The following is an example of one inmate's ordeal with shackles.

In September 2005, although still two weeks from her due date, Samantha Luther, incarcerated in Wisconsin, was allegedly taken in handcuffs and leg shackles to the local hospital, and informed that labor was going to be induced. She told a reporter, "I was in shock. . . . I felt like all of my rights had been taken away." Reportedly, her handcuffs were taken off, while her shackles remained on providing 18 inches between her ankles. The doctor ruptured her amniotic sac, and had her pace the hospital hallway for several hours. "It was so humiliating. My ankles were raw," Luther said. Luther was given drugs to induce labor, when it did not begin, and reportedly was left in her shackles until just before birth. She reported, "I had shackles on up until the baby was coming out and then they took them off for me to push. . . . It was unbelievable. Like I was going to go anywhere." She gave birth to a son. Reportedly, it is common to induce inmates before term, however, according to DOC officials, an inmate must sign a consent form. (Prisontalk.com)

Some states have enacted policies or laws prohibiting the use of restraints on pregnant inmates. "Only 2 states have legislation regulating the use of restraints on pregnant women. These are Illinois and California" (Liptak, 2006; Doetzer, 2008). In August 2009, Governor David Patterson of New York signed into law an antishackling bill for pregnant prisoners. In the other 47 states, the District of Columbia, and the Federal Bureau of Prisons, no such laws exist.

The American College of Obstetricians and Gynecologists states that "Physical restraints have interfered with the ability of physicians to safely practice medicine by reducing their ability to assess and evaluate the physical condition of the mother and the fetus, and have similarly made the labor and delivery process more difficult than it needs to be, thus overall putting the health and lives of the women and unborn children at risk" (Hale, 2007). In Doetzer's (2008) article "Hard Labor: The Legal Implications of Shackling Female Inmates During Pregnancy and Childbirth," she discusses lawsuits filed by women who received poor treatment while they were shackled. She states that nationally about 2,000 women in custody give births each year. After their births, some infants are allowed to stay with their mother. In New York State, "Bedford Hills Correctional Facility nursery has a capacity of 25 beds . . . that allows mothers to keep their infants with them for a year to 18 months (depending on their release date) . . . it provides mothers with the opportunity to nurture family bonds during a critical developmental time in their child's life" (Margolies & Kraft-Stolar, 2006).

Determining how many infants are born with health issues due to poor health care during labor and delivery could open a litigation gate that could cost state governments millions if they were found to be negligent in their care of shackled pregnant inmates. As mentioned, the literature is silent on this subject, with the exception of Amnesty International. Other women who need health services for minor health complaints are handled during "sick call," where inmates' complaints of a problem are placed on a list for the next day's clinic. However, chronic health conditions could be life-threatening if treatment is delayed. Emergency care is usually provided by onsite medical personnel or in a local hospital emergency room. However, many prisons are located in rural communities far from major medical centers. Albion Correctional Facility is located in Orleans County, New York, approximately one hour north of Buffalo. Lengthy travel time to a location where comprehensive medical care may be provided could prove fatal if the facility is not reached in time. If an inmate needs to deliver or has other serious complaints requiring skilled medical and nursery care, a local hospital provides this backup resource. To manage the growing prison population and prisoner/patients complaints, some prison systems have begun using telemedicine. New York State did so in 1997: "Interactive teleconferencing connect[s] physicians in prison with community medical centers. . . . [It] is used on a limited basis to enhance emergency triage, broaden specialty services and minimize the cost and security risks of inmate transportation to off-site providers" (Wynn, 2000, p. 21).

As women enter the various levels of prison bureaucracy, prison health-care providers are now required to solve the health problems brought on in part by the nation's social problems. The Eighth Amendment to the U.S. Constitution prohibits "cruel and unusual punishments," and can be interpreted as a requirement that all prisoners be provided with humane treatment.

Another crisis facing the corrections industry is the constant influx of mentally ill inmates. During the 1960s, hundreds of mental health hospitals closed, and thousands of mentally ill patients were released into community residential (halfway house) settings. Deinstitutionalization of the mentally ill without sufficient support is believed to have caused prisons and jails to become packed with hundreds of mentally ill inmates (Marquart, Merianos, Herbert, & Carroll, 1997; Lamb & Weinberger, 1998). With the advent of new psychotropic drugs, health-care providers believed that patients could be released to the community, be closer to their loved ones, and pose no threat to themselves or the public. Apparently what has happened is that many of these mentally ill patients exhibited inappropriate behavior that landed them in the arms of the law. James and Glaze (2006) reported that at "mid-year 2005, more than half of all prison and jail inmates had a mental health problem, including 705,600 inmates in State prisons, 78,800 in Federal prisons, and 479,900 in local jails." In addition, "female inmates had higher rates of mental health problems than male inmates (State prisons: 73 percent of females and 55 percent of males; local jails 75 percent of females and 63 percent of males"; and federal female prisoners 61 percent and males 44 percent (p. 1–2). Many of these inmates have a mental health and substance abuse dual diagnosis. In New York State, 11 percent of inmates have a mental health diagnosis (Wynn, Szatrowski, & Warner, 2004, p. 9) and at New York State's Bedford Hills Correctional Facility, "as of January 2007, more than 50 percent of Bedford's total population was on the Office of Mental Health caseload" (Margolies & Kraft-Stolar, 2006).

Inmates in the national population and in state facilities have similar mental health diagnoses: schizophrenia, major depression, and bipolar disorder, among others. To manage the symptoms and behavior of the illnesses, inmates must receive medication at scheduled intervals or they can decompensate, acting out through fighting or other disruptive behavior.

Another illness that has severely affected the healthcare system and African American women is HIV/AIDS. African American women account for 13 percent of the U.S. female population, and in 2004, they accounted for 67 percent of female AIDS cases. In 2005, of the 126,964 women living with HIV/AIDS, 64 percent were Black, 19 percent were White and 15 percent were Hispanic and the rate of AIDS diagnosis for Black women was 45.5 per 100,000 (CDC, 2007, pp. 1–2).

In addition, infection with HIV was

- The leading cause of death for Black women age 25–34
- The third leading cause of death for Black women age 35–44
- The fourth leading cause of death for Black women age 45–54.

Women who enter state and federal custody may have had multiple sexual partners and exchanged sex for drugs, shelter, or money. Therefore, when they enter these facilities, they may have been exposed to a range of sexually transmitted diseases, including HIV/AIDS. According to Maruschak (2007), the number of HIV/AIDS cases in state prisons among females decreased from 2,402 in 1999 to 1,935 in 2005. New York State is among the 10 states with the highest number of prisoner AIDS cases (Texas, Illinois and California are also included), and 12 percent of women in New York's prisons are HIV positive (*HIV/AIDS surveillance report* 2006; Correctional Association of New York, 2008). Some women may have been exposed to hepatitis C (HCV). Hepatitis C is a chronic, life-threatening blood-borne infection contracted from infected needles used by drug-dependent women, or when receiving tattoos or body piercings with infected equipment. Approximately 30 percent of all people living with HIV in the general public are co-infected with HCV (Correctional Association of New York State, 2009), and "nobody knows how many inmates have the disease; by some estimates around 40 percent of the 2.2 million in jail and prison are infected" (Mendoza, 2007, p. A6).

Other infectious diseases that may be detected among female inmates are tuberculosis and MRSA. MRSA, or methicillin-resistant *Staphylococcus aureus*, is a bacterium that is resistant to a variety of antibiotics. MRSA has been known in health-care settings for years (Steckelberg, 2008). It is now found in prisons, school buildings, and other places. The bacterium resides in the wounds of an infected person and can be transmitted from an infected person to a healthy person who fails to take precautions like simple hand washing. Prisoners are particularly vulnerable because they share small living spaces (cells). Inmates who have immunosuppressive diseases such as AIDS or HCV may have trouble fighting off the MRSA. In a prison setting where rodents and insects dwell, inmates who are vulnerable face potentially great risk of infections.

The health status of poor African American women is surely affected by poor medical care. Therefore, it can be surmised that when increasing numbers of sick women enter the incarcerated populations, prison health services must become more plentiful and specialized. We must also keep in mind that 2 million prisoners (men and women) move back and forth between incarceration and the community. They may bring home communicable illnesses acquired in the prison facilities. This is a national issue and therefore should receive national as well as local attention and intervention.

## NOTE

1. From *The Imprisonment of African American Women: Causes, Experiences and Effects*, 2nd ed., © 2010 Catherine Fisher Collins by permission of McFarland & Company, Inc., Box 611, Jefferson, NC 28640. www.mcfar landpub.com.

## REFERENCES

Amnesty International USA. (2007). *Excessive use of restraints on women in us prisons: Shackling of pregnant prisoners*. Retrieved from www.prisontalk.com/forums/archive/ind/index.php/t-290478,html

Baker, D. V. (2007). Systemic white racism and brutalization of executed black women in the United States. In R. Muraskin (Ed.), *It's a crime* (pp. 394–443). Upper Saddle River, NJ: Prentice Hall.

Beardsley, E. H. (1990). Race as a factor in health. In R. D. Apple (Ed.), *Women, health, and medicine in America: A historical handbook*. New York: Garland Press.

Belnap, J. (2007). *The invisible women, gender, crime, and justices* (3rd ed.). Belmont, CA: Thomson Wadsworth Press.

CDC. (2007). *HIV/AIDS in the African American*. Retrieved from www.cdc.gov/hiv/topics

Collins, C. F. (1997). *The imprisonment of African American women: Causes, condition, and future implications*. Jefferson, NC. McFarland.

Correctional Association of New York. (2009). *Women in prison project: Incarcerated women and HIV/Hepatitis C fact sheet*. Retrieved from www.correctional association.org/publications/download/wipp/factsheets/HIV_Hep_C_Fact_ Sheet_2009_final_pdf

Correctional Association of New York. (2008). *Women in prison project: Women in prison substance abuse fact sheet*. New York: Correctional Association. Retrieved from http://www.correctionalassocation.org/publication/download/wipp/factsheets/women_and-substance_abuse_fact_sheet_2008.pdf

Day, P. J. (1989). *A new history of social welfare*. Englewood, NJ: Prentice Hall.

Doetzer, G. (2008). Hard labor: The legal implications of shackling female inmates during pregnancy and childbirth. *William and Mary Journal of Women and the Law, 14*(2), 363–392.

Greenfield, L. A., & Snell, T. L. (1999). *Women offenders.* NCJ 175688. Washington, D.C.: U.S. Department of Justice. Retrieved from http://bjs.ojp.usdoj.gov/content/pub/pdf/wo.pdf

Hale, R. (2007, June 12). Correspondence from the executive vice president of American College of Obstetrics and Gynecology to Malika Saada Saar, the executive director of the Rebecca Project for Human Rights.

HRSA. (2007). *Women's health USA 2007* (7th ed.). Rockville, MD: U.S. Department of Health and Human Services.

James, D. J., & Glaze, L. E. (2006). *Mental health problem of prison and jail inmates.* NCJ 213600. Washington, D.C.: U.S. Department of Justice. Retrieved from http://bjs.ojp.usdoj.gov/content/pub/pdf/mhppji.pdf

Lamb, R. H., & Weinberger, L. E. (1998). Persons with severe mental illness in jails and prisons: A review. *Psychiatric Services, 49*(4), 483–492.

Liptak, A. (2006, March 2). Prisons often shackles pregnant inmates in labor. *The New York Times,* A16.

Margolies, J. K., & Kraft-Stolar, T. (2006). *When "Free" means losing your mother: The collision of child welfare and the interaction of women in New York State.* New York: Correctional Association.

Marquart, J. W., Merianos, D. E., Herbert, J. L., & Carroll, L. (1997). Health conditions and prisoners: A review of research and emerging areas of inquiry. *The Prison Journal, 77*(2), 184–208.

Maruschak, L. M. (2007). *HIV in prison, 2005.* NCJ 218915. Washington, D.C.: U.S. Department of Justice. Retrieved from http://bjs.ojp.usdoj.gov/content/pub/pdf/hivp05.pdf

Mendoza, M. (2007, March 15). "Silent Killer" hepatitis C emerging from prison as a public health threat. *Buffalo News,* A6.

National Commission on Correctional Health Care. (2005). Position statement: Women's health care in correctional settings (2005 update)." *Journal of Correctional Health Care, 11*(4), 381–389.

Steckelberg, J. (2008). *MRSA: Understanding your risk factor and prevent infections.* Retrieved from www.mayoclinic.com/health/mrsa/ID00049

Washington, H. A. (2006). *Medical apartheid: The dark history of medical experimentation on black American from colonial times to present.* New York: Doubleday.

Women Shackled During Labor. Retrieved From http://prisontalk.com/forums/archive/index.plp/t-290478html

Wynn, J. R. (2000). *Health care in New York State prisons: A report of findings and recommendations.* New York: Correctional Association. Retrieved from http://www.prisonpolicy.org/scans/healthcare.pdf

Wynn, J. R., Szatrowski, A., & Warner, G. (2004). *Mental health in the house of corrections: A study of mental health care in New York State prisons by the Correctional Association of New York.* New York: Correctional Association. Retrieved from http://www.correctionalassociation.org/resource/mental-health-in-the-house-of-corrections-a-study-of-mental-health-care-in-new-york-state-prisons-by-the-correctional-association-of-new-york

# Index

# About the Editor and Contributors

## Editor

**CATHERINE FISHER COLLINS**, D.Ed, RN, NP, is a writer, teacher, nurse practitioner, former registered nursing school Director, and former Buffalo School Board member. She began her writing career to fill a gap in the literature on women, especially African American women. Her doctorate and master's degrees are from the State University of New York (SUNY) at Buffalo, where she also graduated from the School of Nursing, nurse practitioners program.

Collins is a respected author of many published books, including *Sources of Stress and Relief for African American Women* (2003), *The Imprisonment of African American Women: Causes, Conditions and Future Implications* (1997, winner of the 1997 Outstanding Academic and Scholarly Award), *African American Women's Health and Social Issues*, 1st edition (1996), *African American Women's Health and Social Issues*, 2nd edition (2006), and *The Imprisonment of African American Women: Causes, Experiences and Effects*, 2nd edition (2010). She is the host of Women's Health Radio show that airs on WWWS 1400 AM with a focus on women's health issues and wellness. Dr. Collins is an Oxford University Round Table Fellow and SUNYs' Best Academic Alliances Fellow. She was recently inducted into the Western New York Women's Hall of Fame. Dr. Collins is currently an associate professor at SUNY's Empire State College, where she has taught graduate courses and currently teaches undergraduate courses that deal with women's health and criminal justices.

## Contributors

**FUNMI A. AIYEGBO-OHADIKE,** RN, DNP, FNP-BC (pronounced IYABOW), is a family nurse practitioner who has established herself as an expert clinician with over 17 years of experience. She graduated from Rutgers University with a BS in nursing in 1995, received her MS from Columbia University in 1998, and DNP from Rutgers University in 2010. As a faculty member at Sacred Heart University and University of Medicine and Dentistry, New Jersey, she prepared nursing students on both the baccalaureate and graduate levels for entry to practice. She has particular expertise in geriatrics, pharmacology, and home care. She has presented at both regional and national conferences on topics ranging from dementia to a trial fibrillation.

**PATRICIA K. BRADLEY,** PhD, RN, FAAN, is an associate professor of psychiatric mental health nursing at College of Nursing, Villanova University. She was inducted as a fellow in the American Academy of Nursing in 2011. She received her bachelor's degree in nursing from Temple University. She earned both her master's degree and her doctorate in nursing from the University of Pennsylvania.

Dr. Bradley is an active participant in several advisory committees that focus on health issues of the unserved. She is the president of the board of directors of Linda Creed Breast Cancer.Org, a nonprofit organization located in Philadelphia, and the trainer of their Safe Circle program, offering breast health information to the African American community. She has a particular expertise in the psychosocial aspects of breast cancer screening, diagnosis, treatment, and survivorship among African American women, and has developed training programs and materials focusing on the needs of the African American community. Her collaborations include developing an educational booklet for African American breast cancer survivors, *Getting Connected: African Americans Living beyond Breast Cancer*, with the nonprofit organization Living Beyond Breast Cancer. Her volunteer work with the American Cancer Society spans over 25 years. Dr. Bradley currently serves on several national committees of the American Cancer Society including the National Board of Directors, the National Nominating Committee, the National Awards Committee, and the Talent Strategy Advisory Group. She recently completed several terms as chair of the National Diversity Advisory Group.

**PORTIA JOHNSON,** EdD, RN began her nursing career as a licensed practical nurse on a medical–surgical unit, and continued her education to obtain an AAS from Mercer County Community College with honors. With a bachelor of science (BSN) from William Paterson College, she knew the value of education and obtained a master's in nursing (MSN) from Hunter College in New York. Her doctoral education at Columbia University, Teachers College, New York City positioned her to add to the body of knowledge that governors nursing practice.

Parallel to her educational journey, Dr. Johnson held the title of senior drug safety associate at Hoffmann La-Roche Pharmaceutical Company for 18 years. After completing her doctorate, her career path flowed toward teaching; she is presently an assistant professor in the College of Nursing at Seton Hall University in South Orange, New Jersey.

Dr. Johnson has contributed to numerous courses in the College of Nursing. Most of her impact has been with the undergraduate sophomore generic BSN students. However, she has also added to the lives of students in the RN to BSN online program.

Dr. Johnson shares her expertise on campus as well as in the community. While serving on the College of Nursing's Faculty Development Committee, she was instrumental in strengthening faculty engagement by hosting a networking opportunity for adjunct faculty to meet and greet full-time faculty. Most recently, she was appointed as secretary of the Faculty Development Committee.

In addition, Dr. Johnson is chair of the Obama Obesity Initiative for Concerned Black Nurses of Newark (CBNN), and is the newly elected vice president of CBNN. She is also working on a meta-analysis on childhood obesity, two manuscripts on obesity among Black women, and is writing a chapter on obesity.

Due to her ability to network and form collegial relationships, Dr. Johnson was recently aired on the radio talk-show Solid Gold Soul at WWWS 1400 AM, and was interviewed by the radio host and author Dr. Catherine Fisher Collins, Associate Professor at Empire State University. The listening audience from Western New York gained valuable information about obesity and healthy eating.

Dr. Johnson's high standards and value for education sets an example and provides guidance for her students. Her love for nursing is evident as she is a role model for today's professional nurses.

**DENISE M. LINTON,** DNS, FNP-BC, is an assistant professor in the College of Nursing at the University of Louisiana at Lafayette, where she is a member of the graduate faculty. She earned her master of science degree in nursing with a family nurse practitioner certification from Columbia University's School of Nursing in New York and her doctorate in nursing science from the Louisiana State University Health Sciences Center's School of Nursing in New Orleans. Her area of interest is women's health with a focus on cervical cancer prevention. She serves the profession of nursing by volunteering as a family nurse practitioner at a local community health clinic, disseminating information related to cervical cancer prevention in various peer-reviewed nursing journals, and at local, regional, and national nursing and nurse practitioners conferences. Additionally, she is a member of various nursing and nurse practitioner organizations such as Sigma Theta Tau International Honor Society of Nursing, American Nurses Association, National Black Nurses Association, American College of Nurse Practitioners, and Oncology Nursing Society. She reviews abstracts and manuscripts and is the editor of *Southern Connections*, the Southern Nursing Research Society newsletter.

**LISA M. LOURY-LOMAS,** PhD has worked in the field of psychology for nearly 25 years and is an expert in human relations and development. She has received a BS in psychology, an MA in clinical psychology focusing on father absence and the effect on self-esteem, and a PhD in general psychology with particular emphasis on applied social psychology and the impact of the impostor phenomenon and self-esteem on development, motivation, and success.

She has served the judicial branch of government as well as academia and the private sector. As a 13-year solo practitioner, her practice, which spans the Midwest and the East Coast, involves conducting individual, couples, and family counseling sessions, as well as developing and facilitating corporate workshops and seminars, and public speaking. Her conflict resolution expertise has exposed her to various methods of gaining insight, problem solving, and communicating.

Dr. Loury-Lomas's mission is to assist individualism attaining inner peace and true happiness by identifying barriers and limitations, recognizing strengths and skills, and implementing personal power to reach personal and professional goals. Her diverse educational and professional background has given her great insight into human behavior, information processes, and information exchange.

**JULIANNE MALVEAUX,** is a writer, economist, and the president emerita of Bennett College for Women.

**JAMESETTA A. NEWLAND,** PhD, RN, FNP-BC, FAANP, DPNAP, is a clinical associate professor at New York University's (NYU) College of Nursing. In addition to her role as director of the Doctor of Nursing Practice program, she maintains an active practice as a family nurse practitioner in the college's Faculty Practice, providing primary care to a diverse group of clients in an urban setting. She is sought nationally and internationally for consultation on nurse practitioner education and practice, and particularly nurse-managed health centers. Her passion for scholarly endeavors finds an outlet through service on editorial boards, presentations and publications, mentoring, and community involvement. Her contributions have been recognized through many professional and community awards, including the

2011 American of Academy of Nurse Practitioners New York State NP of Excellence. For the past seven years, she has led *The Nurse Practitioner: The American Journal of Primary Healthcare* as editor-in-chief. She strives to make a small difference in the lives of everyone she meets.

**LORRAINE E. PEELER,** PhD is an associate professor of human development at SUNY's Empire State College in Buffalo, New York. She has a PhD from the university at Buffalo in counselor education. Her research/teaching focus is counseling, cultural competency, and community violence and its outcomes. She has conducted research in the areas of African American attitudes toward the police, psychosocial impact of HIV and African American women, and the intersection between community violence and intimate partner violence for African American women. In addition to her academic work, she is a pastor and conference speaker. She has written numerous books and workbooks to empower and inspire people to become all they were destined by God to be. Some of her titles include *Your Empowerment Zones, Anger! What Is It Good For*, and her recent soon to be released book *Now . . . Your Faith Is a Process.*

**MATTIE L. RHODES,** PhD, RN, CNS, earned her PhD in medical sociology at the State University of New York at Buffalo. She also received her master's degree in adult health clinical nurse specialist and her bachelor's degree in nursing from the SUNY at Buffalo. She is currently a clinical associate professor on faculty at the SUNY at Buffalo. She is a retired naval officer, lieutenant commander and served in the U.S. Naval Reserve for over 13 years. She holds a permanent certification in teaching from State College of New York.

Her commitment to education is evident in many years teaching and mentoring numerous students from diverse backgrounds in various nursing programs and most recently at SUNY at Buffalo for over 25 years. She is often sought after as a speaker regarding cardiovascular disease especially, as it is manifested in women. She has served as past advisor to the Nursing Student Organization and most recently served as an advisor to the Minority Nursing Association. Eight years ago, as a part of undergraduate program, she spent time in Tortola, British Virgin Isles, where she participated in educating registered nurses to achieve their baccalaureate degree in nursing. She taught the nursing leadership/management course. She also presented community education on Women and Heart Disease. While on the Island, she also set up a "mentoring program" with the nurses. This program resulted from a collaborative effort with the university's School of Nursing and British government health officials.

Her research interest includes women and heart disease, "Using the Human Patient Simulator to Teach Clinical Judgment Skills in a Baccalaureate Nursing Program," "Examining Medication Errors in a Tertiary Hospital," "Nurses Perceptions of Violence in the Workplace in a Major Trauma Center," "Use of Graduate Record Exam to Predict Success in a Baccalaureate Nursing Program" and "Evaluation Outcomes of a Dedicated Education Model as a Clinical Teaching Model."

Dr. Rhodes has presented locally and nationally on "innovative teaching models" and recently published "Evaluation Outcomes of a Dedicated Education Unit in a Baccalaureate Nursing Program." She has also published several articles in refereed journals. She holds membership in several professional and public service organizations including Sigma Theta Tau, Nursing Honor Society, Gamma Kappa Chapter, Delta Sigma Theta Sorority Incorporated, Buffalo Alumnae Chapter, and The Links Incorporated Links Erie County Chapter. She participates on several community boards.

**SHUANA K. TUCKER,** PhD is the director of Adult & Continuing Education in Danbury Public Schools and an adjunct professor of Educational Leadership at the University of Connecticut. She has a PhD in educational policy studies from the University of Illinois at Urbana-Champaign, a master's in public administration from Louisiana State University, and a BS in psychology from Xavier University of Louisiana.

Dr. Tucker has conducted research on African American philanthropy and education, Black women's organizations and their philanthropic impact on education, Black women leaders, and women's health issues. She has published work in the *Journal of School Leadership*, the *Journal of African American History*, and other venues. She holds membership in several educational organizations: American Educational Research Association, Association for African American Life & History, and Phi Delta Kappa. Prior to joining Danbury Public Schools, she worked at the U.S. Department of Education, the McKenzie Group, Texas Instruments, and Hartford Public Schools. She also holds membership in Alpha Kappa Alpha Sorority, Inc.; The Links, Inc.; Jack & Jill of America, Inc.; and The Girl Friends, Inc.

**YVONNE WESLEY,** RN, PhD, FAAN, earned her PhD in nursing from NYU, where her focus was on research and theory development. With her master's degree in nursing from Rutgers University in Newark, she specialized in maternal/child health and has numerous publications in peer-reviewed journals. Currently, she is an independent health consultant and an adjunct associate professor in the College of Nursing at NYU and Kean University. Prior positions include vice president of community relations at Meridian Health, vice president of research and development at the Northern New Jersey Maternal–Child Health Consortium, and director of nursing at Newark Community Health Center.

Dr. Wesley started her nursing career at Newark's Martland Hospital in 1978, now known as University of Medicine and Dentistry of New Jersey. As her career progressed, she became the perinatal HIV research manager, where she demonstrated her ability to share complex research protocols with some of Newark's most vulnerable populations—i.e., low-income drug-using pregnant women with HIV. As an established voice on the issue of health care for the underserved, she went on to become the director of nursing services at Newark Community Health Center, Inc.

Her personality and style of leadership quickly caught the eye of regional health planning agencies and she assumed the position of vice president for research and development at the Northern New Jersey Maternal–Child Health Consortium. While in this position, then-Governor Christine Todd-Whitman appointed Dr. Wesley as cochair of the Blue Ribbon Panel on Black Infant Mortality. Holding meetings across New Jersey, she provided a medium for stakeholders to address issues related to Black infant mortality. At the conclusion of the initiative, she was appointed by the Commissioner of Health Len Fishman in 1997 as cochair of the Advisory Council to advise the Department of Health and Senior Services on implementation of the panel's recommendations. Resultantly, state policy changed providing more than 2 million dollars for Black infant mortality reduction.

Dr. Wesley also serves in numerous leadership roles including Association of Women's Health, Obstetrics and Neonatal Nursing's (AWHONN) Research and Review Advisory Panel in Washington, D.C. and the New Jersey Governor's Council on the Prevention of Mental Retardation & Developmental Disabilities. Her work in developing numerous community-based projects exemplifies a mix of nursing research principles and clinical practice. These projects were created with input from community members as well as published scholars.

Due to this work, she has received numerous awards, including Rutgers College of Nursing Outstanding Alumna Award in 2006 and AWHONN's *Nurse of the Year* for outstanding contributions in women's health, obstetrics, and neonatal nursing in 1999. Her high academic achievement has opened the door for her induction into two international honor societies: Kappa Delta Pi and Sigma Theta Tau. And, in recognition of her collective accomplishments and contributions to health care, she was inducted into the American Academy of Nursing as a fellow in 2004.

Dr. Wesley has lectured both nationally and internationally. Moreover, she has appeared on local and national network televisions as she continues to promote wellness. Based on an article published by the *Minority Nurse Magazine*, Dr. Theresa Fulmer, dean of the College of Nursing at NYU, became interested in Dr. Wesley's skill to create a leadership institute. It was her commitment to promoting wellness and eliminating health disparities that has brought them together to conceptualize, implement, and evaluate the NYU College of Nursing's Leadership Institute for Black Nurses. The Leadership Institute has now grown global and will train its first cohort of nurses from Ghana this summer.